A YEAR WITH JESUS

A Five Day a Week Devotional through the Gospels

Jacob Hudgins

A Year with Jesus: A Five Day a Week Devotional through the Gospels
Copyright © 2020 by Jacob Hudgins. All Rights Reserved.

All rights reserved. No part of this book may be reproduced in any form or by any electronic or mechanical means including information storage and retrieval systems, without permission in writing from the author. The only exception is by a reviewer, who may quote short excerpts in a review.

Unless otherwise indicated, all Scripture quotations are from The ESV® Bible (The Holy Bible, English Standard Version®), copyright © 2001 by Crossway, a publishing ministry of Good News Publishers. Used by permission. All rights reserved.

Cover designed by Damonza

Visit my website at www.jacobhudgins.com

Printed in the United States of America

ISBN-13: 978-1-7352970-1-9

Also by Jacob Hudgins

The School of Christ: Learning Character from Jesus

Humility Practice: 27 Ways to Think Less of Yourself—and of Yourself Less

INTRODUCTION

I AM FASCINATED BY JESUS. Even when I remove religious considerations, I find him to be the most important, interesting, and challenging person who ever lived. I am continually surprised by the way he views and describes God. I am intrigued by his care for people who are overlooked and marginalized—long before it was cool to care. I am impressed by his work with his apostles, whom he gradually develops from bumbling and corrupt to bold men of integrity. His blend of brilliant teaching, confrontation of sin and hypocrisy, and tender compassion is without peer anywhere. He is indescribably unique.

Matthew reminds us that Isaiah prophesied of a Messiah like this: *"Behold, my servant whom I have chosen, my beloved with whom my soul is well pleased. I will put my Spirit upon him, and he will proclaim justice to the Gentiles. He will not quarrel or cry aloud, nor will anyone hear his voice in the streets; a bruised reed he will not break, and a smoldering wick he will not quench, until he brings justice to victory; and in his name Gentiles will hope"* (Matt 12:18-21, quoting Isa 42:1-3). Long before Jesus lived, God promised a Savior who would have this mixture of kindness and holiness. He would nurture the weak believer and stand up to injustice, all at once. We will emerge from observing this messiah with one overriding emotion: *"in his name Gentiles will hope."* We will be refreshed in hope.

We have four gospels that give us the details of the life, words, friends, enemies, habits, death, and resurrection of Jesus. The more we immerse ourselves in them, the deeper our fascination grows. Seeing Jesus awakens a hunger to know and understand more—deeper—better. We begin to hope.

In 2017, our local church (the Fairview Park Church of Christ in Little Rock, AR) began a daily devotional series. Our goal was to provide a steady diet of exposure to the words of the Bible. Along with a daily reading, I wrote some brief comments to help us think through, pray about, and apply the things we studied. This book collects those readings and comments.

This devotional book is a guide to reading through the four gospels in one year. There are five readings for each week—one for each weekday—and devotional thoughts to follow along with the reading. My comments are not meant to stand alone; it is best to read the passage carefully prior to my applications.

After the devotional comments, I have included two short categories to help meditation and prayer. "One thing to think about" is a question (or two) that will require introspection and evaluation. "One thing to pray for" is a direction that the thoughts can take in prayer. These are ways we can take the example, words, and deeds of Jesus and make them a part of a period of serious devotion. I would especially encourage setting aside time for reflection and meditation on the readings. Just a few moments of intentional thought can change the course of our days and lives.

I am fascinated by Jesus. Further study of his life and deeds has only deepened my admiration. My prayer is that these words will help you to know Jesus better—and be not just fascinated, but moved to faith and emulation of him.

May God bless you as you read and meditate on his word!

WEEK 1 – MONDAY

Reading: Luke 1:1-25

A People Prepared

John the Baptist is a miracle child. His parents are too old to expect a baby. His birth is announced by an angel. His father is struck mute for not believing the incredible news. Yet all this drama is not just about God blessing a godly older couple. God has a purpose for John. *"He will be great before the Lord"* and *"he will be filled with the Holy Spirit, even from his mother's womb"* and he will *"turn the hearts of the fathers to the children."* All of this is *"to make ready for the Lord a people prepared"*(Luke 1:15-17).

John comes before Jesus to prepare the way for him. God refuses to send his Son into a world that is not ready for him. Things need to change. God's people must get their lives in order. John will be a shock to the nation's system. He will remind people of the need for personal piety and excite messianic fervor, anticipating the one who would come after him. His bold, forceful preaching will rouse God's people from their complacency.

Jesus has promised to come to earth again (Acts 1:11, John 14:3), but in his second coming there will be no forerunner. Over and again he warns us not to be caught unprepared—like the foolish virgins (Matt 25:1-13) or the wicked servant (Luke 12:35-48). There will be no warning, no dramatic birth announcements, and no warmup period. All the changes in my moral character, my commitment to my Savior, and my relationships with others need to happen *now* so that I can be ready for the Lord.

Am I prepared for the coming of Jesus? What will I work on today?

One Thing to Think About: Why do we struggle to remain continually prepared?

One Thing to Pray For: Patience to remain faithful to my Savior while I wait for him

WEEK 1 – TUESDAY

Reading: Luke 1:26-38

He Will Reign

Mary is just an ordinary girl, but this day her life will change forever. An angel appears to her, announcing that she will soon have a child despite being a virgin. Mary does what Zechariah could not: she believes the angel even though he promises things physically impossible. "*For nothing will be impossible with God*"(Luke 1:37).

Gabriel says some amazing things about the child. "*He will be great and will be called the Son of the Most High*"(Luke 1:32). These are not words commonly spoken over a new baby, much less one yet to be conceived. "*And the Lord God will give him the throne of his father David, and he will reign over the house of Jacob forever, and of his kingdom there will be no end*"(Luke 1:33). Despite his lowly, ordinary parentage, Jesus will be a king who will reign forever because his kingdom will never be destroyed.

We think of Jesus in many ways—as Savior, as Rabbi, as Shepherd—but we tend to forget that one of the essential meanings of the word *Messiah* is king. Jesus teaches repeatedly about the kingdom of God (Matt 4:17) and is dogged by accusations that he aspires to be king (Matt 27:11, 29, 36). If we miss the reign of Jesus, we neglect one of the most important aspects of his work.

Jesus *reigns*, which means he is a king who deserves my honor. Jesus *reigns*, which means he is worthy of my obedience and submission. Jesus *reigns*, which means that citizens of his kingdom follow him rather than their own will. Jesus is more than my friend, more than my sacrifice, more than my religion of choice. Jesus is my king.

One Thing to Think About: How would I respond if I were Mary?

One Thing to Pray For: A submissive heart to do the will of God

WEEK 1 – WEDNESDAY

Reading: Luke 1:39-56

My Soul Glorifies the Lord

Elizabeth and Mary have both had their worlds dramatically altered in recent days. Unexpected babies, angelic visits, and suddenly mute husbands must make for some interesting conversations. God is unfolding his eternal plan by appearing to two unknown, unimportant Jewish women.

As Elizabeth (and her baby!) recognize the tremendously valuable cargo Mary carries, Mary sings a hymn of praise to God. It is notable that when Elizabeth begins to praise Mary ("*blessed is she who has believed*") that Mary turns to praise God ("*my soul glorifies the Lord*"). She celebrates that Jehovah is a God of reversals. He brings down the mighty and exalts the humble. He fills the hungry and sends the rich away empty. He works to balance the injustices and pride in the world, proving his goodness and power.

But Mary particularly glorifies God *because of how he has blessed her personally*. Mary knows she does not deserve the tremendous blessing of bearing the Son of God, yet of all the godly women in the world, God chose *her*. God "*has looked on the humble estate of his servant*" and "*from now on all generations will call me blessed; for he who is mighty has done great things for me*"(Luke 1:48-49). There is something deeper about praise that springs from personal blessing. It moves from a recitation of facts about God to a heartfelt, emotionally charged statement of gratitude. Mary grasps the full breadth of what this will mean for her and sings out in praise.

There is a place for acknowledging abstract things about God—for praising his holiness and wisdom and love. But God is not just good. He is good *to me*. Can I say it with Mary: "*My* soul magnifies the Lord"?

One Thing to Think About: Why does God seem to enjoy working through obscure and unimportant people?

One Thing to Pray For: Willingness to seek praise for God instead of myself

WEEK 1 – THURSDAY

Reading: Luke 1:57-80

Salvation in the Forgiveness of Sins

After months of being unable to speak, Zechariah suddenly has a lot to say! Having seen the angel's prophecy fulfilled in his new son John, *"immediately his mouth was opened and his tongue loosed, and he spoke, blessing God"* (Luke 1:64). Luke records the lengthy text of a Spirit-inspired prophecy from his mouth.

Zechariah sees John's birth as a part of God's movement to save his people. God *"has visited and redeemed his people"* (Luke 1:68) and *"raised up a horn of salvation for us"* (Luke 1:69), so that *"we should be saved from our enemies"* (Luke 1:71) and *"delivered"* (Luke 1:74). At this stage, Zechariah's words fit well with the expectations of the period—a Messiah sent to conquer and rule in the style of David.

But Zechariah sees something different as well. John would go before the Messiah *"to give knowledge of salvation to his people in the forgiveness of their sins"* (Luke 1:77). John relates all this language of salvation and deliverance to *sins* rather than a physical war. "Enemies" is redefined from military opponents to our greatest spiritual enemy, Satan. Zechariah envisions God's Messiah acting to deliver and save through forgiveness. This is a rescue mission of epic proportions.

If Jesus' victory was military, we would rejoice, praise, and retell the story. How much more a spiritual victory which we could never achieve for ourselves? We have terrible, powerful enemies. We need *"salvation in the forgiveness of sins."*

One Thing to Think About: Do I think sin is as big a deal as God does?

One Thing to Pray For: Awareness of sin and desire to leave it

WEEK 1 – FRIDAY

Reading: Luke 2:1-21

The Sign of a Baby in a Manger

Luke has already pointed out the miraculous nature of Jesus' parentage. As he recounts the story of his birth, what is surprising is that he is born away from home and laid in a feeding trough. It is hardly a glorious beginning.

The first witnesses are shepherds (the wise men will come later). Sitting in the quiet darkness in the pasture, they must be unbelievably startled to see the glory of the Lord and hear the heavenly host. The angels declare that the Messiah has been born this day. *"And this will be a sign for you: you will find a baby wrapped in swaddling cloths and lying in a manger"*(Luke 2:12). The miracle that proves the truth of their words is the presence of a baby in a completely unexpected place—swaddled and lying in an animal's food trough.

"And they went with haste and found Mary and Joseph, and the baby lying in a manger. And when they saw it, they made known the saying that had been told them concerning this child"(Luke 2:16-17). Realizing that their vision is legitimate, they begin to tell others. Meanwhile things are starting to add up for Mary—she *"treasured up all these things, pondering them in her heart"*(Luke 2:19).

This aspect of Jesus' birth reminds us that God doesn't require glamor to accomplish his work. His way is often dirty and unappreciated, with little fanfare. The point of this is that it leads to people glorifying him (Luke 2:14, 20) rather than people or circumstances.

It is also a reminder that the most important things in life—character, truth, relationships—are not determined by popularity, money, or appearance. This is not the way we would announce the birth of God's Son and the world's Savior—but isn't that precisely the point?

One Thing to Think About: If God wasn't that concerned about Jesus' comfort, is he very concerned about mine?

One Thing to Pray For: God, not me, to be glorified

WEEK 2 – MONDAY

Reading: Luke 2:22-38

Jesus Causes a Stir in the Temple

God chooses righteous parents to raise his Son. Joseph and Mary are serious about obeying the provisions of the Law of Moses: circumcision of the baby (Luke 2:21), purification offerings for Mary (Luke 2:22), and presentation of Jesus before the LORD (Luke 2:23-24). Even when these acts mean that they must travel all the way to Jerusalem and the temple, they are determined to obey.

Also in the temple is Simeon—a *"righteous and devout"* man *"waiting for the consolation of Israel"*(Luke 2:25). As the Spirit has revealed to him that he will see the Messiah, he enters the temple just as the baby Jesus and his parents do. Taking the child in his arms, he praises God, foreseeing that God will bring salvation to both Jew and Gentile through this baby. This is probably not how these ceremonies typically go. After a private word to Mary (surprisingly not to Joseph), Simeon exits the stage (Luke 2:33-35). Anna, a prophetess who *"did not depart from the temple,"* now also comes to praise God and speak to those with messianic expectations (Luke 2:36-38).

The spiritually aware in Israel take note of Jesus, even as a baby. The Holy Spirit is involved as well, ensuring that the right people know what God is doing in this moment. Jesus will produce *"the fall and rising of many"*(Luke 2:34) and the revealing of many hearts (Luke 2:35). Those waiting on God and his work will rejoice. Others won't react so favorably.

Have things changed so much today? Jesus still causes a stir. There is no neutrality or half-heartedness in evaluating him. Is God working through him? Is he truly who he claims to be? I will learn much about myself in the answers I give to such questions. He will cause a stir in my life.

One Thing to Think About: What has Jesus revealed about my heart?

One Thing to Pray For: A heart to celebrate God's work (Luke 2:28-32)

WEEK 2 – TUESDAY

Reading: Luke 2:39-52

Jesus Causes a Stir in the Temple (Again)

We have lots of questions about Jesus' youth. How much does he understand? Can he work miracles? Does he ever say childish things? We are not the first to entertain such questions; some of the apocryphal writings of the first few centuries show imaginations gone wild about young Jesus. This makes it truly remarkable that this era of his life is not really treated at all by the gospel writers.

What we do have is this scene: Jesus immersed in the rituals, law, worship, and house of Jehovah God. He is there for a God-ordained feast commemorating Jewish deliverance from Egypt. He sits among the teachers in the temple—listening, asking, and answering questions about the Mosaic law. We learn that Jesus is thoroughly Jewish, yet exceptional—even as a boy.

Jesus' family dynamic is also intriguing. He seems completely unconcerned about the impact of his absence on his parents (Luke 2:48-49). This foreshadows Jesus declaring that those who hear and do God's word as his true family (Luke 8:20-21).

The key to the text is Jesus' question: *"Did you not know that I had to be in My Father's house?"* or *"Did you not know that I must be about my Father's business?"* (Luke 2:49, NKJV). Jesus speaks about God's work with *urgency*. He is not simply interested in being a Bible nerd who can answer all the questions perfectly. God's will will be his north star throughout his life.

If we know God like Jesus does, we will be urgently about his business too. Learning God's word is an essential part of that. Jesus' intensity about God's things causes a stir in the temple and in his family. Does mine?

One Thing to Think About: Am I urgently concerned with God's word, work, and people?

One Thing to Pray For: Single-minded focus on my Father's business

WEEK 2 – WEDNESDAY

Reading: Luke 3:1-9

No Salvation by Association

John's preaching effort centers around preparing the people for the coming of Jesus. He channels the people's general spiritual interest into specific life changes (v. 8-9, 10-14). "*And do not begin to say to yourselves, 'We have Abraham as our father'*"(Luke 3:8). John cuts to the heart of the contemporary Jewish mentality: We're fine because we're us! We're Abraham's kids! Their belief is in salvation by association—Abraham's goodness equals my goodness (and salvation).

John attacks this view with vigor. "*For I tell you, God is able from these stones to raise up children for Abraham*"(v. 8). The fact that we were born into a certain line means nothing about the kind of people we are. God does not owe us. "*Even now the axe is laid to the root of the trees. Every tree therefore that does not bear good fruit is cut down and thrown into the fire*"(Luke 3:9). People are like trees; we are evaluated on a tree-by-tree basis. If we do not bear fruit—if we are unwilling to hear God's pleas that we change our ways—then we will be cut down, whoever our ancestors are.

Others can help us learn, encourage us to be righteous, and build us up. But others cannot bear fruit for us. There is no salvation by association in families, where a particularly devout patriarch (or matriarch) is somehow a substitute for the faith of others. There is no salvation by association in a local church, where healthy spiritual leaders somehow take others to heaven on their coattails.

There *is* salvation by association in one sense, though. We can only be saved by our association with Jesus! Yet here we come around to the same point, because *Jesus too demands repentance*! There is just no way around looking in a mirror! Are we assuming we are right with God despite life-evidence to the contrary? Does something need to change?

One Thing to Think About: What crutches do I use to avoid self-examination and change?

One Thing to Pray For: Courage to face my need to change

WEEK 2 – THURSDAY

Reading: Luke 3:10-22

His Winnowing Fork

Repentance looks different in every life. As the crowds come to John, they ask for specific guidance from God for their situations. The one with two tunics or food is to share with others (v. 11). Tax collectors are to quit skimming off the top (v. 13). Soldiers must not threaten and be happy with their pay (v. 14). The reign of God is not a dry theological concept; it will always mean that things must change to get our lives ordered under God's rule.

John declares that Jesus will baptize with "*the Holy Spirit and fire.*" He will judge and sift. "*His winnowing fork is in his hand, to clear his threshing floor and to gather the wheat into his barn, but the chaff he will burn with unquenchable fire*"(Luke 3:17). The winnowing fork is a device (like a pitchfork) used to throw the wheat into the air so that the wheat falls (being heavier) and the chaff floats on the air. The fork separates what is worthwhile from what is useless. Jesus will distinguish those who genuinely desire to trust and obey the Father from those who trust themselves. No one slides by Jesus unevaluated.

The standard of Jesus' judgment is faith. Already we have seen much of this faith: in Zechariah, Mary, the shepherds, Simeon, and Anna. Those who believe God can act to redeem find it a short leap to believing in Jesus as God's instrument of redemption. Judgment has begun with Jesus, but it is not yet complete. He is sifting, even today. When complete, we will find ourselves in the barn—or in unquenchable fire. How does the fact of judgment change you today?

One Thing to Think About: Does the thought of judgment frighten me? Why?

One Thing to Pray For: Patience to deal with the division caused by Jesus' separation

WEEK 2 – FRIDAY

Reading: Luke 3:23-38

What Good is a Genealogy?

Genealogies are a challenge for the modern reader. There is no story here—just a host of names that are hard to pronounce, attached to people long dead whose lives we know almost nothing about. It is obvious that Luke's genealogy is different from Matthew's (Matt 1:1-17). Luke's works backward while Matthew's moves forward. There are many different names in the two lists. Most notably, Luke's genealogy goes back all the way to Adam, the son of God, while Matthew begins with Abraham. It is likely that Luke is tracing Mary's genealogy while Matthew is documenting Joseph's, which would account for many of these differences.

The genealogy shows that Jesus is thoroughly Jewish. These records remind us that though Jesus would become a Savior for all peoples, he comes from a distinct lineage and people. Jesus grows up steeped in the traditions and worship of Judaism and completely fulfilled the purpose and vision of the Jewish law. That would be impossible if he were an outsider. These documents are his bona fides.

The genealogy shows that Jesus is a descendant of David. Many of the messianic prophecies hinge on the seed of David. Isaiah speaks of a root of Jesse (David's father), Jeremiah a branch of David. If Jesus were not from this line, he could only lay claim to such promises in a figurative sense.

The genealogy shows that Jesus is a descendant of Abraham. This is vital because God made promises to Abraham to be fulfilled through his descendants (seed) (Gen 22:18). The New Testament makes clear that these promises are fulfilled in the salvation Jesus brings (Gal 3:16-18, 29). The genealogies position Jesus as a legitimate fulfillment of all the Old Testament promises. They form an essential bridge between the testaments. Genealogies simply show us that God has kept his word.

One Thing to Think About: Would Jesus be the Messiah if he wasn't from David's line?

One Thing to Pray For: Gratitude to God for planning and keeping his word

WEEK 3 – MONDAY

Reading: Luke 4:1-13

A Chess Match with Satan

In this reading we return to the story of Jesus, freshly baptized, 30 years old, led by the Spirit to the wilderness. For forty days he is tempted by the devil, fasting as he does so. Luke highlights three particular temptations. *"If you are the Son of God, command this stone to become bread"*(Luke 4:3). In this temptation the devil hones in on Jesus' hunger and his divine power. Why should God's Son be hungry? But Jesus hears in the appeal the idea of using power for selfish purposes and reaffirms his devotion to the Father and his will. *"It is written, 'Man shall not live by bread alone'"*(Luke 4:4).

Next he shows Jesus all the world's kingdoms at once and promises them to him: *"if you, then, will worship me, it will all be yours"*(Luke 4:7). It is not clear whether this is actually Satan's to give, but it is the nature of the proposition that is problematic. Jesus hears in it the idea of worshiping something besides God, for any reason. *"It is written, 'You shall worship the Lord your God, and him only shall you serve'"*(Luke 4:8).

Finally he places Jesus on the temple pinnacle, quotes Psalm 91 at him, and urges him to jump and let the Father prove his loyalty and prevent injury to Jesus. It is a challenge: if you are so devoted to the Father, prove it! God will save you! Yet in this offer Jesus hears the idea of testing God, forcing him to keep his word. *"It is said, 'You shall not put the Lord your God to the test'"*(Luke 4:12).

Jesus sees through the lies of Satan to his agenda: attacking Jesus' relationship with God. Jesus balks at the devil's ideas and relies on Scripture for his reasoning. What is particularly striking in the story is Jesus' perception; he sees right through these seemingly reasonable requests to the spiritual dangers they camouflage. For us, this story shows our need for discernment to hear Satan's voice in the cacophony around us—and sometimes from within us. We need knowledge (to see the real issue) and courage (to resist Satan and obey God).

One Thing to Think About: What approaches would the devil devise against me?

One Thing to Pray For: "Lead us not into temptation, but deliver us from evil"

WEEK 3 – TUESDAY

Reading: Luke 4:14-30

With or Without You

It is a bittersweet homecoming for Jesus. He enters the synagogue and sees the old crowd he grew up with. He reads the Scripture from the Isaiah scroll and begins to preach from it (Luke 4:21). We can picture the gleam of hometown pride in the eyes of the townsfolk. They have heard of Jesus doing great things in Capernaum (Luke 4:23) and they are impressed at his teaching, marveling that they have known him from early days (Luke 4:22).

But something is missing. It is not a fair hearing. As impressed as they are by Jesus, they have reservations. *"Is this not Joseph's son?"* they ask, struggling to make the connection. *"And he said to them, 'Doubtless you will quote to me this proverb, 'Physician, heal yourself.' What we have heard you did at Capernaum, do here in your hometown as well"*(Luke 4:23). Jesus picks up on a strain of unbelief and rejection in the crowd that culminates in them trying to throw him off a cliff (Luke 4:29).

Jesus takes this rejection in stride, reminding them of the example of Elijah and Elisha. Both these prophets were rejected by their people (Luke 4:24) and were sent to a Gentile widow and healed a Gentile leper, respectively. If his people reject him, God can work in Zarephath and Syria instead. If Nazareth says no to the Messiah, he will move on to places that will accept him.

God is not bound to work *only* with Jews—and never has been. God will find people of faith wherever they are—and reject unbelievers wherever they are. Nazareth's rejection will just make them a tragic footnote in the glorious story of the Messiah. God's work will go on with or without you. Our rejection does not stop God. However, the difference in whether I accept or reject him makes all the difference in the world to *me personally*. It is a choice with eternal consequences for me.

One Thing to Think About: Am I responding in faith to the way God is working today?

One Thing to Pray For: Praise to God for his unstoppable power

WEEK 3 – WEDNESDAY

Reading: Luke 4:31-44

His Word Possessed Authority

The series of events Luke narrates in this section tie together by an emphasis on Jesus' *word*. The gospel writers often note that people marvel at the authority of Jesus' words. Jesus knows what he is talking about and his tone reflects it. He tells Nicodemus, *"Truly, truly, I say to you, we speak of what we know and bear witness to what we have seen"*(John 3:11). Jesus knows men and knows God. There is no need to stand on another's authority.

Jesus' word is authoritative not just by its truthfulness, but also by the power that accompanies it. The same mouth that teaches about God bosses around demons. *"And they were all amazed and said to one another, 'What is this word? For with authority and power he commands the unclean spirit,s and they come out!'"*(Luke 4:36).

The demons know him. He needs no incantations or special formulas to cast them out. He rebukes fevers as if they are real people (Luke 4:39) in the same way that he will later rebuke the wind and waves. This is his creation and he directs and redirects it as he sees fit.

When God speaks, things move ("Let there be light," Gen 1:3). When Jesus speaks, things move ("Come out of him," "Peace! Be still!"). When I hear Jesus' words, do I move?

One Thing to Think About: If all of God's creation obeys when he speaks, what does he expect me to do?

One Thing to Pray For: The ability to be freshly astonished by Jesus

WEEK 3 – THURSDAY

Reading: Luke 5:1-11

Depart from Me, for I am a Sinful Man

Jesus is accompanied by a huge crowd at the shore of the Sea of Galilee (called Gennesaret here). He gets into Peter's boat and preaches to the people on the shore. Yet when the sermon ends, Jesus turns to Peter and tells him to put the net out and catch some fish. Peter is a professional fisherman. Jesus is a carpenter. Expertise is an issue here. There is also a pressing reason for Peter to object: *"Master, we toiled all night and took nothing!"*(Luke 5:5). Yet, however reluctantly, Peter consents: *"But at your word I will let down the nets"*(v. 5). Upon his obedience, a great haul of fish begins to break his nets and fills two boats to the point of sinking.

"But when Simon Peter saw it, he fell down at Jesus' knees, saying, 'Depart from me, for I am a sinful man, O Lord.' For he and all who were with him were astonished at the catch of fish that they had taken"(Luke 5:8-9). Peter swiftly acknowledges that Jesus is someone amazing. But with this realization comes another on its heels: because of his sin, he is not worthy to be with a person so lofty. And so he responds with the odd combination of being astonished by Jesus and then asking him to go away.

Like Isaiah (Isa 6:5), as Peter finds himself in the presence of God, he becomes more aware of his own sin and sinfulness. Being around people and focusing on our relationships with them leaves us feeling like we're "pretty good." Not so God.

Peter doesn't really want Jesus to depart. In fact he leaves everything to follow him (v. 11). What he really wants is Jesus to accept him despite his sinfulness. This is the greatest gift. Am I aware of my sin? Am I humbled by what I see in Jesus?

One Thing to Think About: Am I a sinful person?

One Thing to Pray For: Heightened awareness of my sinfulness in order to appreciate the holiness and power of God

WEEK 3 – FRIDAY

Reading: Luke 5:12-26

You Can Make Me Clean

Leprosy was the dreaded disease of the ancient world. There was no cure. Because it was contagious, quarantine was the only treatment. The provisions of the Law of Moses were particularly harsh on lepers, demanding that they live alone outside the camp (Lev 13:46). Worse than the physical symptoms was the fact that they were deemed unclean.

When this man "full of leprosy" approaches Jesus, he begs him "*Lord, if you will, you can make me clean*"(Luke 5:12). This is in strong contrast to the man who asks Jesus "*if you can do anything, have compassion on us and help us*"(Mark 9:22), calling into question Jesus' ability. The leper is confident Jesus can heal him; the only question is about Jesus' willingness to do so. "*You can make me clean.*" In the gospels, lepers are not said to be *healed* but *cleansed*. The man is begging Jesus to make him so that he is no longer defiled by this disease. In pity (Mark 1:41) Jesus touches the man: "*I will; be clean*"(v. 13).

Life begins in a sense of innocence and purity, yet as time passes, we are contaminated by what we hear, see, think, and do. Something within us yearns for that time of cleanness to return. We have a deep desire to feel clean, innocent, pure again. How long has it been since you felt that way?

In a way we come to Jesus with the same request. "*You can make me clean.*" This is what Jesus offers. He has compassion on us in our helpless, defiled state. He reaches out. He heals. He cleanses.

One Thing to Think About: Have I done things that still haunt me, so that I feel unclean months or years later?

One Thing to Pray For: Purity that comes from forgiven sin (1 John 1:9)

WEEK 4 – MONDAY

Reading: Luke 5:27-39

Doctors are for Sick People

Jesus calls Levi the tax collector to follow him. Tax collectors are notorious in Jewish society for dishonesty and collusion with Rome. Calling Levi is a bad move in the eyes of the Pharisees, who think Jesus' influence is hurt and compromised by his bad associations. They "*grumbled*" and ask the disciples "*Why do you eat and drink with tax collectors and sinners?*"(Luke 5:30). They cannot imagine a reason for this behavior because it is something they would never do.

"*And Jesus answered them, 'Those who are well have no need of a physician, but those who are sick'*"(Luke 5:31). I'm here to help. I'm the doctor and I'm here for the sick. That's what doctors are for. We don't criticize doctors for hanging around sick people. We know that they are trying to help and so such associations are necessary. But the whole purpose of doctors is to mend and heal the sick. Without sick people, why have doctors at all?

Jesus then speaks to his divine mission in coming to earth. "*I have not come to call the righteous but sinners to repentance*"(Luke 5:32). The point of the incarnation, virgin birth, and preaching efforts of Jesus is to call sinners. People who are doing fine don't need Jesus' help. They are not his target (although do such people really exist?). To miss Jesus' fixation on sinners is to miss entirely his reason for coming. Misunderstanding Jesus' love for sinners means misunderstanding him completely.

For us, this text doesn't just tell us of Jesus' love for sinners like us. It reminds us that Jesus puts a higher value on trying to *help* sinful people than to just stay away from them in the name of "purity." Are we like Jesus—willing to brave accusations like these for the sake of lost souls?

One Thing to Think About: Do I interact with lost people regularly? What is my goal for these interactions?

One Thing to Pray For: Open doors to lead others to repentance

WEEK 4 – TUESDAY

Reading: Luke 6:1-19

Just What Is Lawful?

In this section, Jesus twice tangles with the Pharisees about the Sabbath. On the first occasion, the disciples pluck heads of grain and rub them in their hands. The Pharisees dub this work. The second time it appears they have laid a trap for Jesus, watching closely to see whether he will heal a man with a withered hand at the synagogue service. In both instances they are trying to bust Jesus on technicalities.

It is plain that neither of these "violations" really violate God's goal in prohibiting people from work on the Sabbath. Shouldn't hungry and sick people be helped on the Sabbath? "*And Jesus said to them, 'I ask you, is it lawful on the Sabbath to do good or to do harm, to save life or to destroy it?'*"(Luke 6:9). Just what *is* lawful? Is it lawful to do harm (by neglect)? To destroy life?

More frustrating is the fact that the Pharisees' seeming dedication to the law does not apply when it comes to things *they* care about. Jesus later asks, "*Which of you, having a son or an ox that has fallen into a well on a Sabbath day, will not immediately pull him out?*"(Luke 14:5). Where is the concern for the Sabbath law then? It is (rightly) set aside for the emergency.

The root problem here is not about the Law of Moses. It's that the Pharisees care more about condemning others than about people and their needs. The Sabbath is just the current pretext for their rejection of Jesus. Notably absent from these examples is any concern by the Pharisees for hunger, sickness, or suffering—unless it happens to be *their* ox or son.

It is possible for us to fixate on Scripture and miss people. When urgent needs arise, we can spend time and energy debating what is "lawful" and opportunities pass by. Is this what God really wants? Just what is lawful?

One Thing to Think About: Do I ever neglect people?

One Thing to Pray For: A heart of obedience AND compassion

WEEK 4 – WEDNESDAY

Reading: Luke 6:20-36

Sons of the Most High

Jesus presents us with a high calling in this text. He boldly challenges us to love those who oppose and harm us. For emphasis he repeats it in different ways: pray, bless, offer, give, do good (Luke 6:27-31). It is a direct repudiation of the worldly ethic of "dog eat dog." Our world warns us not to show weakness and to respond to aggression with stronger aggression. Jesus teaches us to respond to evil with good.

We recoil from this. It just won't work, we think (though we may not dare say it). That's not real life. The inclusion of *"give to everyone who begs from you"*(Luke 6:30) and *"lend"*(Luke 6:35) only add another layer of resistance from us. Jesus presses forward, though. Our resistance is *exactly the point*.

"If you love those who love you, what benefit is that to you? For even sinners love those who love them"(Luke 6:32). Is there virtue in loving those who already love us? Is that a challenge? Responding kindly to kindness requires no effort or spirituality whatsoever. It is shocking when people *don't* respond well to kindness.

But he drives home the point in a way we can't miss. When we love enemies and do good and lend, we *"will be sons of the Most High, for he is kind to the ungrateful and the evil"*(Luke 6:35). God is like this. This is how we prove that we are his children. It is more than by virtue of his creation. It is more than baptism. This is likeness. If we are going to be anything like God, Jesus tells us it should be in the way we respond to opposition, threats, pain, demands, injustice. We do not only bless and pray for the good people. Does God do that?

These are not the people we *want* to love. There is no reciprocating and no advantage here. But that's what love is.

One Thing to Think About: Why do I feel I need to get a benefit from my relationships?

One Thing to Pray For: Mercy and strength to respond to hostility with kindness—like my Father

WEEK 4 – THURSDAY

Reading: Luke 6:37-49

Can the Blind Lead the Blind?

Jesus wants us to think through the implications of leadership. If I am going to lead you, you assume some things about me: that I know where I'm going and that my understanding surpasses yours and will help you. You assume I can see. *"Can a blind man lead a blind man? Will they not both fall into a pit?"* (Luke 6:39).

The troubling part of the blind leading the blind is not the blind follower. It's natural that a blind man understands his need for help and seeks to be led. The troubling part is that in his blindness he has enlisted the help of someone no better off than himself. *"A disciple is not above his teacher, but everyone when he is fully trained will be like his teacher"* (v. 40). We will not rise above our teacher; we will only become like him. Implicit in Jesus' words is the fact that we must choose those to whom we listen. There is danger in following others who are just as blind as we are.

In our time, there are so many voices vying for our attention and allegiance. Scientists, political figures, and religious thinkers are seeking adherents. These are in addition to the arrogance of the "ordinary" man who assures himself and others that he has things figured out. But how can the blind lead the blind?

What about Jesus? Jesus gives divine wisdom and testifies of things beyond this world which he has experienced (and we have not). More, he is exactly who we would like to be. We will not do better than our teacher, but what if we could become like Jesus? Isn't that the worthiest goal for our lives?

One Thing to Think About: Where are the voices I'm listening to leading me?

One Thing to Pray For: Guidance from God (Prov 3:5-6)

WEEK 4 – FRIDAY

Reading: Luke 7:1-17

The Compassion of Jesus

This is a tender scene. A widow weeps as her only son is laid to rest. It seems as though all of this small town has come out to grieve with her (Luke calls the crowd "considerable"). Yet this crowd meets a "great crowd" surrounding this rabbi whose name is on everyone's lips. Instead of passing by, Jesus takes note of her. "*And when the Lord saw her, he had compassion on her and said to her, 'Do not weep'*"(Luke 7:13). Jesus interrupts this funeral to speak to her—and then to her son, raising him from the dead. This miracle springs from Jesus' compassion for her.

Jesus is touched by the suffering of people, particularly the suffering and helplessness that accompanies death. It is at the tomb of Lazarus, observing other grieving family members, that Jesus is "*deeply moved*"(John 11:33, 38) and weeps with them (John 11:35) even though he knows he will shortly raise Lazarus. Jesus cares what we feel.

Jesus is not a robot. He does not chide grieving people as too worldly-minded or mouth empty platitudes ("God just needed another angel"). He just cares. Never does Jesus grow too busy with his mission to notice the grief and hurt of the little people.

Jesus' actions remind me how deeply he cares for *me*. He understands what I am feeling and feels it with me. My pain matters to him. But Jesus also shows me that I must get over my fixation on myself. There is a world full of pain around me and I must learn to see what others are experiencing, feel with them, and act to help.

One Thing to Think About: Am I deeply touched by the suffering of others?

One Thing to Pray For: A heart of compassion like his

WEEK 5 – MONDAY

Reading: Luke 7:18-35

Children in the Marketplace

John the Baptist sends messengers to Jesus (since John is languishing in prison, Luke 3:20) asking again whether he is the Messiah. After answering their question indirectly, Jesus addresses the crowd's response to John. In doing so, he gives tremendous endorsements of John (Luke 7:26, 28). Yet there is also tremendous criticism of the people. *"What then did you go out to see?"* Jesus asks three times. What did you want from John? *"A reed shaken by the wind?"*(v. 24). Someone weak? That doesn't fit John. *"A man dressed in soft clothing?"*(v. 25). A pampered aristocrat? Not hardly. *"A prophet?"*(v. 26). This is nearer to the mark. They went out to see a wild man and prophet of God—yet they found him not quite to their taste.

Jesus compares the crowd to children in the marketplace who cannot agree on a game that suits them. They won't play "wedding" and they won't play "funeral." How does this relate? *"For John the Baptist has come eating no bread and drinking no wine, and you say, 'He has a demon.' The Son of Man has come eating and drinking, and you say, 'Look at him! A glutton and a drunkard, a friend of tax collectors and sinners!'"*(Luke 7:33-34). John the Baptist was too weird. Now Jesus is too normal! Jesus and John use very different approaches, but the people find something to criticize in both of them. Just what *would* make them happy?

At times we are critical of God's methods: "I wish God had done it this way" and "I don't like this about the Bible" and "How could God allow…". Jesus is saying that the problem is not with God (or John or Jesus or the Bible), but with *us*. There is a broader point here about complaining. When we develop the spirit of discontentment, we can learn to be unhappy in any circumstance (the reverse of Philippians 4:11). There is always something to complain about and if we develop a taste for it, we may wind up rejecting God. God has worked the way he has to *help* us, not to *please* us.

One Thing to Think About: Do I complain about God or the people he has placed in my life?

One Thing to Pray For: Contentment with God and the situation in which he placed me

WEEK 5 – TUESDAY

Reading: Luke 7:36-50

Forgiveness Is the Difference

This woman has made a scene, barging into the Pharisee's house while he is hosting a dinner party. She stands behind Jesus, crying onto his feet and putting ointment on them. She is overwhelmed with emotion. Not everyone shares her feeling. Simon the Pharisee just can't believe Jesus is letting her *touch* him. "*If this man were a prophet, he would have known who and what sort of woman this is who is touching him, for she is a sinner*"(Luke 7:39). Simon believes that even the physical touch of a sinner contaminates others.

Jesus responds by telling a story of two debtors forgiven two different amounts. The one forgiven more loves his master more. The forgiven person acts differently. He acts from gratitude, passion, relief, and freedom. This is why the woman pours honor onto Jesus while Simon does not even provide an ordinary welcome (Luke 7:44-47). The one who feels he has been forgiven little has little love.

The lesson to us is that we must remember our great debt before God—and that he has wiped it away in Christ. We cannot afford to ever let that become dry theology. We know what we've done. We do not deserve forgiveness. We do not deserve for Jesus to have anything to do with us. We deserve to be shut out of the banquet of God, the kingdom of God, and the blessings of eternal life. But something changed—something that we did not deserve and can never repay. God gave these things to us through his Son. Our debt has been erased.

So how does the grateful, liberated man or woman act? Our attitude toward sin is transformed because we are no longer slaves to it and do not want to go back under its power. Evangelism is not a rote duty but an impassioned and deeply personal plea to help others find what we have found. Jesus becomes more than an interesting historical figure; he is now the key to our eternal destiny. It is easy to see the difference between spiritual staleness and vibrant faith. Forgiveness is the difference.

One Thing to Think About: Just what have I been forgiven?

One Thing to Pray For: Love that springs from gratitude

WEEK 5 – WEDNESDAY

Reading: Luke 8:1-15

Why the Gospel Doesn't Always Work

Jesus describes four types of soil. Three of them are inhospitable to the seed. As he explains, these soils represent reactions to the message of the gospel. *"As he said these things, he called out, 'He who has ears to hear, let him hear'"*(Luke 8:8). It is an admonition to better, more productive hearing.

The wayside soil pictures a man who hears the word but has it taken from him by the devil (in Matthew Jesus adds that he "does not understand it"). The gospel doesn't sink into this heart. It is hard—uninterested or unwilling to understand. The stony soil shows us a man who hears and receives the message joyfully for a time but withers in times of difficulty. In this heart the gospel produces a shallow faith—emotions without depth. It is an improvement from the first soil, but there is still no permanent effect. The thorny ground tells us about a busy faith. All the *"cares and riches and pleasures of life"* compete with the word and effectively overrule it. Attention and allegiance are divided. There is depth here, but so much depth that too many things are growing in the ground.

Then there is the good ground. The gospel is only truly successful in properly cultivated environments—the *"honest and good heart"*(v. 15) that bears fruit *"with patience."* This man is productive in what he learns; he cleans out the clutter of his life in pursuit of what really matters (Luke 10:42).

The gospel doesn't always "work" not because of any failure in the message, but due to the poor soil it encounters. What about me? How do I listen? Is the word having God's expected effect in my heart? Do I care about it? Do I let it sink in? Am I in it for the long haul, ready for tests and challenges? Do I need to make more room? Is life intruding on life? Where do I fit in Jesus' parable?

One Thing to Think About: Am I paying attention to how I *listen* to God's word?

One Thing to Pray For: Honesty to see myself rightly and obey God's word

WEEK 5 – THURSDAY

Reading: Luke 8:16-39

Jesus' Real Family

At this stage a great crowd is surrounding Jesus (Luke 8:4), to the degree that his family cannot get to him (Luke 8:19). I wonder what they think of this scene. Are they proud, surprised, or mocking? *"And he was told, 'Your mother and your brothers are standing outside, desiring to see you.' But he answered them, 'My mother and my brothers are those who hear the word of God and do it'"*(Luke 8:20-21). This response sounds rude. What harm is there in going out to see family?

Jesus is not anti-family. He promotes fidelity in marriage (Matt 19:3-9) and tells his disciples to let the little children come to him (Matt 19:14). Jesus has faithful parents and he submits himself to them while young (Luke 2:51). Jesus speaks rudely to his family not because he hates them, but because he has a point to make. Jesus' real family—his closest kin—are not his blood relations. He is most like those who *"hear the word of God and do it"*—this crowd of people thronging him to draw closer to God. We can be included in their number if we are willing to hear and obey the Father.

That also means that *I* now have brothers and sisters that are not fleshly relations. We are unified by our interest in and passion for God. In fact, we should not be surprised when this commonality of passion makes us more like them than our physical families. None of this means that we no longer have responsibilities to family—or that we cannot have physical kin who are spiritual kin as well. Jesus is simply showing that the *real* family is about commonality of passion for God. Spirit is thicker than blood.

One Thing to Think About: Do I feel a closer bond to my physical family or my spiritual family? Why?

One Thing to Pray For: The unity of my spiritual family

WEEK 5 – FRIDAY

Reading: Luke 8:40-56

Desperation

These two healing stories show us how desperation can change our behavior in positive ways. First we have Jairus, a ruler of the synagogue. *"Falling at Jesus' feet, he implored him to come to his house, for he had an only daughter, about twelve years of age, and she was dying"*(Luke 8:41-42). In what other circumstance would a synagogue ruler ask Jesus for something, especially in this humble, begging manner? Then we have the woman with the hemorrhage who *"though she had spent all her living on physicians, she could not be healed by anyone"*(Luke 8:43). All other avenues of aid have failed, so in her desperation she touches the fringe of Jesus' garment.

Jesus is careful to connect the actions of both to *faith*. He tells them, *"Daughter, your faith has made you well"*(Luke 8:48) and *"Do not fear; only believe, and she will be made well"*(Luke 8:50). He draws a spiritual lesson from what might appear a purely physical concern. We are left simultaneously amazed by Jesus and thankful for his help for the helpless (a demographic that includes us).

Desperation shortens the gap of faith. We are more willing to believe because our need is pressing and obvious. We feel its urgency. We sense that all other options are inadequate, including our own resources. In these moments of weakness God shines. Faith becomes real.

What do we do in our times of desperation? Where do we go when we reach our limits? How do we deal with adversity and suffering? Are we connecting with Jesus through faith in our times of desperation?

One Thing to Think About: Am I in desperate need of Jesus?

One Thing to Pray For: Faith that overcomes my fear

WEEK 6 – MONDAY

Reading: Luke 9:1-17

Take Nothing for Your Journey

For the first time the twelve leave Jesus. He sends them out to *"proclaim the kingdom of God and to heal"*(Luke 9:2) with power over demons and disease. The move is genius: he is spreading the message of the kingdom *and* training his men all at once. It is a reminder that evangelism is good for everyone involved—teacher and learner alike.

"And he said to them, 'Take nothing for your journey, no staff, nor bag, nor bread, nor money; and do not have two tunics'"(Luke 9:3). This is not how we plan for journeys. No luggage or transportation or wallet. They have no option but to rely on God. At every step, Jesus wants this to be faith-building. God will provide, God's message will be taught (even in Jesus' absence), God's power will be demonstrated, and God will be the one accepted or rejected (Luke 10:16).

Against all odds, this ragtag group of Galileans gets the message out. Luke notes that *"Herod the tetrarch heard about all that was happening"*(Luke 9:7). The word gets around. They are successful in telling about the kingdom of God—even though they have no resources or formal plan.

This story teaches us to trust God to provide. When we turn our energy and attention to the real stuff of life and the spiritual work that awaits us, God takes care of us (Matt 6:33). The good news is that we don't have to pry open all the doors, formalize the perfect evangelism plan, or have an ideal presentation. We simply have to seize the opportunities before us.

One Thing to Think About: Since God seems to enjoy using small, everyday people and things to accomplish amazing things, what little things is he using in my life?

One Thing to Pray For: Trust in God's provision, purpose, and power

WEEK 6 – TUESDAY

Reading: Luke 9:18-27

Taking Up Our Cross Daily

This is a critical moment for the disciples. In response to Jesus' question about his identity, they voice their unspoken belief: he is *"the Christ of God"*(Luke 9:20). Confession is a big step because it means they are going public with their faith, opening themselves up to contradiction or ridicule. But Jesus has a startling reaction to their confession: *"And he strictly charged and commanded them to tell this to no one"*(Luke 9:21). He tells them he's going to be rejected and killed (Luke 9:22). Then he tells them that if they want to come after him, they need to take up their cross and follow him (Luke 9:23).

Taking up a cross does not mean simply carrying a burden. The emphasis is on what happens when the cross is set down. One who carries a cross knows that he will die on it. To *choose* to take up our cross is to sign up for the possibility of death.

God's work deserves my whole being, by death or life. *"Let him deny himself"* involves letting go of my willfulness and my own plans for my life. Having surrendered my life, what else is there to hold back? *"For whoever would save his life will lose it, but whoever loses his life for my sake will save it. For what does it profit a man if he gains the whole world and loses or forfeits himself?"*(Luke 9:24-25). Physical life is *not* the highest priority. Some things are worth dying for. This is fundamental to following Jesus because this is the way he thought.

The challenge for us is that we live in comfort. We have wealth, medicine, and entertainment. We seem to resent even mild inconveniences. Will I sacrifice my whole life for Jesus? Am I willing to be killed, jailed, badmouthed, derided? Will I give up my time, my dreams, my family for him? To follow Jesus, I embrace suffering and loss *"daily."* It's what he did.

One Thing to Think About: Is there something I'm unwilling to go through for Jesus?

One Thing to Pray For: Strength to daily take up my cross, ready to suffer, for Jesus

WEEK 6 – WEDNESDAY

Reading: Luke 9:28-45

Jesus is Heaven's Front-Page News

Peter, James, and John are privy to witnesses from heaven. Jesus brings them along for a simple time of prayer (Luke 9:28), as he surely had done at other times. Yet as he prays, he is changed (Luke 9:29) and they see "*his glory*"(Luke 9:32). Moses and Elijah appear in glory too (Luke 9:30-31), though we are not told how the three disciples recognize them.

Luke records an interesting detail: as Moses, Elijah, and Jesus converse, they speak of "*his departure, which he was about to accomplish at Jerusalem*"(Luke 9:31). What a discussion that must have been! Jesus is shortly to finish his "exodus"(the Greek word for "departure" here) through the cross, resurrection, and ascension. Moses and Elijah are here as very interested onlookers (and perhaps encouragers?). These two great prophets of the Jewish Scriptures acknowledge Jesus and talk mission with him.

Peter wants to honor all three (Jesus, Moses, and Elijah), but the Father speaks: "*This is my Son, my Chosen One; listen to him!*"(Luke 9:35). Establishing Jesus' superiority—even to such great figures as Moses and Elijah—is a big deal in heaven. Jesus is heaven's front-page news. The heavenly host rejoices at his birth (Luke 2:13). The gospel involves "*things into which angels long to look*"(1 Pet 1:12). Jesus even says that "*many prophets and righteous people longed to see what you see, and did not see it, and to hear what you hear, and did not hear it*"(Matt 13:17). We are truly blessed—truly, deeply blessed—to have a fuller vision of the purpose and work of God through Jesus, what all heaven and creation has itched to see.

When we see front-page news in our world, we take note. We remember important events. We talk about them with others. We want to know more. Do we feel the same about Jesus?

One Thing to Think About: If I could talk directly to Jesus about any one thing, what would it be?

One Thing to Pray For: Appropriate honor for Jesus and respect for his word in my own heart

WEEK 6 – THURSDAY

Reading: Luke 9:46-62

Jesus and the Sons of Thunder

Jesus has just brought the room down with a prediction of his death (Luke 9:44-45). Now he "*(sets) his face to go to Jerusalem*"(Luke 9:51) because he is determined to die there. He will teach along the way, but perhaps not for as lengthy a time as his audience would like. His haste may explain why a Samaritan village rejects him: "*But the people did not receive him, because his face was set toward Jerusalem*"(Luke 9:53).

James and John are none too happy about this news. "*And when his disciples James and John saw it, they said, 'Lord, do you want us to tell fire to come down from heaven and consume them?'*"(Luke 9:54). Is this reaction more intense because the people are Samaritans? James and John, excited by their new powers, perhaps with visions of Elijah, want to vindicate Jesus. "*But he turned and rebuked them*"(Luke 9:55). Jesus makes clear that these brothers have it all wrong.

It is easy to have James and John's mentality. We take the nuclear option into our relationships. If you don't act the way you should—the way I'd prefer—the way that benefits me—I might just blow the whole thing up. I might stop talking to you, stab you in the back, or run you down to others. If I could, I would "call down fire" on you because you have treated me so wrongly. In particularly toxic moments, we allow that one wrong we have suffered to poison our thinking and grow out of proportion to its real import. Jesus' response reminds us that this is improper.

Jesus' patience—not just with the Samaritans, but also with James and John—bears fruit as these brothers are slowly transformed into better people. This is the same John whom we refer to as the "apostle of love". We are all thankful that Jesus never uses the nuclear option with them, blasting them for their evil hearts and expelling them from his presence. We require patience and Jesus gives it. Do we give it to others?

One Thing to Think About: Do I become angry easily—whether justified or not?

One Thing to Pray For: Patience with people—like Jesus has

WEEK 6 – FRIDAY

Reading: Luke 10:1-24

The Right Kind of Joy

As Jesus continues his trek toward Jerusalem, he sends his men (70 or 72) ahead of him to preach to the cities he will visit. Though Luke does not record a specific empowering of these men, Jesus tells them to "*heal the sick*"(Luke 10:9). "*The seventy-two returned with joy, saying, 'Lord, even the demons are subject to us in your name!'*"(Luke 10:17). They are exultant—perhaps even surprised—at the powers he has given them. Demons were a huge problem in the ancient world—frightening, unpredictable, and with no known solution. Jesus stresses that the disciples' powers reflect his dominion over Satan ("*I saw Satan fall like lightning from heaven*") and that the disciples have significant authority ("*over all the power of the enemy*", Luke 10:18-19). Particularly striking is the fact that Jesus corrects their joy. "*Nevertheless, do not rejoice in this, that the spirits are subject to you, but rejoice that your names are written in heaven*"(Luke 10:20). Their joy needs to come from a different source—not just their powers, but what they mean. Joy is appropriate, but it needs to be the *right kind* of joy.

The right kind of joy springs from a relationship with God. "*Rejoice that your names are written in heaven.*" When the novelty of this power wears off, when Jesus has left earth, when life wears us down, this kind of joy continues. My name is still written there! Praise God! The right kind of joy springs from what God has done. In the next verse, Jesus rejoices that God has revealed his will to little children (Luke 10:211). God, in his brilliance, has stumped the world and accomplished all his will. I rejoice because I benefit from God's good works!

We tend to enjoy the gift rather than the giver. We love the experience rather than taking time to think about what it means. Here Jesus pushes us toward something more permanent. He cautions us against being overly enamored with the current spiritual moment.

One Thing to Think About: How does it make me feel to know that my name is written in heaven?

One Thing to Pray For: Joy in my relationship with God and his wonderful works

WEEK 7 – MONDAY

Reading: Luke 10:25-42

Martha, Martha!

People often try to engage Jesus in their personal disputes. "Tell my brother to divide the inheritance with me!" "Who is the greatest?" Here two sisters invite Jesus into their house. Mary stops serving to sit at Jesus' feet and this bothers Martha. *"And she went up to him and said, 'Lord, do you not care that my sister has left me to serve alone? Tell her then to help me'"*(Luke 10:40). Jesus, how can you allow this unfairness?

Jesus' answer is powerful. On one level, it is a no. *"Mary has chosen the good portion, which will not be taken away from her"*(Luke 10:42). Jesus will not stop her from hearing God's word, whatever Martha may say. On another level, it is insightful. *"Martha, Martha, you are anxious and troubled about many things"*(Luke 10:41). Jesus sees Martha's anxiety, worrying about every detail of serving and hosting *except Jesus himself*. He knows her heart's turmoil and still speaks warmly to her.

But most importantly, Jesus' words are about singularity of focus and the danger of distraction (Luke 10:40). *"You are anxious and troubled about many things, but one thing is necessary"*(Luke 10:41-42). Martha must choose from among the many things to find the *one thing* that matters most—hearing the life-giving words of the Savior.

In all our activity (even good activity!) and all our anxiety (even over good things!) we can lose sight of Jesus. It starts when our feet hit the floor in the morning. Our phones alert us to messages and online news and social media. Friends and family need us. Work calls. Our bodies demand our attention. Bills must be paid and yards tended and oil changed and clothes washed. It is easy to forget that *one thing is necessary*.

One Thing to Think About: What makes me feel anxious and troubled?

One Thing to Pray For: Discipline to choose to hear Jesus' teaching over the call of other things

WEEK 7 – TUESDAY

Reading: Luke 11:1-13

Jesus-Style Prayer

The disciples are drawn toward the prayer life of Jesus and ask for more formal instruction. "*Lord, teach us to pray, as John taught his disciples*"(Luke 11:1). Knowing Jesus' role as Son of God, we see prayer here as it truly should be.

Jesus-style prayer is *simple*. This prayer (Luke 11:2-4) is short. He does advocate the long prayers of the hypocrites because it just doesn't take that long to cut to the chase. Simple doesn't mean shallow. This prayer covers God's kingdom, daily provision, our deep need for forgiveness and spiritual guidance. Jesus' prayer hits our essential priorities and calibrates our focus. These are the things that matter.

Jesus-style prayer is *persistent*. The story of the friend at midnight (Luke 11:5-8) shows the value of continual asking. We need a longer-term view of prayer. We can't nag God into submission, but persistence is a sign that we trust he hears (Luke 18:1) and that we need *his* help. Jesus prays this way when he asks the same thing three times in Gethsemane. Given this, perhaps the length of Jesus' prayers is more about persistence and repetition than new topics.

Jesus-style prayer *asks*. He encourages us to ask (Luke 11:9-13) because prayer is predicated on a Father who longs to bless. This is not a blank check, but a reassurance that God *wants* our requests. Prayer is not a "principle of the universe" but an appeal to a loving Father. We don't have to impress God (with lengthy prayers), but we also don't have to be so modest that we don't ask.

One Thing to Think About: In what ways does Jesus' style of prayer challenge me?

One Thing to Pray For: Persistence in my faith to keep asking for what I need

WEEK 7 – WEDNESDAY

Reading: Luke 11:14-26

Plundering Satan's House

As Jesus casts out another demon, some of the onlookers make an accusation: *"He casts out demons by Beelzebul, the prince of demons"*(Luke 11:15). Jesus responds to them to show them that this line of reasoning is not well thought-out.

First, if Jesus casts out demons by Satan's power, then Satan would be attacking himself—a mark of tremendous instability. *"And if Satan also is divided against himself, how will his kingdom stand?"*(Luke 11:18). Divided kingdoms fall. Beyond that, Jesus is not the only one casting out demons. Many other Jews (like the 72, Luke 10:17) share this power. *"And if I cast out demons by Beelzebul, by whom do your sons cast them out?"*(Luke 11:19). Are they in league with Satan too?

But if this is *God's* power, then it marks a decisive victory over Satan (Luke 10:18). Now Jesus plunders his house. His power over demons shows that Jesus is greater, stronger, and wiser than Satan. We see it in demons cast out. We see it in healings. We see it in Jesus retaking the people Satan has taken captive.

Satan is at work in our world—corrupting, destroying, and attacking. He is powerful and we cannot beat him alone. Seeing Jesus rightly starts with acknowledging Satan's power and our helplessness. But it must culminate in *celebrating Jesus' victory* over Satan and the liberation that brings us! We were in Satan's house, but praise God that Jesus has plundered Satan's house!

One Thing to Think About: How have I experienced Satan's power?

One Thing to Pray For: Diligence to not let sin reign again in my mortal body

WEEK 7 – THURSDAY

Reading: Luke 11:27-36

Lamps

Jesus uses lamps to illustrate both how light (righteousness) and darkness (evil) spread and grow. *"No one after lighting a lamp puts it in a cellar or under a basket, but on a stand, so that those who enter may see the light"*(Luke 11:33). Lamps rely on strategic positioning. They spread light by being in a place where their good is maximized (stands instead of cellars).

The eye is the same way. *"Your eye is the lamp of your body"*(Luke 11:34). Because of its strategic positioning, everything is impacted (for good or evil) by the eye. Jesus is not simply concerned about eyes and physical bodies. I believe the point here is about *focus*. What we fixate on—our *input*—has an impact on the rest of our being (Luke 10:42). Have you ever been so embittered toward someone that you couldn't even entertain a positive thought about them? Have you ever grown so negative in your thinking that you could not count a single blessing? When your eye is bad, your body is full of darkness (Luke 11:34).

But the opposite is true too. *"If then your whole body is full of light, having no part dark, it will be wholly bright, as when a lamp with its rays gives you light"*(Luke 11:36). If we focus on and keep taking in the good, *we* become the lamp! We become "*wholly bright*," able to pass on what is good to others. We are suddenly strategically positioned to influence others toward God.

Negative thinking consumes and pollutes. We must choose positive inputs and focus on what is good (Phil 4:8). As we shine with good, others are drawn toward our God.

One Thing to Think About: Do I tend to dwell on negative things? What impact does this focus have?

One Thing to Pray For: A healthy eye and a body full of light

WEEK 7 – FRIDAY

Reading: Luke 11:37-54

Woes

Jesus again agrees to eat at a Pharisee's house, but this time they don't even get to dinner before Jesus launches in on his host. The man is shocked that Jesus doesn't wash his hands (Luke 11:38) and Jesus blasts him and other guests with a series of woes. Woes are statements of condemnation that attach to promises of judgment. They are a prophetic tool that Jesus uses to criticize the Pharisees and lawyers with God's authority.

Jesus pronounces woes because of their *failings in personal piety*. They look clean outwardly but "*inside you are full of greed and wickedness*"(Luke 11:39). They "*love the best seat in the synagogues and greetings in the marketplaces*"(Luke 11:43). They tithe passionately but "*neglect justice and the love of God*"(Luke 11:42). These men are religious figures, but what good is religion if it is only skin deep?

Jesus pronounces woes because of their *failings in working with others*. They are like unmarked graves (Luke 11:44), which made Jews ritually unclean without their knowledge. Others are contaminated by these men without even realizing it. They also "*load people with burdens hard to bear*"(Luke 11:46), teaching things they don't even plan to practice themselves. They take away the key of knowledge and hinder others from entering the kingdom (Luke 11:52). It is bad enough to not be close to God yourself; to hurt others and prevent them from coming to him is worse.

The danger of a text like this is that we read only to criticize these men without personal introspection. We fail in *our* personal piety when we only serve to impress others, when we major in minors, and when we seek praise from people instead of God. We fail in *our* working with others when we overload others with requirements God never gave and when we contaminate them with our own corruption.

One Thing to Think About: What failings does Jesus notice in me—and what am I doing about them?

One Thing to Pray For: Humility to see myself—and God—and others—rightly

WEEK 8 – MONDAY

Reading: Luke 12:1-21

Rich toward God

Jesus raises the stakes here. He speaks about those who kill the body (Luke 12:4) and the threat of rulers and authorities (Luke 12:8-12). There is both challenge and reassurance in this. The challenge is to be ready to confess, not to fear. The reassurance is that God is greater than men and will provide words for these situations.

It is then particularly out of place for this man to ask Jesus to settle an argument about his father's inheritance (Luke 12:13). Jesus makes an example out of the man (Luke 12:14-15). He *should* be embarrassed. Covetousness has blinded him. To illustrate covetousness, Jesus tells a story that could be ripped from the headlines of 21st century America.

The "rich fool" does not appear a fool to the world. He is a cunning businessman. In our time, he would be profiled in industry magazines as a visionary. *"I will do this: I will tear down my barns and build larger ones, and there I will store all my grain and my goods"*(Luke 12:18). He plans, schemes, and expands, but he has no thought of the real tomorrow. All his plans are intended to win himself the right to relax (Luke 12:19). But God's edict is urgent: *"This night your soul is required of you, and the things you have prepared, whose will they be?"*(Luke 12:20). Jesus summarizes: *"So is the one who lays up treasure for himself and is not rich toward God"*(Luke 12:21). His hoarding does not last. There are no pockets in a shroud. As several have noted, our life is like a game of Monopoly. When all our accumulation has ended, the game is over, and all our wealth goes back in the box.

Am I "rich toward God"? Does my money leave a trail of good—or just a trail of selfishness and consumption? Can I admit that "relaxing" is the opposite of the disciple's disposition?

One Thing to Think About: What do my finances say about my faith in Jesus?

One Thing to Pray For: Courage to live above the world's fixation on "now" and "relaxation"

WEEK 8 – TUESDAY

Reading: Luke 12:22-34

Fear Not, Little Flock

Jesus is still discussing money here, following his response to the man asking about his inheritance. In this section, though, his teaching is less about what we *do* with money and more about how we *view* it. "*Do not be anxious*"(Luke 12:22) and "*Fear not*"(Luke 12:32) show us that our view of money and the necessities of life can reveal the nature of our faith.

One problem with a materialistic fixation is that it supplants God and makes him unnecessary. We live like Gentiles (Luke 12:30)—planning, worrying, and fixing problems by ourselves without any God to provide. There is no one to comfort us and no one we can trust. We are on our own—so we *must* be anxious!

Jesus reassures us: "*Fear not, little flock, for it is your Father's good pleasure to give you the kingdom*"(Luke 12:32). God wants to bless you! Even if we live without great possessions, God wants to give us something great. Even if we are a "little flock"—a small, unnoticed group in the world's eyes—God bestows his kingdom on us. And (this is both vital and difficult) even if we give to the point that our livelihood is threatened, God will take care of us (Luke 12:31-32).

"*Sell your possessions, and give to the needy. Provide yourselves with moneybags that do not grow old, with a treasure in the heavens that does not fail*"(Luke 12:33). It would be a major step for us to so trust God that we give *beyond* what is comfortable. Read the verse again. Jesus is encouraging us to do something financially extreme to help others, stepping out in faith rather hunkering down in fear and anxiety. And at the end of that, we learn that trust is more appropriate to our position as his "little flock."

One Thing to Think About: Why do I get so anxious about my life?

One Thing to Pray For: Courage to give sacrificially, painfully, wholeheartedly

WEEK 8 – WEDNESDAY

Reading: Luke 12:35-48

The Discipline of Watchfulness

Throughout this chapter Jesus warns of difficult times on the horizon. Things will soon be revealed (Luke 12:2). Some will soon try to kill the disciples (Luke 12:4) and they will be tested as to whether they will confess Jesus (Luke 12:8-9) when arrested and brought before rulers (Luke 12:11). It is true with money too—whether God is saying *"this night your soul is required of you"*(Luke 12:20) or reminding us of the threat of thieves and moth taking our money (Luke 12:33).

Jesus' disciples live with a constant awareness of a future in which difficulty may surface and in which God has promised to act. We are *"waiting for the master"*(Luke 12:36). So Jesus warns us: *"stay dressed for action"*(Luke 12:35) and be *"awake"*(Luke 12:37) and be *"faithful and wise"*(Luke 12:42) in the absence of direct leadership while awaiting the master. The concern is that we grow lazy, forgetting the promise of the return of the master, and are caught unprepared (Luke 12:45-46). Our willful abuse of others and lack of faith will be exposed. *"You must also be ready, for the Son of Man is coming at an hour you do not expect"*(Luke 12:40).

Watchfulness takes *discipline*. It is hard to remain continually alert. We must choose to refresh ourselves, mentally prepared for the length of our wait. We cannot afford for our focus to waver but must retrace the promises we cling to. Most of all, we must remember that our preparation (or lack thereof) *will be exposed*—whether by hard times we encounter or by Jesus' "coming."

Will I stick it out—or will I give up because waiting is hard?

One Thing to Think About: Am I really in it for the long haul?

One Thing to Pray For: Determination to remain watchful

WEEK 8 – THURSDAY

Reading: Luke 12:49-59

I Came to Cast Fire

Here Jesus works to correct misconceptions about his impact. "*I came to cast fire on the earth, and would that it were already kindled! I have a baptism to be baptized with, and how great is my distress until it is accomplished!*"(Luke 12:49-50). Jesus is on a divine mission of bringing judgment and difficulty that he finds personally distressing. His point is not that he *wants* to cast fire on the earth, but that this is the *impact* of his work. Jesus himself will be "*baptized*," a term he uses to describe his suffering (Mark 10:38), and he is challenged by it. This is a rare glimpse into Jesus' personal anguish about his mission. This is hard for him!

"*Do you think that I have come to give peace on earth? No, I tell you, but rather division. For from now on in one house there will be five divided...*"(Luke 12:51-52). Jesus says plainly that he will bring division, specifically within families. It is the separation between believers and unbelievers.

Jesus' words are jarring to us. They clash with our view of him as uniting and bringing peace. Perhaps they even belie that fact that we long to construct a middle-class Jesus supporting happy, well-mannered families.

Following Jesus will require stout conviction that serves him no matter what family does. The point here is not about shunning our families, but about cultivating a commitment level that is not derailed by such deeply painful divisions. We must be prepared for the pain and unpleasantness that has *always* accompanied discipleship because our Master has come to cast fire on the earth.

One Thing to Think About: What has following Jesus meant for my relationships?

One Thing to Pray For: Faithfulness to Jesus in every circumstance

WEEK 8 – FRIDAY

Reading: Luke 13:1-9

Interpreting Tragedy

Some in the crowd share the news of an awful tragedy (Luke 13:1). Pilate, for reasons not revealed, kills some Galileans and mixes their blood with the blood of lambs for sacrifice. Jesus gives us a clue about how to interpret tragedies like this. "*Do you think that these Galileans were worse sinners than all the other Galileans, because they suffered in this way? No, I tell you; but unless you repent, you will all likewise perish*"(Luke 13:2-3). We shouldn't *assume* this is a statement about their lives. A grisly end does not necessarily mean a corrupt life. Instead, Jesus points the focus inward (*"unless you repent, you will all likewise perish"*). *I* will suffer similarly if I am evil. They didn't necessarily suffer this for their evil, but *I* will suffer something for mine.

Jesus brings up another tragedy to emphasize the point. "*Or those eighteen on whom the tower in Siloam fell and killed them: do you think that they were worse offenders than all the other who lived in Jerusalem? No, I tell you; but unless you repent, you will all likewise perish*"(Luke 13:4-5). This incident is slightly different because it is not caused by people, but Jesus' teaching is the same. Don't assume it is because of their sin. Look inside yourself. Jesus' parable of the fruitless fig tree (Luke 13:6-9) ties in with the "repent" theme. One more year is promised—one more chance to bear fruit—and then judgment comes.

Jesus teaches us to interpret tragedy by not spending too much time asking if victims "deserved" it, but instead looking within ourselves. What do I deserve? What do I need to change? Such events bring us up short. They remind us of the brevity of life, the reality of God, and what really matters—*my* standing before God.

One Thing to Think About: What tragedies have I observed that raise deeper questions?

One Thing to Pray For: God's patience as I change to better conform to his will

WEEK 9 – MONDAY

Reading: Luke 13:10-21

Not One More Day of Slavery

It is the Sabbath. God's people are gathered in the synagogue for prayer and study. As Jesus teaches there, a woman enters who is bent over and unable to straighten herself. Jesus calls her over, lays his hands on her, and declares her *"freed from your disability"*(Luke 13:12). She is healed.

The synagogue ruler is furious: *"There are six days in which work ought to be done. Come on those days and be healed, and not on the Sabbath day"*(Luke 13:14). Notice Jesus' reply: *"You hypocrites! Does not each of you on the Sabbath untie his ox or his donkey from the manger and lead it away to water it? And ought not this woman, a daughter of Abraham whom Satan bound for eighteen years, be loosed from this bond on the Sabbath day?"*(Luke 13:15-16). If you untie animals on the Sabbath, can't I free a woman from Satan's bonds today?

Jesus is declaring emphatically that he will not resign her to one more day of slavery! Can we imagine the Allies liberating Auschwitz—and then waiting before releasing the prisoners? Can we imagine American slavery ending, yet no one actually being allowed to go free? Isn't this just taunting? Wouldn't it be ignoring the reality of suffering?

Jesus declares that God—and his work—doesn't take a break for the Sabbath (John 5:17). The fact that man needs rest is not intended to keep us from doing good. Do we discourage people from doing God's work because they do it in the "wrong" way? How do we handle unorthodox expressions of zeal? Do we miss the big, good thing—commitment to Christ or praise to God—because we focus on the seeming impropriety?

One Thing to Think About: Are the needs and suffering of others a priority for me?

One Thing to Pray For: A sense of the urgency of doing God's work

WEEK 9 – TUESDAY

Reading: Luke 13:22-35

Will Those Who Are Saved Be Few?

"*And someone said to him, 'Lord, will those who are saved be few?'*"(Luke 13:23). It is an odd question because it is hard to know the intent of the asker. What does he mean by "saved" and why would he wonder if they would be "few"? Jesus takes this as an opportunity to speak of unexpected candidates for kingdom entry. His answer is yes.

"*Strive to enter through the narrow door. For many, I tell you, will seek to enter and will not be able*"(Luke 13:24). "*Strive*" emphasizes intensity of effort; it is a word we have borrowed as "agonize". Narrow means hard (see Matt 7:14). The way is hard, the gate is narrow, and the people are few. Jesus warns us not to assume that we'll float into the kingdom with ease because just about everyone will. We should expect difficulty.

"*For many, I tell you, will seek to enter and will not be able*"(Luke 13:24). Many will not enter because they only "seek" and do not "strive". Jesus protests "*I do not know you*" despite the fact that they eat and drink with him and hear him teach (Luke 13:25-26). He warns that the kingdom will proceed without them (Luke 13:28) and will be filled with Gentiles in their place (Luke 13:29). His words pack a punch because these people seem to be very close to Jesus.

We cannot afford to reason right or wrong based on numbers. Kingdom entry is not based on majority rule. The many can be wrong. Further, Jesus is not merely saying "try harder" here. It is more akin to "take it seriously." When following Jesus matters most to us, effort takes care of itself.

One Thing to Think About: Am I tempted to take comfort in the fact that other people agree with me or are pleased with me?

One Thing to Pray For: Focus to strive to enter by the narrow door

WEEK 9 – WEDNESDAY

Reading: Luke 14:1-11

Honor Is Given, Not Taken

Jesus eats at a Pharisee's house again. He observes the way the guests choose the places of honor around the table. In ancient society, this was a big deal. The closer you get to the host, the more honor you have. These men are trying to slip into the highest places.

"When you are invited by someone to a wedding feast, do not sit down in a place of honor"(Luke 14:8). Why not? Jesus focuses on the fact that changes can be made in seating. What if you get demoted in favor of someone greater than you (Luke 14:8-9)? How shameful is that? *"But when you are invited, go and sit in the lowest place, so that when your host comes he may say to you, 'Friend, move up higher.' Then you will be honored in the presence of all who sit at table with you"*(Luke 14:10). Jesus' advice is to take the lowest place. Perhaps the host will honor you, but no matter what, you won't be shamed.

"For everyone who exalts himself will be humbled, and he who humbles himself will be exalted"(Luke 14:11). We *will* be humbled or exalted. This is not really about seating. It is about seeking honor, reaching for it, trying to take it. Honor is given, not taken. *"Let another praise you, and not your own mouth; a stranger, and not your own lips"*(Prov 27:2).

In fact, honor comes by *not* seeking it, by giving up on the pursuit of it, and by reaching for (and being content with) the lowest place. Often we are desperate for approval, validation, and applause. We overextend. We compromise. We get distracted. We remain discontent. There is peace in this humility. We are calm and quiet in the lowest place. Only then are we ready to be honored.

One Thing to Think About: Am I more concerned with the approval of others—or of God?

One Thing to Pray For: Courage to willingly choose the lowest place

WEEK 9 – THURSDAY

Reading: Luke 14:12-24

God's Great Feast

Jesus is still eating at the Pharisee's house (Luke 14:1) when someone exclaims, "*Blessed is everyone who will eat bread in the kingdom of God!*"(Luke 14:15). This turns the conversation to God's great feast—the common picture of God's kingdom as a messianic banquet.

Jesus tells a story of a great feast prepared with many invitations offered. Yet the invitees all give lame excuses like needing to see fields, look at oxen, or just hang out with a new wife. The master is angry (Luke 14:21), rescinds his invitation (Luke 14:24), and gives it to others (Luke 14:21-23).

Jesus' teaching refers to Jews who make every excuse and pretext not to hear him. Whether the excuse is the Sabbath, or that he is empowered by Beelzebub, or that his disciples don't fast, or that he eats with tax collectors and sinners, or that he eats and drinks too much, it all sounds the same to God. They are rejecting his offer. They judge themselves unworthy of a place at God's table. He will go to the Gentiles if he must.

To us, it is a reminder that a tremendous gift is offered to us and that it is the height of ingratitude and foolishness to excuse ourselves. Excuses for our disobedience to God are rejections, not reasons. They don't hold water before God.

There is also a reminder here of the offer given to us: a place at God's table with Abraham, Isaac, and Jacob (Luke 13:28-30). Will you be there—or do you have something "better" to do?

One Thing to Think About: What excuses do I tend to make when I disobey God?

One Thing to Pray For: A soft heart to accept God's invitation—even over other things

WEEK 9 – FRIDAY

Reading: Luke 14:25-35

A Decision You Can't Make Standing Up

As great crowds attend Jesus (Luke 14:25), he gives sharp words. To follow him, a disciple must *"hate his own father and mother and wife and children...and even his own life"*(Luke 14:26). He must also *"renounce all that he has"*(Luke 14:33). Jesus is setting discipleship requirements to the crowd: if you think you like me, are you ready to give up *everything*—to surrender *all*? Especially he urges them not to answer too quickly, but to count the cost.

"For which of you, desiring to build a tower, does not first sit down and count the cost, whether he has enough to complete it?"(Luke 14:28). When we build something, we *sit down* and count the cost. We don't rush it. *"Or what king, going out to encounter another king in war, will not sit down first and deliberate whether he is able with ten thousand to meet him who comes against him with twenty thousand?"*(Luke 14:31). Before we go to war, we *sit down* and strategize.

Jesus' repeated use of "sit down" in these verses illustrates the seriousness of this decision. It is the difference between considering buying a pack of gum and buying a car. For the latter, I need to sit down, get my calculator out, and make sure I'm really ready. It's a big decision and I don't want to regret it later. I love Jesus for not pulling the wool over my eyes. He doesn't use sales pitches or fine print. If I follow him, I do it with eyes wide open. In fact, he assures me that *it will cost me*.

Sometimes we get the wrong idea from the stories of the New Testament—that people always made life-changing decisions immediately. Jesus here encourages thought and consideration. Sit down. As teachers, we must give people space to count the cost and make the wise choice, even if it takes a while. It's that important.

One Thing to Think About: Am I truly all in for Jesus—or have I committed more than I'm willing to give?

One Thing to Pray For: Perseverance to remain true to Jesus when my commitment is tested

WEEK 10 – MONDAY

Reading: Luke 15:1-10

God's Great Joy

The Pharisees are again unhappy with Jesus because of his companions. *"This man receives sinners and eats with them"*(Luke 15:2). His proximity to sinners is a problem at Levi's house, at Simon's house, and later at Zacchaeus' house. Their logic is clear: these sinners taint Jesus by association. In this chapter, Jesus tells three stories to recalibrate their view of the lost—especially the thought that they are irredeemable.

"What man of you, having a hundred sheep, if he has lost one of them, does not leave the ninety-nine in the open country, and go after the one that is lost, until he finds it?"(Luke 15:4). This is a human emotion. "What man of you" doesn't drop what we're doing and find our sheep? *"And when he has found it, he lays it on his shoulders, rejoicing. And when he comes home, he calls together his friends and his neighbors, saying to them, 'Rejoice with me, for I have found my sheep that was lost'"*(Luke 15:5-6). When found, we feel tremendous relief and joy. We even want to celebrate with others. The story of the lost coin emphasizes the same elements—loss, search, relief, joy, celebration.

The key connection is this: *"Just so, I tell you, there will be more joy in heaven over one sinner who repents than over ninety-nine righteous persons who need no repentance"*(Luke 15:7). This is how God feels! God rejoices! God celebrates! When God's lost ones come home, there is *"joy in heaven"*! This is God's great joy—and he wants us to celebrate *with* him (Luke 15:6, 9). Can we consider ourselves close to God if we are unmoved by his great joy? Jesus is cultivating in us a compassion for the lost, a desire to join in the search, and a willingness for there to be joy on earth, as there is in heaven.

One Thing to Think About: What is my great joy? Is it God's?

One Thing to Pray For: A shift in my priorities so that God's joy is also mine

WEEK 10 – TUESDAY

Reading: Luke 15:11-32

The Older Brother Syndrome

Jesus has been criticized for receiving tax collectors and sinners (Luke 15:2). He responds by telling three stories where something valuable is lost, then found. But sheep and coins pale in comparison to a son who *"was lost, and is found"*(Luke 15:32). A son leaves home, lives wastefully and sinfully. He is lost. He hits rock bottom and crawls home. Jesus shows us a father who loves, forgives, and rejoices that his son has returned (Luke 15:22-24). These tax collectors (Luke 15:1) are the prodigals. They have lived in evil but have finally come home. God rejoices!

Then there is the older brother. *"But he was angry and refused to go in"*(Luke 15:28). He is resentful of the attention his younger brother gets and what it means—that he is unrewarded and unappreciated. This is the Pharisees—definitively out of step with God and his great joy.

The older brother syndrome means that we (like Jonah) think others are unworthy of God's grace (conveniently forgetting that we are too!). We resent others and the inconvenience they are. We doubt their sincerity, grow frustrated with their weaknesses, and feel a little jealous of the attention they receive from God and others. Or perhaps the syndrome reveals itself most clearly when we—instead of rejoicing with God—reserve judgment to see whether the sinner is really worthy of our kindness.

We should rejoice with God! Connecting to God's heart means celebrating with him when his lost children come home!

One Thing to Think About: Do I ever react skeptically when I see people come (or come back) to God?

One Thing to Pray For: Selfless joy when God's purposes are realized

WEEK 10 – WEDNESDAY

Reading: Luke 16:1-9

The Sneaky Manager

Jesus' odd story features a bad manager who is called to account because he is about to lose his job. This lights a fire under him (Luke 16:3-4). He is suddenly obsessed with the *future*—"what shall I do?"—and uses his master's money to make some friends for the time when he's out of work. He cuts deals, taking huge discounts off of people's bills to make sure they love him (Luke 16:6-7).

His master can't helped but be impressed, even though he has been defrauded. *"The master commended the dishonest manager for his shrewdness"*(Luke 16:8). He has been wise and forward-thinking—although certainly "*dishonest.*"

Jesus tells us the lesson is *not* that we should do business this way. *"And I tell you, make friends for yourselves by means of unrighteous wealth, so that when it fails they may receive you into the eternal dwellings"*(Luke 16:9). We must learn the importance of making friends *before* the time when we need them. Wealth is just one of several tools we can use *now* to prepare for *tomorrow*. The manager's urgency means that he is not worried about managing at the moment, just about impressing the right people.

Jesus expects us to use our wealth in a way that prepares us for the time when wealth fails, anticipating *"the eternal dwellings."* He wants his disciples to leverage wealth to build relationships, bless others, and honor the God who will receive them into eternal dwellings. Do we feel the pressure of what is coming? When all our money and accomplishments fade? When all that will count is the "friends" we have made who can help us in eternity? Are we preparing?

One Thing to Think About: Am I thoughtful for the future *beyond* this life?

One Thing to Pray For: Wisdom to use money rightly

WEEK 10 – THURSDAY

Reading: Luke 16:10-18

God Knows Your Hearts

Jesus follows up his story about the sneaky manager with more discussion of money. "*One who is faithful in a very little is also faithful in much, and one who is dishonest in a very little is also dishonest in much*"(Luke 16:10). Faithfulness—meaning dependability and trustworthiness here—is the key. Our use of money shows God he can trust us. It also reveals whether God has rivals in our hearts: "*You cannot serve God and money*"(Luke 16:13).

This produces a fascinating reaction. "*The Pharisees, who were lovers of money, heard all these things, and they ridiculed him*"(Luke 16:14). They mock Jesus and his message challenging their view of money. He has struck a nerve. Perhaps they think that if they silence him, his words will be less true.

"*And he said to them, 'You are those who justify yourselves before men, but God knows your hearts. For what is exalted among men is an abomination in the sight of God'*"(Luke 16:15). You are worried about what people think, but *God knows your hearts*. God is the one who is measuring your faithfulness. God is the one who will reward. God knows whom you're serving. We can reject Jesus and his words, argue down those who would challenge us, and salve our own consciences, but God knows our hearts.

There is also a positive to this. God knows my heart. People can assign bad motives to my actions. People can misunderstand my words and best efforts. People can criticize and fail to show me compassion. But God knows my heart, and honest, sincere service to him is always noticed.

One Thing to Think About: Is my service to God honest and sincere?

One Thing to Pray For: Faithfulness to God's purposes in the little things

WEEK 10 – FRIDAY

Reading: Luke 16:19-31

A Glimpse behind the Veil

Still with money on his mind, Jesus tells a chilling story that pulls back the veil of what happens after death. A rich man enjoys his riches (Luke 16:19) while Lazarus leads a miserable, poor, needy life (Luke 16:20-21). The shocking part is that their states are *reversed* after death. The rich man is in torment while Lazarus is comforted. This outcome goes strongly against the grain of popular Jewish thought, which held that riches indicate God's favor.

Abraham explains to the rich man, *"Child, remember that you in your lifetime received your good things, and Lazarus in like manner bad things; but now he is comforted here, and you are in anguish"*(Luke 16:25). He also tells the rich man that there is a gulf fixed between comfort and torment with no transfers allowed (Luke 16:26). Our decisions now determine eternity and there are no mulligans or do-overs. These facts lead the rich man to ask for someone to go back and warn his brothers (notably he still sees Lazarus as an errand boy, Luke 16:24, 27).

This parable is a warning shot across the bow of those whose main pursuit in life is *comfort*. God takes our uses of comforts and treatment of others extremely seriously. It is time for introspection. Where do I fit in this story? Am I too concerned about my comfort—physically, spiritually, financially, socially? Do I use for myself resources that others need, turning a blind eye to their desperation?

One Thing to Think About: Am I too comfortable?

One Thing to Pray For: Vision to accept hardship now in anticipation of God's comfort

WEEK 11 – MONDAY

<u>Reading</u>: Luke 17:1-19

The Anti-Entitlement Mantra

Jesus knows the underlying issues in the hearts of his disciples—then and now. In this section he teaches us a mantra to remind us of how we should think about ourselves. *"We are unworthy servants; we have only done what was our duty"*(Luke 17:10).

<u>The servant eats last</u>. *"Will any of you who has a servant plowing or keeping sheep say to him when he has come in from the field, 'Come at once and recline at table'? Will he not rather say to him, 'Prepare supper for me, and dress properly, and serve me while I eat and drink, and afterward you will eat and drink'?"*(Luke 17:7-8). The servant is not the focus and not the honored one. Christ's kingdom means willingly taking a backseat to others, forfeiting our pursuit of personal honor.

<u>The servant doesn't wait for gratitude or praise</u>. *"Does he thank the servant because he did what was commanded?"*(Luke 17:9). When a servant serves, there is nothing exceptional about it. He does not expect anyone to point out what a great job he is doing.

<u>The servant only does his duty</u>. *"We are unworthy servants; we have only done what was our duty"*(Luke 17:10). Duty has become an old-fashioned word in our age because it connotes higher obligations than our age wants to acknowledge. Servants do what they should because they *should*. If so much has been done for us—if we have a place in the kingdom—then high ambitions are entirely uncalled for.

This mantra is anti-entitlement. It eliminates thinking that is centered on "what I deserve" and "my rights" and replaces it with a sense of humble service and doing our duty. If we can apply this mindset to our lives—to our conflicts, our ministry to others, our marriages, our brothers in Christ—think how it will transform us!

<u>One Thing to Think About</u>: Am I prepared to think of myself as an unworthy servant?

<u>One Thing to Pray For</u>: Humility to accept my role

WEEK 11 – TUESDAY

Reading: Luke 17:20-37

The Completely Unexpected Kingdom

Jesus has come to earth during a time of tremendous messianic expectation. It is an era of Roman occupation of Israel, many would-be messiahs, and John the Baptist's "revival" preaching. Jesus' message is consonant with this: *"Repent, for the kingdom of heaven is at hand"*(Matt 4:17).

The common view among the Jews of Jesus' day seems to be that a new golden age is coming and the only mystery is when and where. *"Being asked by the Pharisees when the kingdom of God would come"*(Luke 17:20). Jesus corrects their misconception that they will be able to clearly observe it: *"The kingdom of God is not coming in ways that can be observed, nor will they say, 'Look, here it is!' or 'There!' for behold, the kingdom of God is in the midst of you"*(Luke 17:20-21).

It is staggering to consider that a kingdom could be established and *no one notice*. It is *"in the midst of you"* or *"within you"*—already present, but in a different way than we expect. This explains Jesus' repeated attempts to liken the kingdom of God to some *physical* thing—wheat and weeds (Matt 13:24) or treasure or leaven or a mustard seed or a dragnet (see Matt 13). If it is only a kingdom, why not liken it to a kingdom? Jesus is teaching us about a kingdom that is not physical, but a relationship with God through the reign of Christ. The kingdom is within us.

The rest of this section details another unexpected aspect of this kingdom: it is marked by physical judgment. It will catch people unawares, as in the days of Lot and Noah, and must be greeted by believers with a willingness to suffer for Christ if need be (Luke 17:33). These are not the notes being sounded by the Jews of Jesus' day about the kingdom—and they remain unexpected today.

One Thing to Think About: Is it hard for me to think of the kingdom as real because it's not physical?

One Thing to Pray For: Spiritual perception to see Jesus at work—even in ways I don't expect or foresee

WEEK 11 – WEDNESDAY

Reading: Luke 18:1-14

What Self-Righteous Worship Looks Like

Jesus teaches on prayer here as a demonstration of faith. When we continually ask (Luke 18:5), we show faith (Luke 18:8) and Jesus wants us *"always to pray and not lose heart"*(Luke 18:1). He then tells a story about two men with different kinds of prayers.

"He also told this parable to some who trusted in themselves that they were righteous, and treated others with contempt"(Luke 18:9). Jesus illustrates the worship of the self-righteous and why it doesn't please God. *"The Pharisee, standing by himself, prayed thus: 'God, I thank you that I am not like other men, extortioners, unjust, or even like this tax collector'"*(Luke 18:11). His only need to address God is to thank him that he is different (meaning "better"). *"I fast twice a week; I give tithes of all that I get"*(Luke 18:12). His "prayer" only recounts his deeds of righteousness. He supposedly has come to worship, but this is not about God at all because *he doesn't feel he needs God in order to be righteous*. In fact, there is no need whatsoever in his prayer.

Meanwhile the tax collector has no illusions that he is righteous. That's why he's praying! *"God, be merciful to me, a sinner!"*(Luke 18:13). Jesus pronounces the verdict: *"I tell you, this man went down to his house justified, rather than the other. For everyone who exalts himself will be humbled, but the one who humbles himself will be exalted"*(Luke 18:14). Self-righteousness is merely exalting ourselves. God will correct.

The danger is that over time we begin to trust more in our own goodness—our resumé—than our God. We forget the great need and passion that prompted us to say "God, be merciful to me, a sinner!" We begin to feel pretty good about ourselves ("I'm a pretty good guy!"). We view God less as a fount of every blessing and more as a referee, who only declares that I'm better than others.

One Thing to Think About: Do I tend to think that I am righteous in myself?

One Thing to Pray For: Humility to not look down on others

WEEK 11 – THURSDAY

Reading: Luke 18:15-30

Losing to Gain

The rich young ruler has a lot going for him, but Jesus informs him *"one thing you still lack"*(Luke 18:22). He needs to transfer his treasure from the earthly to the heavenly, specifically by giving to the poor and coming to follow Jesus. He leaves sad, seemingly unwilling to listen to Jesus about this. *"Jesus, seeing that he had become sad, said, 'How difficult it is for those who have wealth to enter the kingdom of God!'"*(Luke 18:24). Wealth can hinder kingdom entrance. In fact, it almost certainly *will* hinder—just as a camel will be hindered from passing through a needle's eye.

Peter responds to Jesus' dire predictions: *"See, we have left our homes and followed you"*(Luke 18:28). Jesus agrees and blesses their willingness: *"Truly, I say to you, there is no one who has left house or wife or brothers or parents or children, for the sake of the kingdom of God, who will not receive many times more in this time, and in the age to come eternal life"*(Luke 18:29-30). When you lose something for the kingdom, you gain it many times more—*and eternal life!* What a deal!

It is only in forsaking things that would hinder our kingdom pursuits that we find them in greater measure. As a Christian, I have far more houses than I can amass by my own wealth—a larger family—all that I need and far more—*and eternal life!* When I lose, I gain.

This leads to yet another examination of my wealth. Have I left anything to follow Jesus? We cannot think that because Jesus is not physically present that he doesn't expect us to leave behind hindrances to the kingdom, even if (*especially* if) they mean a lot to us. Has my perspective been changed to where I know this is truly the *best* way—that when I lose most, I gain most?

One Thing to Think About: When have I seen the "lose to gain" principle work—in my life and others'?

One Thing to Pray For: Vision to see short-term losses as long-term gains

WEEK 11 – FRIDAY

Reading: Luke 18:31-43

A Faith that Won't Be Silenced

Jesus approaches Jerusalem and is well aware of what is about to happen there (Luke 18:31-33). Jericho is near Jerusalem and as he passes through, a great crowd is with him. A blind man by the roadside hears the ruckus. He begins to yell, "*Jesus, Son of David, have mercy on me!*"(Luke 18:38). "Son of David" indicates a high view of Jesus and perhaps a budding belief that he is the Messiah.

Not everyone is pleased with the blind man's shouts. "*And those who were in front rebuked him, telling him to be silent. But he cried out all the more, 'Son of David, have mercy on me!*"(Luke 18:39). The people feel he is an intrusion and a distraction—certainly not what everyone had come to see. Yet the more they try to shut him up, the louder he gets. "*But he cried out all the more.*" So Jesus stops, brings him closer, asks for the specifics, and heals him. "*Your faith has made you well*"—a faith that won't be silenced.

I am struck by the way people would have hindered him—just as the disciples tried to hinder people bringing little children to Jesus (Luke 18:15-16). They would have kept him from Jesus and healing. Yet there is something within him so desperate and determined that he gets louder rather than quieter.

Sometimes people try to hinder us from Jesus. They try to talk us out of it. They try to shame us for our faith. They try to forcibly stop us. Some discourage us through their hypocrisy. We can allow people and their failings to keep us from Jesus. It is doubly tragic for someone else's failure to hinder not just them, but me too. I need Bartimaeus' spirit: *no one will come between me and my Savior!*

One Thing to Think About: What kinds of people, situations, temptations, and thoughts hinder me from coming to Jesus?

One Thing to Pray For: A life that will bring others to Christ—not hinder them

WEEK 12 – MONDAY

Reading: Luke 19:1-10

Seeking Out Zacchaeus

Of all the people in Jericho, Jesus singles out this *"chief tax collector"*(Luke 19:2). He is rich, hated, and viewed as a sinner (Luke 19:7). Yet Jesus tells him, *"I must stay at your house today"*(Luke 19:5). There is urgent business there. For his part, Zacchaeus is interested and excited—he climbs trees and opens up his home (Luke 19:3-4, 6). Perhaps he has been waiting for something like this.

The key issues are clear: *"And Zacchaeus stood and said to the Lord, 'Behold, Lord, the half of my goods I give to the poor. And if I have defrauded anyone of anything, I restore it fourfold'"*(Luke 19:8). How does Zacchaeus use his wealth? How does Zacchaeus react when he sins? His statement reads to me like a new resolution—a statement of repentance. It also could be a declaration of his regular policy (which the people don't understand), in which case Jesus' statement (Luke 19:9) is more focused on the fact that God accepts godly people, even if they are tax collectors.

"For the Son of Man came to seek and to save the lost"(Luke 19:10). Jesus' mission is to seek out the Zacchaeuses of the world and tease out their faith. How many Zacchaeuses are there in my life right now? How many people do I know that are close to the kingdom, ready for a change, only needing a little interest and a push in the right direction? Will I seek them?

One Thing to Think About: Do I find it easier to label people than to reach out to them?

One Thing to Pray For: Thick skin to brave the insults that come with seeking the lost

WEEK 12 – TUESDAY

Reading: Luke 19:11-27

The Quiet Rebellion

As Jesus and the crowd near Jerusalem, some are thinking that the consummation of the kingdom is about to happen. Jesus tells another parable to correct this misconception about the kingdom (remember Luke 17:20-21). The problem in this case is timing because some are thinking that the kingdom *"was to appear immediately"*(Luke 19:11).

In the story, it is plain that some time passes while the nobleman receives the kingdom (Luke 19:12, 15). This was typical in ancient times. An aspiring leader would travel to Rome to get confirmation of his rule, often over the protests of his enemies (Luke 19:14). In the meantime, the king gives money to his servants and upon his return calls them to give account. For what they have earned, they get authority over a city. One servant does nothing, *"for I was afraid of you"*(Luke 19:21). Angry, the king gives his mina to the man with ten minas. Then he deals with his enemies (Luke 19:27).

Jesus describes two types of rebellion and rejection. One is outright: *"we do not want this man to reign over us"*(Luke 19:14). Another is more subtle, and thereby more dangerous. It is the quiet rebellion of laziness and distraction. We rest in our belief in the king, while doing precious little with his blessings while we await his return. Despite his clear expectation that we use his gifts, we rebel in our own quiet way.

You and I are in a similar waiting period. What will the king say to us when he returns?

One Thing to Think About: What am I doing to honor Jesus with all he has given me?

One Thing to Pray For: A spirit of faith (rather than fear) to use my gifts to serve him and others

WEEK 12 – WEDNESDAY

Reading: Luke 19:28-48

The Stones Would Cry Out

Jesus enters Jerusalem riding on a new colt. A multitude of disciples surround the road, calling him king. As we've seen, the thought is common that Jesus is going to Jerusalem for a coronation (Luke 19:38). There is great excitement. Meanwhile the Pharisees are, as ever, nervous. This talk of kings is going too far! *"Teacher, rebuke your disciples"*(Luke 19:39). *"He answered, 'I tell you, if these were silent, the very stones would cry out'"*(Luke 19:40).

Jesus *must* be praised. This is an absolute necessity. This moment, when the Son of God enters the city where God put his name to accomplish God's eternal purpose to redeem mankind, is *so significant* that it *cannot* pass without notice. If people do not praise him, the stones will.

God's people *must* be aware of the times. Jesus weeps over the city for what is going to happen there (Luke 19:41-44). The real shame is that this punishment is *"because you did not know the time of your visitation"*(Luke 19:44). The inanimate creation has more awareness than the people! Something huge is happening and the stones know it, even if God's own people do not.

Jesus still must be praised. Am I praising him?

His people still must be aware of the times. Am I?

One Thing to Think About: What part of this crowd would I have been in?

One Thing to Pray For: Awareness of what God is doing in our time (and a heart to respond accordingly)

WEEK 12 – THURSDAY

Reading: Luke 20:1-26

Truth Is Not Political

Jesus has entered Jerusalem. He is there to die. As he enters the temple, he drives out the buyers and sellers, encroaching on the turf of the chief priests and religious authorities. They take notice and challenge him: *"Tell us by what authority you do these things, or who it is that gave you this authority"*(Luke 20:2). He responds: *"Was the baptism of John from heaven or from man?"*(Luke 20:4). What was John's authority? Answer mine and I'll answer yours!

The question is not difficult to understand or answer, but they have a hard time with it. *"If we say, 'From heaven,' he will say, 'Why did you not believe him?' But if we say, 'From man,' all the people will stone us to death, for they are convinced that John was a prophet'"*(Luke 20:5-6). They aren't concerned about the *true* answer. They only consider the *political dimensions and impact* of their answer. Their opinions are malleable enough to consider either option. They are willing to say whatever will make them look best. So they say *"we do not know."* Jesus rejects this mentality (Luke 20:8). They are not worthy to have their question answered because they are not honest about spiritual things.

Truth is not political. The answers do not change based on who we talk to. We must beware of compromising truth because of the situation. We must remember that our reasoning about spiritual things has an impact, both practically (get baptized by John or not?) and in our understanding (*"we do not know"*). When we are wrong, we must admit it whether it is popular or face-saving or not. To be committed to truth is to accept the consequences of telling the truth, whatever they may be.

One Thing to Think About: When am I tempted to compromise or play down my convictions?

One Thing to Pray For: Courage to speak truth all the time

WEEK 12 – FRIDAY

Reading: Luke 20:27-47

There Will Be a Resurrection

In this last week before his crucifixion, several groups bring their most difficlut questions—their stumpers—to Jesus. He answers them all. The Sadducees deny the resurrection and think they have a "what if" that destroys resurrection theory. There are seven husbands for one woman, with no children. They add legitimacy to the hypothetical by pointing out that this was *Moses'* writing (Luke 20:28). Tell us, Jesus: whose wife will she be in the resurrection?

"But those who are considered worthy to attain to that age and to the resurrection from the dead neither marry nor are given in marriage"(Luke 20:35). Things are different in the resurrection. In particular, there is no death (Luke 20:36). There is no changing states from single to married to widowed to married.

Yet there is something here that must be affirmed. *"But that the dead are raised, even Moses showed, in the passage about the bush, where he calls the Lord the God of Abraham and the God of Isaac and the God of Jacob. Now he is not God of the dead, but of the living, for all live to him"*(Luke 20:37-38). God speaks of himself as the God of many people who are physically dead—yet he continues to be their God. This has staggering implications. Death is not the end of existence or consciousness or our relationship with God.

There *will be* a resurrection. And even if we are unsure of the exact specifications of that body or what that will mean, we trust this because of Jesus. Thankfully, God is not limited by my understanding. That means my loved ones who have passed on still live. It means my own death is not the end. It means I need to be preparing for what is coming *after* this life.

One Thing to Think About: How does my perspective change when I realize that I'm going to live forever?

One Thing to Pray For: Comfort when I face death—and comfort to pass on to others who face it

WEEK 13 – MONDAY

Reading: Luke 21:1-19

An Opportunity to Bear Witness

Jesus has arrived in Jerusalem. As the disciples admire the temple, Jesus makes a disturbing pronouncement: *"As for these things that you see, the days will come when there will not be left here one stone upon another that will not be thrown down"*(Luke 21:6). The disciples scramble: When? How will we know? Jesus gives a long discourse on the destruction of Jerusalem and its temple.

Jesus aims to prepare the disciples for difficult times. Not only will there be the typical troubles of life—wars, earthquakes, famines—but there will also be threats personal to them. *"But before all this they will lay their hands on you and persecute you, delivering you up to the synagogues and prisons, and you will be brought before kings and governors for my name's sake. This will be your opportunity to bear witness"*(Luke 21:12-13). Jesus wants them to determine now that they will not prepare how to answer but simply allow God to speak through them (Luke 21:14-15).

It is notable that amidst all these awful circumstances, Jesus tells them to see it as an *opportunity* to bear witness. No matter what the outcome, when disciples handle persecution for the gospel, they have borne witness. Rather than focusing on mistreatment, worrying about whether they will be saved, or even preparing elaborate speeches, Jesus insists that they focus on their opportunity to advance the message.

If you are like me, the difficulty is in being calm enough to handle the situation with God's wisdom rather than in an emotional way. Even in tough times, our actions have an impact. People are watching.

One Thing to Think About: What opportunities to bear witness has God given me? Do I have a hard time seeing them as opportunities?

One Thing to Pray For: Faith that God will help me know how to answer in a way that honors him

WEEK 13 – TUESDAY

Reading: Luke 21:20-38

My Words Will Not Pass Away

Jesus is predicting the coming destruction of Jerusalem (Luke 21:20). He is warning his people to get out of town when they see armies surrounding the city (Luke 21:21) and read the signs that trouble is brewing (Luke 21:29-31). He also binds the prophecy to the *very* near future: *"Truly, I say to you, this generation will not pass away until all has taken place"* (Luke 21:32).

"Heaven and earth will pass away, but my words will not pass away" (Luke 21:33). Jesus uses the words "pass away" in three ways in this text. 1) The generation will not "pass away" or cease to live before this word is accomplished. 2) Heaven and earth will "pass away" or come to an end. There is a thought-provoking expectation that the current order is not eternal. 3) By contrast, Jesus' words *"will not pass away,"* meaning they will never end, be unfulfilled, or be proven untrue. Jesus is the word that created heaven and earth (John 1:1-3) and his word will continue true even when his creation does not.

We are constantly bombarded by words. We have access to more than ever before. Yet precious few words have staying power and permanent importance. Jesus is telling us that his words are *ironclad* and certain. It is a preposterous claim if he is not God.

His words are not mere suggestions. They are not simply interesting observations about human nature. They are not vague guesses about the future. They are not just reflective of contemporary Jewish thought. They are eternal and will outlive the world. Will I listen? Will I respect his word—follow it—obey it?

One Thing to Think About: Have I ever said anything that won't "pass away"?

One Thing to Pray For: Passion to hear and follow Jesus' words

WEEK 13 – WEDNESDAY

Reading: Luke 22:1-23

Satan Entered Judas

The leaders are looking for a way to kill Jesus but are afraid of upsetting the people, who had lined the roads for his entry and are now hanging on his words (Luke 19:48). They are at an impasse. Something changes in our text: *"Then Satan entered into Judas called Iscariot"* (Luke 22:3).

This has been brewing. Much earlier in his ministry, Jesus asks, *"Did I not choose you, the Twelve? And yet one of you is a devil"* (John 6:70). Just a few days earlier, Judas scolded Mary for "wasting" her ointment on Jesus because he wanted to steal that money out of the moneybox (John 12:1-6). In response to this growing problem, Jesus puts him in charge of the moneybox and invites him to the Passover meal—yet gives him a stern warning (Luke 22:21-22).

We've read several stories of Satan entering and possessing people throughout Luke. Yet most of these are examples of *involuntary* possession, done against the will of the possessed person. When Satan enters Judas here, it is *voluntary* possession. Judas allows himself to be taken over. He has certain characteristic weaknesses—a desire for money, an unwillingness to apply warnings to himself, and an inability to see reality until it is too late. All of these weaknesses conspire—at just the wrong time—to bring about Judas' horrible betrayal.

Voluntary possession—Satan entering us—is still possible today (Rom 6:13, 16). Jesus warns Judas, but he makes it clear that he will not force himself on us if we're willing to surrender ourselves to Satan. If we do, the results will be tragic.

One Thing to Think About: Have I ever surrendered myself to Satan? How did that turn out?

One Thing to Pray For: Strength to resist Satan and heed warnings

WEEK 13 – THURSDAY

Reading: Luke 22:24-46

Praying in Crisis

It is the last night before Jesus' crucifixion and he is keenly aware of what is happening. He teaches the disciples through the Passover meal that what they are sharing has deeper significance because of what is about to happen to him (Luke 22:19-20). He corrects them again about their desire to be the greatest (Luke 22:24-30), warns Peter about his coming denial (Luke 22:31-34), and tells them to bring swords (Luke 22:35-38), probably to highlight the danger coming.

I want to call attention to a thread running through Luke's record: prayer in a time of crisis. Jesus gives thanks (Luke 22:17, 19). He tells Peter, "*I have prayed for you*"(Luke 22:32). He gives instruction: "*Pray that you may not enter into temptation*"(Luke 22:40, 46). And of course, Jesus himself prays in the garden. He kneels and repeats his prayer three times. "*Being in agony, he prayed more earnestly*"(Luke 22:44).

In times of crisis, we often feel *too busy* to pray. In times of crisis, we often feel *too distracted* to pray. Jesus is busy too. And he clearly has something heavy on his mind. *Yet these facts motivate him to pray!* People of faith lean hard on God in times of crisis. Jesus finds strength and comfort—even answers—in his prayers.

In my times of crisis, do I still give thanks? Do I still pray for others? Do I ask God's help with the elephant in the room—the thing that's dominating my mind and heart?

One Thing to Think About: Who do I *long* to talk to when things get hard? Is God on that list?

One Thing to Pray For: Steadfastness to keep talking to God in my difficulties

WEEK 13 – FRIDAY

Reading: Luke 22:47-71

Something Bigger than Fairness

The gospel writers record details that emphasize the innocence of Jesus and the shame and injustice of his seizure, trial, and execution. He is arrested secretly: "*Have you come out as against a robber?*"(Luke 22:52). He is abandoned by his "loyal" followers, denied by his right-hand man, and betrayed by one of the twelve. He is beaten and mocked *pre-trial* (Luke 22:63-65). They trap him in the council with false witnesses and make him testify against himself.

Reading this account leaves me sad and angry all at once. It is so unfair! It isn't right! How could they do this? How could God let this happen? As hard as this has to be for Jesus, his mind has been made up since Gethsemane. Something is driving him that is bigger than fairness. The Hebrew writer says Jesus "*for the joy that was set before him endured the cross, despising the shame*"(Heb 12:2). Jesus has bigger things on his mind in this moment than getting fairness for himself.

Unfairness makes me frustrated and angry. Jesus teaches us that there are more important things than our personal justice. Am I showing mercy? Am I obeying the Father? Am I pursuing God's purposes? Wrongs that need to be righted will be his domain. It is when I try to take my justice into my own hands that the real problems start.

One Thing to Think About: Why do I feel that I must always be treated fairly?

One Thing to Pray For: Vision to see what matters more than personal justice—like Jesus

WEEK 14 – MONDAY

Reading: Luke 23:1-17

Sending Jesus to Herod

The Jewish leaders bring Jesus to Pilate with a different sort of accusation than the night before: *"We found this man misleading our nation and forbidding us to give tribute to Caesar, and saying that he himself is Christ, a king"*(Luke 23:2). Yet very quickly, Pilate declares, *"I find no guilt in this man"*(Luke 23:4). What to do? *"And when he learned that he belonged to Herod's jurisdiction, he sent him over to Herod, who was himself in Jerusalem at that time"*(Luke 23:7). Herod is glad (Luke 23:8) and this exchange helps ease tensions between the two men (Luke 23:12). Pilate is so desperate to dump this decision on someone else that he does something kind to his enemy.

In this week before Jesus' death, everyone is tested—the apostles, the Sanhedrin, the Jewish people, and Pilate himself. All of them must face the question of what they will do with Jesus—and no one else can answer for them. Sadly, all of them fail.

Sending Jesus to Herod reminds me of how we try to avoid making crucial decisions with difficult consequences. Like Pilate, we see the difficulty coming. And like Pilate, we try to foist it (and the responsibility for it) off on others. But the fascinating thing about Jesus is that he insists that *we* make those choices about him. *"Who do you say that I am?"*(Luke 9:20). *"Count the cost"*(Luke 14:28). *"But these are written so that you may believe that Jesus is the Christ, the Son of God, and that by believing you may have life in his name"*(John 20:31).

We can stall, equivocate, and consider, but eventually, choices must be made. I must make them. My morality, my doctrine, my practice, my faith, and my approach to my death are determinations I must make. We can try to outsource these choices, but Jesus won't let us avoid the key questions of life.

One Thing to Think About: Do I try to avoid difficult decisions—especially in my spiritual life?

One Thing to Pray For: Boldness to choose to follow Jesus—especially when the stakes are high

WEEK 14 – TUESDAY

Reading: Luke 23:18-38

Forgive Them, for They Know Not What They Do

The chief priests and rulers have ramrodded Jesus' conviction through and are here at the side of his cross to watch the whole affair end. The cries on the air of "crucify him" and the weeping of many underscore the gloom of the moment. Yet from the cross comes a shocking word: *"Father, forgive them, for they know not what they do"* (Luke 23:34).

He finds compassion for them in their *ignorance*. *"They know not what they do."* They don't understand the significance of this moment. They think they are doing right. They cannot possibly see. This doesn't make them innocent, but it affects the nature of their sin and his view of them.

This is the heart of forgiveness: finding a place to feel compassion, even though others hurt (or kill!) us. Certainly not all of these people will change and find forgiveness. But perhaps Jesus sees in this crowd some who will become his followers. Perhaps there are others who will wrestle internally with the rightness of this act. As he watches them commit this awful deed, he can look forward and see the way this day will haunt so many of them for the rest of their lives. So he prays for their forgiveness.

When we forgive, we must search for this place of compassion. We seek commonality, understanding, and reason for hope.

One Thing to Think About: Is there someone I need to extend forgiveness to—or even pray that they'll be forgiven?

One Thing to Pray For: Reconciliation with those who have wronged me

WEEK 14 - WEDNESDAY

Reading: Luke 23:39-56

The Thief on the Cross

It is absolutely staggering that as Jesus is enduring such pain and shame while dying for the sins of the world, he is still evangelizing. This thief pleases Jesus with his statements of genuine faith. First he rebukes the other thief for mocking Jesus (Luke 23:40). He understands that Jesus is innocent (*"but this man has done nothing wrong"*) while the thieves are not.

But there is one sentence that changes this man's eternal destiny: *"Jesus, remember me when you come into your kingdom"* (Luke 23:42). As he watches Jesus dying, he is confident that he will still come into his kingdom. He asks Jesus to remember *him* even as Jesus is dying. The man believes Jesus is king and that his kingdom will continue through and beyond death. Jesus replies, *"Truly, I say to you, today you will be with me in Paradise"* (Luke 23:43). Jesus promises him, with confidence, that *today* he will be with him in Paradise.

Obviously this is not a pattern for evangelism today. The focus is on Jesus rewarding and producing faith, even in his last moments. Jesus is thoughtful of others and their spiritual state, even as he is dying.

Death is a rubber-meets-road moment in our faith. Do we trust like this? Do we have faith like the thief on the cross?

One Thing to Think About: Do I really believe that Jesus has power over death?

One Thing to Pray For: An obedient faith in King Jesus

WEEK 14 – THURSDAY

Reading: Luke 24:1-12

The Unexpectedly Empty Tomb

After resting on the Sabbath after Jesus' death, the women return to the tomb to anoint his body. But there is no body! Confused (Luke 24:4), they are frightened by men (angels) who explain that Jesus told them all this. *"Remember how he told you"*(Luke 24:6)—and as they remember, they rush back to tell the others, who also don't believe. Peter goes to check it out himself and leaves marveling (Luke 24:12).

It is notable that every disciple here is caught off-guard. They are *"perplexed"*(Luke 24:4), *"frightened"*(Luke 24:5), *"did not believe"*(Luke 24:11), and are left *"marveling"*(Luke 24:12). The empty tomb is not expected. There is no vigil, no sea of witnesses, no "told-you-so"s. They must be reminded of what Jesus said—and *even then* they struggle to believe.

There is comfort in this. It puts to rest the idea that they made this story up. Even the Jewish leaders have a better handle on it than the apostles (see Matt 27:63-66). It is a reminder that *Jesus' words don't rely on our understanding to be true.* Real is real—whether we see it or not.

The empty tomb is something we would not dare to hope for after such an awful death. Yet it is the ultimate statement that the ugliness of this world will not last forever—that there is a happy ending still in store after death.

One Thing to Think About: Would it have been hard for me to believe the tomb was empty?

One Thing to Pray For: Joy at the empty tomb!

WEEK 14 – FRIDAY

Reading: Luke 24:13-35

The Budding of Hope

This is a tender scene of Jesus appearing (after his resurrection) to two disciples walking to another town. As they walk, they are sad (Luke 24:17). When Jesus comes to them, they tell Jesus about Jesus. "*But we had hoped that he was the one to redeem Israel*"(Luke 24:21). Note the past tense: "*we had hoped.*" They are sad because hope is gone. Jesus has died.

Jesus speaks to them about the Scriptures. "*Was it not necessary that the Christ should suffer these things and enter into his glory?*"(Luke 24:26). Jesus broadens the possibilities. Maybe this was all part of the plan! They want to talk more. They recognize Jesus and he disappears. They have been changed by this encounter ("*did not our hearts burn within us while he talked to us*") and they rush back to Jerusalem to tell the others they have seen Jesus.

It is a stark difference between walking and moping—and rushing back with joy. It is the difference between hopelessness and hope. The possibility that something could be true—that something good will happen—motivates and energizes us. It makes *now* better because it holds the promise of a better *future*.

Jesus changes things—for us too—by giving us hope! Could it be? Could it really be?

One Thing to Think About: Am I energetically anticipating something great?

One Thing to Pray For: The "burning heart" set aflame by hope

WEEK 15 – MONDAY

Reading: Luke 24:36-53

A Piece of Broiled Fish

Up to this point, we have only seen quick glimpses of the resurrected Jesus. The angels have declared that he is risen. He appears in veiled form on the road to Emmaus. Peter sees him (Luke 24:34), but we don't read about it. Here, at last, Jesus appears to the whole gathering (Luke 24:36-37). They are afraid and think he is a spirit.

Jesus gives two proofs to convince them. *"See my hands and my feet, that it is I myself. Touch me, and see. For a spirit does not have flesh and bones as you see that I have"*(Luke 24:39). He invites them to touch his hands and feet, marred by the marks of crucifixion. He invites them to see and to touch. This proves he is not a spirit and that he is the same person, bearing the marks they had watched Jesus suffer.

The second proof is food. *"They gave him a piece of broiled fish and he took it and ate before them"*(Luke 24:42-43). After the physical examination, they are still reluctant to believe (for joy, Luke 24:41). This is not an ordinary fish dinner. Jesus eats this fish because it is a concrete proof that he really did appear. It is about *Jesus eating* because a spirit doesn't eat.

In the future, they can always point back to this moment. I felt his hands. I saw him eat. This really happened. It is something concrete. John will say, *"that...which we have seen with our eyes, which we looked upon and have touched with our hands"*(1 John 1:1). The resurrected Jesus is a concrete person—not a spirit—and I watched him eat fish. My hope is rooted in a real bodily resurrection, vindicating Jesus' claims.

One Thing to Think About: Would it be hard for me to believe if I was there?

One Thing to Pray For: Understanding of Jesus' resurrection and the Scriptures

WEEK 15 – TUESDAY

Reading: Mark 1:1-15

The Kingdom of God is at Hand

Mark's writing is spare and fast-moving; 15 verses into his gospel, we have covered Jesus' forerunner, baptism, temptation, and first preaching efforts. We learn quickly that Jesus is an impressive figure. John the Baptist tells us he is "*mightier than I*"(Mark 1:7), he is beloved of the Father (Mark 1:11), and angels minister to him as he resists Satan (Mark 1:13). Everything points to Jesus knowing *exactly* what he is talking about.

"*Jesus came into Galilee, proclaiming the gospel of God, and saying, 'The time is fulfilled, and the kingdom of God is at hand; repent and believe in the gospel*"(Mark 1:14-15). The essence of Jesus' message is that God's kingdom is here. The kingdom of Daniel's and Isaiah's prophecies—the throne of David described throughout the Old Testament—is established. There is restoration and blessing—and the emergence of a kingdom that shall never be destroyed (Daniel 2:44). The heart of Jesus' message is that God is acting in a new way that fulfills all of preceding history in a culminating moment.

It is shocking that many argue that Jesus failed in establishing the kingdom that Mark says characterizes his message. Jesus *is* a king. His followers (or subjects) are his people—his disciples, later described as his church. Jesus ushers in something new, but old—the idea of God saving again, but in a newer, deeper way.

One Thing to Think About: Does picturing Jesus as my *king* change my view of him?

One Thing to Pray For: Faith in and submission to God's new way of acting through Jesus

WEEK 15 – WEDNESDAY

Reading: Mark 1:16-34

Fishers of Men

This is likely not Jesus' first encounter with Peter, Andrew, James, and John. At the very least we know that Andrew previously was a follower of John the Baptist (John 1:40-42). That helps explain why they follow so readily when Jesus calls. Jesus calls "*and immediately they left their nets and followed him*"(Mark 1:18). James and John "*left their father Zebedee in the boat with the hired servants and followed him*"(Mark 1:20). They are leaving behind careers to walk with Jesus.

"*Follow me, and I will make you become fishers of men*"(Mark 1:17). This is a unique appeal for fishermen. He does not simply say that they will catch men, but that "*I will make you become*" men-fishers. Jesus is promising to change them into something they are not yet. Jesus has the power to alter our character and personality to make us into what we are not. This especially occurs as we shift our priorities to mirror his.

To be fishers of men—bringing men in to God, casting nets for men—is a higher work than mere fishing. It connects men to God. Jesus offers personal transformation, a higher purpose, and a connection with God. He makes good on his offer to the disciples—and offers the same to us.

One Thing to Think About: How has Jesus changed my life—my character—my personality?

One Thing to Pray For: A part in God's great work of men-fishing

WEEK 15 – THURSDAY

Reading: Mark 1:35-45

An Early Morning Prayer

Things are moving quickly in Jesus' ministry. His fame has spread throughout Galilee (Mark 1:28)—particularly in Capernaum, where the whole city has just gathered to be healed (Mark 1:33).

"And rising very early in the morning, while it was still dark, he departed and went out to a desolate place, and there he prayed" (Mark 1:35). Though probably exhausted, he gets up very early—in the dark—to go somewhere to be alone and pray. The crowds are great, but they make it hard to pray and focus. Jesus is not neglecting people by doing this. For him, prayer is something that *must* be done.

Peter and the others search for him and tell him that *"everyone is looking for you"* (Mark 1:37). There is work to do! People want more of you! Surely the disciples are breathlessly excited at the growing popularity of Jesus. *"And he said to them, 'Let us go on to the next towns, that I may preach there also, for that is why I came out'"* (Mark 1:38). Jesus informs them that on the heels of his success in Capernaum, it is (surprisingly?) time to move on.

Prayer is a time to reconnect with God and his purpose, silencing the voices of the world. It is no coincidence that Jesus emerges from prayer with a clearer sense of mission (*"this is why I came out"*). Prayer is a time to gain perspective, to remember what's important, and to pace ourselves in our lives. Reread that sentence and it becomes clear why prayer is essential for God's people—including Jesus.

Jesus makes time to pray in a busy schedule. We will have to make time as well.

One Thing to Think About: Why do I find other things more important than prayer?

One Thing to Pray For: Proper perspective on life

WEEK 15 – FRIDAY

Reading: Mark 2:1-12

Which Is Easier?

In this section, Jesus returns to Capernaum, his "home base." He is "*at home*"(Mark 2:1)—perhaps referring to Peter's house (Mark 1:29)—and a great crowd has gathered again. As he preaches, there are sounds from above as someone is busting a hole in the roof. There is urgency in their action. It cannot wait until tomorrow (and who knows when Jesus will leave again?).

"*And when Jesus saw their faith, he said to the paralytic, 'Son, your sins are forgiven'*"(Mark 2:5). Jesus deliberately provokes those around him by speaking of sins rather than healing. The scribes reject this ("*Who can forgive sins but God alone?*", Mark 2:7). Jesus responds: "*Which is easier, to say to the paralytic, 'Your sins are forgiven,' or to say, 'Rise, take up your bed and walk'?*"(Mark 2:9). Which is easier to say? It is easier to talk about sins being forgiven because sins are invisible and forgiveness is impossible to prove. But...

"'*But that you may know that the Son of Man has authority on earth to forgive sins'—he said to the paralytic—'I say to you, rise, pick up your bed, and go home'*"(Mark 2:10-11). If I can do the harder thing I say, I can do the easier thing I say too. If I can tell a paralyzed man to walk and he does, then what about when I tell someone their sins are forgiven? Jesus is asserting power over both the body and the soul.

Jesus' healing power is amazing, but that's not the real story. The people he heals will eventually die. The real story is about a power affecting *eternal* states—spiritual cleansing, forgiveness. Reading this story reminds me of the old hymn "Victory in Jesus," where after singing about Jesus healing the lame and the blind, we declare, "Then I cried, dear Jesus, come and heal my broken spirit." This is the healing we all seek—easier to say, but harder to do—that will truly matter forever.

One Thing to Think About: If I saw Jesus heal someone with a word, would it help me believe his teaching?

One Thing to Pray For: Forgiveness—the healing I need most

WEEK 16 – MONDAY

Reading: Mark 2:13-22

Follow Me

This section takes us back to Jesus' call of Peter, Andrew, James, and John—"*follow me.*" Here it is Levi (Matthew), a Jew sitting in the tax booth. He is working for the Romans. Has he compromised his integrity, as so many tax collectors did? Has he betrayed his people? If the others are a pattern, then this is likely not the first time he has seen Jesus. Perhaps he knows Jesus and his teaching, making this call a challenge to give his life over to what he has heard. Mark's emphasis is on *what they left* (nets, boats, tax booth) and *why* (to follow Jesus).

"Follow me" means *priority*. Levi physically leaves his tax booth (Mark 2:14). Nothing matters more than answering this call. Our society denigrates this kind of action, decrying it as out of balance. How can you leave your job? How will you provide for yourself? But for Levi (as well as the rest of the apostles), the spiritual sets the tone. It is the highest priority and the call that must be answered first. Everything else must adjust to its supremacy. This priority is symbolized by leaving, usually with great urgency.

"Follow me" means *commitment*. Jesus is not simply asking for a statement of faith, but the embrace of a new lifestyle. "Follow" is continual. These men will walk, study, and grow. They will learn to teach, to trust, and to pray. This pushes against the transactional view of Christianity that asks "what do I get if I follow Jesus?" and instead asks "What can I do for him?".

We follow—and as we follow, we are changed, deepened, matured, and re-created.

One Thing to Think About: Am I a follower of Jesus?

One Thing to Pray For: God's growth as I follow Jesus

WEEK 16 – TUESDAY

Reading: Mark 2:23-3:6

The Sabbath Was Made for Man

In the middle of this set of passages emphasizing the hostility, complaints, and rejection Jesus receives, his disciples walk through the fields on the Sabbath and pluck heads of grain. *"And the Pharisees were saying to him, 'Look, why are they doing what is not lawful on the Sabbath?'"*(Mark 2:24). Technicality! This is not lawful! Jesus responds that David did something similar (Mark 2:25-26), but the Pharisees don't try to condemn *him*.

"And he said to them, 'The Sabbath was made for man, not man for the Sabbath'"(Mark 2:27). God made the Sabbath to *bless* man—to ensure that he rests, isn't constantly fixated on work, and takes care of himself. We need this balance. This is good for us. God had people in mind when he made this law.

But these Jews have twisted the Sabbath, as if man were made for the Sabbath. In their minds, the Sabbath was an inviolable law and our job is simply to keep it, whether it's good for us or not. This is the only explanation for how they accuse hungry men eating and sick men being healed of Sabbath violations.

There is also something deeper than the Sabbath here. Jesus is teaching us that God doesn't give us law to restrict us or bother us, but to *bless* us. His laws are for our good. We keep them, but not as an end in themselves. We keep them as an act of trust in the God behind them, assured that they are an expression of his love.

One Thing to Think About: When have I experienced that God's law is a blessing?

One Thing to Pray For: A deeper understanding of God's intent in his law—like Jesus has

WEEK 16 – WEDNESDAY

Reading: Mark 3:7-19

The Messianic Secret

"*And he strictly ordered them not to make him known*"(Mark 3:12). This ties in with other passages in the gospel where Jesus forbids people telling about him and his deeds (Mark 1:44, 5:43, 7:36, 8:30, Matt 9:30). This strikes us as so strange. If God is acting decisively in history and bringing good news for man, why restrict the message?

One reason is *witnesses*. Jesus doesn't need or want the testimony of demons, as in this passage. The demons will shortly become a problem (Mark 3:22) as onlookers mistakenly think he is in league with Satan. When the time is right, Jesus will have the witnesses he chooses, but in this case silence is preferable. This, however, doesn't account for telling the healed to be quiet.

Another reason is *managing his ministry*. Jesus tells the healed leper not to tell anyone (Mark 1:44). When he tells anyway, the crowds gather so that Jesus "*could no longer openly enter a town*"(Mark 1:45). Jesus' popularity is sometimes a problem for his own peace. It also sometimes inhibits healings—like the paralytic who can't get to him, Bartimaeus who is silenced by the crowds, or even Zacchaeus who must climb a tree to see him. There will come a time when the word spreads all over, but Jesus manages his ministry until then.

Another reason for the secrecy is *approach*. Matthew ties the command of silence to his approach as Messiah (Matt 12:16-21), especially the idea that "*he will not quarrel or cry aloud, nor will anyone hear his voice in the streets*"(Matt 12:19). Jesus is not just seeking a crowd or more concerned about numbers than people. He wants to encourage faith on a personal level. After his resurrection, things change. Now the gospel is preached, constraints are lifted, and nothing is secret. Praise God!

One Thing to Think About: Would I have the discipline to restrict the message if I were in Jesus' shoes?

One Thing to Pray For: Praise for God's wisdom and grace

WEEK 16 – THURSDAY

Reading: Mark 3:20-35

Blasphemy

This scene highlights two derogatory opinions about Jesus. His family concludes that *"he is out of his mind"*(Mark 3:21) and the Jerusalem scribes believe he is both possessed by Beelzebul and empowered by him (Mark 3:22). Jesus hears and knows about these accusations, yet his response does not spring from personal offense.

"Truly, I say to you, all sins will be forgiven the children of man, and whatever blasphemies they utter, but whoever blasphemes against the Holy Spirit never has forgiveness, but is guilty of an eternal sin"(Mark 3:28-29). Jesus makes a distinction between concern about blasphemy against *him* and blasphemy against God and his empowering Spirit. At another time, when a similar accusation is made (John 8:48-50), Jesus acknowledges their dishonor for him but is more concerned about their dishonoring of God.

These men are in danger not just of insulting a Galilean rabbi, but of speaking evil against God and his Spirit. These are serious matters.

Words mean things. They reflect my heart and show respect (or lack thereof). Care must be shown in what I say.

Like Jesus, my primary concern should not be for whether people honor *me*, but whether they honor *God*.

One Thing to Think About: Am I careful with my words—especially in speaking about God?

One Thing to Pray For: The humility of Jesus

WEEK 16 – FRIDAY

Reading: Mark 4:1-13

The Master Parable

The parable of the sower is one of Jesus' best-known. It has the classic features of his parables—it is simple, uses common images to illustrate spiritual truth, and reveals the nature of God's work. *"Do you not understand this parable? How then will you understand all the parables?"*(Mark 4:13). Jesus puts special emphasis on *this* parable. If you can't get this one, how will you get the rest?

The sower is the master parable. It is the most important because it is about *hearing*. If our hearing is damaged, *"how then will you understand all the parables?"* Jesus focuses on the fact that the word is not planted in neutral territory. It lands in a heart (soil) with certain characteristics.

While this information seems primarily intended to help the apostles interpret the results of the gospel as they preach it, Jesus' question points at them. If you don't understand, are you the wayside? Shallow? Overgrown?

It is a call for us to pay attention to the way we listen to the word of God. This is not about a physical act, but how we accept or resist it, how much we let it affect us, and what practical change (fruit) it brings. If we understand and obey, more will be given (Mark 4:24-25). Our understanding deepens and new levels of knowledge and change can be reached. God's word bears fruit.

One Thing to Think About: When was the last time I allowed God's word to make practical changes in my life, attitude, words, or relationships?

One Thing to Pray For: A good heart to bear fruit for God

WEEK 17 – MONDAY

Reading: Mark 4:14-25

The Word-Chokers

As Jesus explains the parable of the sower, he details why the gospel doesn't always have the life-altering effects it should. I want to call attention to the thorns that choke the word: "*but the cares of the world and the deceitfulness of riches and the desires for other things enter in and choke the world, and it proves unfruitful*"(Mark 4:19).

The cares of the world. These are physical concerns. They include all our financial cares—careers, bills, planning for the future. Bodily health and exercise go here as well. These concerns have their place, but like cutting back thorns, we must constantly choose to make them secondary to the growth and nourishing of our spirits.

The deceitfulness of riches. Money makes empty promises; it is deceitful. What initially is concern for survival easily grows into the love of comfort and the desire to live well. God's word is a threat to this (as we have seen throughout the gospels), so we try to serve two masters, blunting the impact of Jesus' teaching.

The desires for other things. This is the heart that just wants to be elsewhere. It loves God, but loves other things more. Hobbies, people, fun—fill in the blank of your favorite thing. Jesus warns that these loves are a threat to the word.

Jesus is not speaking here about people who don't care about the word or God. He is aiming for those who love to hear but have other allegiances that keep them from obeying. Is that me?

One Thing to Think About: What habits, cares, allegiances, or desires do I have that keep me from uninterrupted connection with God?

One Thing to Pray For: Courage to put Jesus first

WEEK 17 – TUESDAY

Reading: Mark 4:26-34

He Knows Not How

Jesus uses lots of agricultural images to explain what the kingdom is like. This is one we often overlook. A man scatters seed, then goes to sleep. The seed sprouts and grows but *"he knows not how"*(Mark 4:27), meaning it is not because of his knowledge or power. *"The earth produces by itself"*(Mark 4:28) and all the man does is reap when it's time (Mark 4:29).

Jesus is teaching us that it is in the nature of the kingdom (and the word of the kingdom) to *grow*. This also seems to be a part of the leaven image (Matt 13:33). God's kingdom is an active, living force that does its work without the knowledge or help of people. We plant the seed and it grows, but we know not how.

Part of the point also seems to be that it is not dependent on man in any way. It will grow no matter what we do. So we can never take credit for the growth of the seed. We are only the person who sows and reaps while God does the work.

Jesus encourages us to have faith in God's work and to give him praise when we see his work in our lives and others'.

One Thing to Think About: How has God been working on people in my life?

One Thing to Pray For: A faith that sows and waits for God

WEEK 17 – WEDNESDAY

Reading: Mark 4:35-41

Peace! Be Still!

This is a significant storm. As experienced as these Galileans are in navigating the sea, they are convinced that they are going to die (*"we are perishing"*, Mark 4:38). They are panicked. Meanwhile, Jesus is asleep.

"And he awoke and rebuked the wind and said to the sea, 'Peace! Be still!' And the wind ceased, and there was a great calm"(Mark 4:39). Peace! Be still! Jesus speaks to the wind and sea as if they are people—underlings, more specifically. He issues commands.

Jesus speaks here as master of his creation, like a parent when his child will obey only his voice. Jesus made all this and it does his bidding. He turns water (his creation) into wine (also his creation). He walks on water. He multiplies bread, violating any number of laws of physics and chemistry (he made those laws too).

We have no control over weather—and precious little control over nature in any way. Power like this outstrips ours. Yet it leaves us astonished that such a God could think so much of *us*—when we are powerless and so often rebellious. If Jesus can still storms with a word, what can he do *to* me? What can he do *for* me?

One Thing to Think About: What in my life do I tend to panic about?

One Thing to Pray For: Peace in trusting the power of God

WEEK 17 – THURSDAY

Reading: Mark 5:1-20

Jesus and the Pigs

Jesus encounters a man with a miserable existence. He is beset by a legion of demons. He breaks the chains intended to help him. He cries out and cuts himself. He must live in the tombs rather than with people. Luke says that he is naked (Luke 8:27). The demons who inhabit him beg Jesus to send them into the pigs, which he does, and they then drown the pigs. It is a strange story.

When the people come out of the city, they see everything. The man is now in his right mind and the pigs are gone—or perhaps their bodies are visible in the water. "*And they began to beg Jesus to depart from their region*"(Mark 5:17). They are presumably disturbed because of this destruction of property—or perhaps they have a nebulous fear of spiritual activity. So Jesus leaves. The man wants to be with Jesus (Mark 5:18-19), but Jesus tells him to go tell his friends. He will be more effective in this place than Jesus.

I can't fully explain why Jesus allows this fate to the pigs, but it is obvious that he acts out of concern for this man. Jesus values this man more than the pigs. He is willing to help people and liberate them from suffering at almost any cost.

It is possible that we act like the townspeople: get rid of our problems, but save our pigs! We tend to not like the inconvenience and cost of Jesus' work to remove our sins. We want blessings without sacrifice. But Jesus balks at this. It is not how he works. Having Jesus free us from Satan's power is worth whatever it costs us.

One Thing to Think About: Is it possible that Jesus has reasons for doing things that I'm not privy to?

One Thing to Pray For: Opportunities to tell how much the Lord has done for me

WEEK 17 – FRIDAY

Reading: Mark 5:21-43

Do Not Fear, Only Believe

Jairus, out of options, comes to Jesus about his 12-year-old daughter. She is at the point of death. He believes Jesus might be able to help and even has a vision of how that would look: *"Come and lay your hands on her, so that she may be made well and live"*(Mark 5:23).

As they travel to his house, a couple of things happen. A woman with a flow of blood draws his attention. Jairus must be encouraged by this, while still frustrated because of the urgency of his daughter's situation. Perhaps Jesus' power is legitimate! Then messengers tell him his daughter has died. He is devastated and probably frustrated by the delay.

At this moment Jesus speaks: *"Do not fear, only believe"*(Mark 5:36). The fear here is of the new reality in which his daughter is dead. It is terrifying and hurtful and sad. Jairus goes into the room with him and watches Jesus raise his daughter. He is overcome with amazement (Mark 5:42).

By saying, *"Do not fear, only believe"*(Mark 5:36), Jesus juxtaposes fear and faith (Mark 4:40). They are incompatible. Fear anticipates bad things, as if anticipation will lessen the pain of them. It can limit faith because faith is optimistic where fear is pessimistic. God is able. Jesus challenges us to trust him instead of our fear.

One Thing to Think About: How do my fears challenge my faith?

One Thing to Pray For: Faith that God really is bigger than the things I fear

WEEK 18 – MONDAY

Reading: Mark 6:1-13

Isn't This the Carpenter?

Jesus has a rough homecoming. Surely word has gotten back to Nazareth of all he has been doing in Capernaum and around the Sea of Galilee. As he teaches in his hometown synagogue, gazing into the faces of his old babysitters and boyhood companions, they are scandalized. *"Where did this man get these things? What is the wisdom given to him? How are such mighty works done by his hands?"*(Mark 6:2). Particularly it is Jesus' wisdom and works that trouble the Nazarenes. They are undeniably awesome, but this is incompatible with the mundane facts about Jesus they already know. *"Where did <u>this man</u> get <u>these things</u>?"*

"'Is not this the carpenter, the son of Mary and brother of James and Joses and Judas and Simon? And are not his sisters here with us?' And they took offense at him"(Mark 6:3). Isn't this the carpenter? Don't we know his family? There's nothing remarkable or notable about Jesus or his family. They are so decidedly ordinary. Jesus responds: *"A prophet is not without honor, except in his hometown and among his relatives and in his own household"*(Mark 6:4). It is hard for us to appreciate spectacular people that we know well. They are known quantities. Sadly, the Nazarenes react in such a way that they cause Jesus to marvel and drive him away.

A couple of lessons for us: <u>There is a difference in knowledge about Jesus and faith in him</u>. These people know him better than anyone (think of the stories they can tell!) but still don't believe. There is a danger that we become masters of the information about Jesus without ever translating it into faith. Further, <u>familiarity can be an enemy of faith</u> (Mark 6:4). We can know Jesus so well—hear his stories so often, sing of his love so regularly—that we lose the sense of awe he is due.

One Thing to Think About: Is it hard for me to believe that an ordinary carpenter from Nazareth was actually God's Son?

One Thing to Pray For: Knowledge that leads to and deepens my faith

WEEK 18 – TUESDAY

Reading: Mark 6:14-29

Up to Half My Kingdom

This is a dark story. A good man stands up for God's law, speaks out as a prophet against evil, and is killed for his efforts. The spotlight in this story is on Herod, a conflicted and contradictory figure. He stops Herodias from killing John for his message because he views him as righteous and holy (Mark 6:19-20). He is perplexed, but hears him gladly (Mark 6:20). He respects John, but doesn't do what he says. It is a stalemate.

"*But an opportunity came*"(Mark 6:21). An opportunity for evil arises when Herodias' daughter dances before the men. The tone of the passage and setting imply that it is more than excellent footwork that impresses the men. It is a sensuous dance which (perhaps combined with alcohol) causes Herod to utter fateful, haunting words: "*Whatever you ask me, I will give you, up to half my kingdom*"(Mark 6:23). Consulting with her mother, she asks—with half the kingdom on the table!—for a man to be killed. This shows the extent of Herodias' hatred.

"*And the king was exceedingly sorry, but because of his oaths and his guests he did not want to break his word to her*"(Mark 6:26). Herod, again a contradiction, does something he is sorry for. And so, for the testimony of God's word—and through the failure of another man—a good man dies.

Herod shows the danger of holding truth at arm's length—and of keeping evil people close by. When an opportunity for evil comes, he stands no chance.

One Thing to Think About: Am I ever reluctant to do what I know is right—hedging my bets?

One Thing to Pray For: Courage to stand like John—not like Herod

WEEK 18 – WEDNESDAY

Reading: Mark 6:30-44

Sheep Without a Shepherd

After the news of John the Baptist's death, Jesus encourages the disciples to withdraw with him so that they can rest and get away. But they can't! People run to get there ahead of them (Mark 6:33). Rather than being annoyed, Jesus has compassion.

"When he went ashore he saw a great crowd, and he had compassion on them, because they were like sheep without a shepherd. And he began to teach them many things"(Mark 6:34). He sees that the reason for their passion is not a lack of boundaries. It springs from deep need. Matthew says they are *"harassed and helpless"*(Matt 9:36). Sheep without a shepherd are pitiful and deeply needy. They are unable to protect themselves and lack direction.

Jesus shows his heart for people. *This* is why he's here! So he teaches (Mark 6:34). His compassion is primarily for *spiritual* need. These people love God but they don't know what God needs and wants from them right now. As it gets late, he wants to provide for the physical needs of people who have sought the kingdom first today. He turns five loaves and two fish into a meal for thousands of seekers.

Jesus sees past the annoyance—past the inconvenience—past the lack of understanding—and continues to work out of a heart full of compassion.

One Thing to Think About: Do I think about others—even the annoying—with compassion?

One Thing to Pray For: Awareness of—and concern for—the spiritual needs of others

WEEK 18 – THURSDAY

Reading: Mark 6:45-56

Confused, Terrified, Astounded

After this intense day of teaching and feeding, Jesus wants to be alone to pray. "*Immediately he made the disciples get into the boat*"(Mark 6:45). He makes them go to the other side of the sea before him. This implies he will meet up with them, but how? When? There are no boats where he is (John 6:22).

After the disciples leave Jesus, the long day gets longer. They are trying to get to Bethsaida, but "*the wind was against them*"(Mark 6:48) to the degree that they are still on the water during the fourth watch (3:00-6:00 A.M.). "*He came to them, walking on the sea. He meant to pass by them, but when they saw him walking on the sea they thought it was a ghost, and cried out, for they all saw him and were terrified*"(Mark 6:48-50). They see him and are terrified. Are they frightened that Jesus is dead? Or just spooked by the possibility of a ghost nearby?

"*But immediately he spoke to them and said, 'Take heart; it is I. Do not be afraid.' And he got into the boat with them, and the wind ceased. And they were utterly astounded*"(Mark 6:50-51). Jesus reassures them. He gets into the boat with them and the wind they've been fighting stops. They are astounded. They have seen something new and unforgettable.

The disciples' reactions to Jesus run the whole gamut—from confused to terrified to astounded. This reminds us that Jesus is not ho-hum. Authentic engagement with Jesus produces emotions—real emotions like confusion, terror, marveling. Is that still happening in my spiritual life?

One Thing to Think About: When was the last time I felt confused, terrified, or amazed by Jesus?

One Thing to Pray For: Fresh eyes to see Jesus' amazing power

WEEK 18 – FRIDAY

Reading: Mark 7:1-23

What Defiles Us?

The Pharisees are concerned that Jesus' disciples are eating with "*defiled*" hands (Mark 7:2, 5) by not washing, as the tradition of the elders instructs. There are two issues here—the issue of following traditions as if they are divine and the nature of what defiles us.

The Jewish mentality (or at least its Pharisaic permutation) on defilement is well documented by Mark: "*When they come from the marketplace, they do not eat unless they wash. And there are many other traditions that they observe, such as the washing of cups and pots and coper vessels and dining couches*"(Mark 7:4). They are consumed with the possibility of accidentally picking up defilement in everyday commerce. Taken to an extreme, this mindset fears the world around it because even unintentional contact has an impact on my worship and standing before God.

Jesus stands against this. "*There is nothing outside a person that by going into him can defile him, but the things that come out of a person are what defile him*"(Mark 7:15). Nothing outside us defiles us. This is not where sin and corruption occur. Mark makes clear that this even applies to food (Mark 7:19). True defilement comes from within, from our hearts (Mark 7:20-23). It is not money or relationships or substances that defile. It is our desire to use those things in evil ways or toward evil ends.

No one—nothing—can *make* me sin. I don't accidentally contract sin. Others can influence me, but it is ultimately my choice and comes from my heart. If my heart is pure and determined to do right, no circumstance can defile me.

One Thing to Think About: Do I tend to blame others—or the situation—or myself—when I sin?

One Thing to Pray For: Pure actions that spring from a purified heart

WEEK 19 – MONDAY

Reading: Mark 7:24-37

He Has Done All Things Well

Mark makes only brief reference (Mark 7:24-30) to Jesus' trip to Tyre and Sidon. As he returns to Galilee, he encounters a man who is deaf and dumb. The text makes clear that these are two separate problems. Jesus tries for privacy (Mark 6:33) and tries to contain the report of the healing (Mark 6:36) but neither is particularly successful.

Jesus does some things with spit (Mark 6:33) but it is his words that produce the real change. "*And looking up to heaven, he sighed and said to him, 'Ephphatha,' that is, 'Be opened'*"(Mark 6:34). Just as he tells the sea to "be still," he tells this man's ears to be opened.

"*And they were astonished beyond measure, saying, 'He has done all things well. He even makes the deaf hear and the mute speak'*"(Mark 7:37). "He has done all things well" focuses on how varied a ministry Jesus has. He is not a one-trick pony. Everyone they bring to him, he heals: demons, paralytics, lepers, blind, deaf, mute, and even the dead! Jesus has no specialty. He does all things well. But clearly this begs deeper inspection for them. Miracles of unexpected or higher order not only astonish, but bring up identity questions. "*Who then is this?*"(Mark 4:41).

Nothing is a throwaway for Jesus and there is nothing outside his expertise. No teaching he gives is unimportant or ignorable. This pushes us toward complete trust. He has done *all things* well.

One Thing to Think About: Have I found anything that Jesus does not do well?

One Thing to Pray For: Trust in Jesus in *all things*—especially the hard things

WEEK 19 – TUESDAY

Reading: Mark 8:1-21

Two Good Ways to Frustrate Jesus

In this section we see Jesus get into an argument with the Pharisees and chew out the disciples. The first causes him to sigh deeply in his spirit (Mark 8:12). The second leaves him exasperated: *"Do you not yet understand?"*(Mark 8:17, 21).

The Pharisees are testing him (Mark 8:11-12), seeking a sign (right on the heels of him feeding the 4000 miraculously). He has produced many signs, but all have been rationalized and explained away. It is <u>insincerity from religious people</u> that frustrates Jesus. They know the right words and talk about the right things, but not from the right heart.

The disciples are in a different boat (pun intended). They are not processing Jesus' spiritual concerns. They take his warnings about the *"leaven of the Pharisees"* to be criticism about their failure to remember to bring bread (Mark 8:15-16). Jesus wants them to trust that he'll take care of bread and to see the danger of the influence and teaching of the Pharisees. It is <u>failing to mature spiritually</u> that frustrates him here.

It is not a stretch to say that these things frustrate Jesus today. Insincerity won't fool him. Immaturity won't please him. Do I mean what I'm saying and doing for Jesus? Is my heart in it? Am I growing and deepening my understanding? Am I walking by faith?

One Thing to Think About: What would it feel like to get chewed out by Jesus?

One Thing to Pray For: Pure motives in my search for truth

WEEK 19 – WEDNESDAY

Reading: Mark 8:22-33

But Who Do You Say That I Am?

As he walks with his disciples, Jesus asks an interesting question. *"Who do people say that I am?"*(Mark 8:27). It sounds like he is asking for a report on popular opinion—the word on the street. How are we doing? Lots of opinions are floating around: *"John the Baptist; and others say, Elijah; and others, one of the prophets"*(Mark 8:28). Most seem to identify Jesus with other figures, seeing certain similarities. The people think Jesus is a big deal and part of God's action in the world—a prophet, at the least.

"But who do you say that I am?"(Mark 8:29). What about you? What do you think? Do you line up with them? Obviously those who once were John the Baptist's disciples know Jesus isn't John the Baptist. Jesus has also talked about John the Baptist being Elijah. *"Peter answered him, 'You are the Christ'"*(Mark 8:29). You are not a prophet, but *the* prophet—the promised Messiah.

I am fascinated by what Jesus does here. By asking *"who do you say that I am?"*, he pushes the question onto *me*. There comes a time when I must decide what *I* believe. I must account for myself. I cannot simply rest on what others say or report on popular opinion or stick with my parents.

The question of Jesus' identity is still vital. It remains the key to everything. What do I believe and say about him?

One Thing to Think About: What do *I* believe about Jesus?

One Thing to Pray For: Courage to confess my faith—no matter what others say

WEEK 19 – THURSDAY

Reading: Mark 8:34-9:13

Profit

Jesus challenges his disciples: "*If anyone would come after me, let him deny himself and take up his cross and follow me*"(Mark 8:34). Following Jesus includes denying our own desires and ambitions. Disciples also must expect suffering because of our connection to Jesus and devotion to the Father's will.

"*For whoever would save his life will lose it, but whoever loses his life for my sake and the gospel's will save it*"(Mark 8:35). "Save his life" here refers to our highest desire. Am I focused on self-preservation or obedience? This question will matter soon for the disciples in the garden—and the gloomy tone of it speaks to us as we remain in a world hostile to Jesus and his people.

"*For what does it profit a man to gain the whole world and forfeit his soul? For what can a man give in return for his soul?*"(Mark 8:36-37). Jesus challenges us to think in terms of profit—a benefit that outweighs a cost. If we cling to our life so strongly that we forsake Jesus, no benefit outweighs the cost. The reason is that we have really *forfeited* our life (Mark 8:35). Jesus' logic is that when we let go of self-preservation and trust God, we gain true life, even if the body dies. But if we forsake him to save our skin, what is the profit?

Persecution is part of our association with Jesus. Will I be ashamed of him?

One Thing to Think About: Am I prepared to suffer for Jesus?

One Thing to Pray For: Perspective to see the proper costs of being ashamed of Jesus

WEEK 19 – FRIDAY

Reading: Mark 9:14-29

I Believe; Help My Unbelief!

The disciples are somehow unable to cast this demon out of a young man. It causes some tension—an argument with the scribes and a disappointed father. This response proves that the disciples are usually very dependable healers, since people are upset when they are unsuccessful.

Jesus expresses exasperation (Mark 9:19), although it's unclear whether it is the disciples or the father who are *"faithless"*. The father explains his son's symptoms to Jesus, then says, *"But if you can do anything, have compassion on us and help us"*(Mark 9:22). Jesus responds sarcastically: *"'If you can'! All things are possible for one who believes"*(Mark 9:23). It is not Jesus' power that is the limiting factor here.

"Immediately the father of the child cried out and said, 'I believe; help my unbelief!'"(Mark 9:24). His statement is both strange and wonderfully fitting. He does believe—that's why he's here. He knows this is possible and trusts that God is able. But even as he says it, he knows that his faith is weak and insufficient. Perhaps he is afraid of disappointment if Jesus can't do it. Maybe he sees that this is possible *theoretically* but has a hard time believing it will happen for his son.

Disciples can relate. We follow Jesus because we believe, yet we are continually aware of ourl imitations and weaknesses. There is honesty and humility here, rolled into one.

One Thing to Think About: Is there unbelief in my heart that I need Jesus' help with?

One Thing to Pray For: I believe; help my unbelief!

WEEK 20 – MONDAY

Reading: Mark 9:30-50

Drownings and Amputations

Jesus' language takes a turn here toward the shocking and violent. The apostles have been arguing about who is the greatest (Mark 9:34). In response, Jesus takes a child in his arms and speaks to them about receiving little ones in contrast to seeking dominance over others. John remembers a man they did *not* receive (Mark 9:38) and Jesus explains that they should welcome him because *"the one who is not against us is for us"*(Mark 9:40).

"Whoever causes one of these little ones who believe in me to sin, it would be better for him if a great millstone were hung around his neck and he were thrown into the sea"(Mark 9:42). If we cause "these little ones"—either children or young, weak disciples—to sin, woe to us! This grisly scene of violent drowning is *better* than the fate awaiting us. Jesus is using graphic language to teach that *causing others to sin is a big deal*.

"And if your hand causes you to sin, cut it off. It is better for you to enter life crippled than with two hands to go to hell, to the unquenchable fire"(Mark 9:43). Now the perspective shifts to something that causes *me* to sin (rather than others). I should *"cut it off"*—even if it hurts and even if it is valuable. It is *better* to enter life without it than hell with it. Jesus is not literally advocating amputation here. He is speaking of the desperate spirit that sacrifices a limb or an eye to save the body. I must be willing to remove anyone or anything from my circle of influence if they cause me to stumble or sin—a bad friend or a computer or a job or money or a habit or a hobby or a TV show or a place. *Causing me to sin is a big deal.*

Jesus is getting our attention with these dramatic images to show us sin is a big deal. Will we hear him?

One Thing to Think About: Am I aware of my impact on others for good or evil—and their impact on me?

One Thing to Pray For: Vision to see bad influences in my life—and courage to remove them

WEEK 20 – TUESDAY

Reading: Mark 10:1-16

Marriage from the Beginning

The Pharisees test Jesus with the age-old controversy: is divorce OK (Mark 10:2)? Jesus explains that Moses allowed divorce *"because of your hardness of heart"*(Mark 10:5), but that *"from the beginning of creation"*(Mark 10:6), God had a different plan.

<u>God made them male and female</u> (Mark 10:6). God created gendered people. Humans are complementary but different, implying different functions but commonalities. This also implies that God wants them to be together, pointing toward marriage as God's general expectation for human behavior.

<u>God wants marriage to create independent families</u>. *"Therefore a man shall leave his father and mother and hold fast to his wife"*(Mark 10:7). In marriage, a man is no longer under the jurisdiction of his parents. God's intent is that he be one with his wife in a new home.

<u>God wants two to be one flesh.</u> *"and the two shall become one flesh. So they are no longer two but one flesh"*(Mark 10:8). Two people are joined together. This implies both sexual unity and the merging of lives. The unity of disparate persons is a work of God (Mark 10:9, Mal 2:15, Eph 4:3).

<u>God doesn't want divorce</u>. *"What therefore God has joined together, let not man separate"*(Mark 10:9). Divorce undoes all God has intended from the beginning and accomplished in marriage.

One Thing to Think About: Am I fulfilling God's plan for marriage by patient faithfulness to my mate?

One Thing to Pray For: Strength to maintain commitments I've made

WEEK 20 – WEDNESDAY

Reading: Mark 10:17-34

A Camel through the Eye of a Needle

Jesus encounters an energetic kingdom prospect (Mark 10:17). Mark notes that Jesus *"loved him"*(Mark 10:21) and tells him his need is to sell all he has, give it to the poor, and follow Jesus. *"He went away sorrowful, for he had great possessions"*(Mark 10:22). Jesus takes it as an opportunity to publicly lament the difficulty riches cause in seeking the kingdom. *"How difficult,"* he declares (Mark 10:23). And in case we missed it, he repeats himself, *"how difficult"*(Mark 10:24)! In case we missed that, *"it is easier for a camel to go through the eye of a needle than for a rich person to enter the kingdom of God"*(Mark 10:25).

It is a vivid image that is purposefully absurd. We would probably overlook it otherwise. First, we must disabuse ourselves of the idea that Jesus is not speaking to us, but strictly to the CEOs of Fortune 500 companies. Even the poorest American is extraordinarily wealthy. Jesus' perspective is that wealth introduces *extreme difficulty*. It competes with God. We cannot serve God and money. We must lay up treasures in heaven, not earth. Here a good man walks away from God's Son because of it.

Money is necessary, but Jesus warns about the grip it tends to hold over those who hold it. Are we suspicious of money and its effect on us? Do we have strategies to prevent our loving, serving, and wasting it? What are we doing for Jesus with our money?

One Thing to Think About: What does Jesus think of my use of my money?

One Thing to Pray For: A heart focused on seeking the kingdom, not money

WEEK 20 – THURSDAY

Reading: Mark 10:35-52

Not So Among You

James and John approach Jesus (presumably out of earshot of the other apostles), asking for the right and left hand in the kingdom. The irony is that this follows on the heels of Jesus saying he's shortly to die (Mark 10:33-34). The other ten are "*indignant*"(Mark 10:41) at the power play. Jesus addresses the situation.

"*You know that those who are considered rulers of the Gentiles lord it over them, and their great ones exercise authority over them*"(Mark 10:42). The Gentiles (godless) are like this. For them, everything is about power. They employ backstabbing and politicking and strategy. Think of modern business culture or of American politics, where there is no "playing nice."

"*But it shall not be so among you*"(Mark 10:43). You will be different. Jesus' people will not be power-obsessed. For them, "*whoever would be great among you must be your servant*"(Mark 10:43). His own example is instructive: "*even the Son of Man came not to be served but to serve, and to give his life as a ransom for many*"(Mark 10:45).

Jesus creates a new culture that is radically different from the dominant one. It critiques what is popular, contrasting it with the divine. Humility and service are not just what Jesus did; they are what *we* do. Even today, the church can become this same sad combination of power, domination, and politicking. A new culture starts with *me*. In Jesus, I learn that others do not exist to serve me and that the closer I get to him, the lower (not higher!) I go.

One Thing to Think About: Do I tend to want to control others or demand their respect and approval?

One Thing to Pray For: A new heart to be like Jesus—and to build a culture of people like Jesus

WEEK 20 – FRIDAY

Reading: Mark 11:1-11

The Triumphal Entry

Jesus has arrived in Jerusalem. We know why he is here (Mark 10:33). As he enters the city, many come and throw their cloaks on his colt (Mark 11:7) and the road (Mark 11:8). They place leafy branches along the road as if rolling out the red carpet. It is a sign of the crowd's honor of Jesus, making the way easier for the coming king.

And they yell: "*And those who went before and those who followed were shouting, 'Hosanna! Blessed is he who comes in the name of the Lord! Blessed is the coming kingdom of our father David! Hosanna in the highest!*"(Mark 11:9-10). They are aware that Jesus comes in the name of Jehovah and of David. They believe their king is coming into Jerusalem to claim his throne.

The question we must ask: where will this crowd be in a week's time? This outpouring of public support will evaporate to nothing when Jesus' enemies come for him. Perhaps even some of these well-wishers will be shouting "crucify him!". It is a reminder that spiritual high points don't guarantee future successes. How good they must feel on this day! How confident the apostles must be! Yet, as with Elijah after Mt Carmel (1 Kings 19), hard times will resurface that will require deeper levels of commitment and faithfulness.

It is the same with us. Spiritual experiences are great, but there will also be a majority of days that are just a spiritual grind—or perhaps even a spiritual challenge. How will we live then?

One Thing to Think About: Do I find it easier to affirm my faith when there are no consequences?

One Thing to Pray For: A faith that follows through

WEEK 21 – MONDAY

Reading: Mark 11:12-26

Fig Trees, Mountains, and Prayer

Jesus finds a fig tree that has nothing on it but leaves. *"And he said to it, 'May no one ever eat fruit from you again'"*(Mark 11:14). The next morning the disciples notice the same tree withered from its roots. Jesus is shortly to tell a parable about fruit (Mark 12:1-12), which reminds us that Israel is often pictured this way. An unfruitful tree is a bad sign.

Jesus uses the tree as an opportunity to teach. *"Have faith in God. Truly, I say to you, whoever says to this mountain, 'Be taken up and thrown into the sea,' and does not doubt in his heart, but believes that what he says will come to pass, it will be done for him"*(Mark 11:22-23). He opens their eyes to the tremendous opportunity prayer presents and the great power God has given access to. Especially notable is the fact that he doesn't attribute this to miracle power, but prayer.

"Therefore, I tell you, whatever you ask in prayer, believe that you have received it, and it will be yours"(Mark 11:24). We push back against this at times because it appears too good to be true. Jesus' point is that the only limiting factor in prayer is my faith. God wants me to ask—even to ask audaciously—for big things. This doesn't obligate God (because prayer is always grace) but encourages me to step out in faith.

One Thing to Think About: When was the last time I prayed a big, daring, audacious prayer?

One Thing to Pray For: Courage to overcome my doubts in prayer

WEEK 21 – TUESDAY

Reading: Mark 11:27-12:12

They Will Respect My Son

Jesus' vineyard story describes God's interactions with the Jewish nation. God is expecting certain actions (fruit) from them and sends prophets (servants) to encourage this. But the people reject, hurt, and kill the prophets.

The crux of the story is what happens next. *"He had still one other, a beloved son. Finally he sent him to them, saying, 'They will respect my son'"* (Mark 12:6). He has one other— one last attempt to reach his people. Jesus also calls him *"beloved."* *"They will respect my son"* shows God's will that his Son be honored and obeyed, even by those who rejected the prophets who preceded him.

Yet when they reject and kill the son, it is the last straw. *"What will the owner of the vineyard do? He will come and destroy the tenants and give the vineyard to others"* (Mark 12:9). There will be a reckoning for how they have treated his son. There is a tremendous difference in a servant and a son. There is an expectation that a son would be treated with all the respect accorded to the father. When this fails to materialize, punishment is due.

Jesus' story indicates that God's Son is the *last* effort by the master (Mark 12:6, "finally" or "last of all"). He is not just another in a line. The point of the parable is that the Jews' rejection of Jesus is not only similar to their rejection of the prophets, but worse. Jesus deserves our respect because of his connection to the Father. He is the beloved Son in whom the Father is well-pleased. I can never afford to ignore or reject him.

One Thing to Think About: How would I have listened to Jesus if I had been alive then? Do I read his words that way today?

One Thing to Pray For: Proper respect for Jesus as God's Son and messenger

WEEK 21 – WEDNESDAY

Reading: Mark 12:13-27

The God of the Living

The Sadducees have a characteristic belief. They *"say that there is no resurrection"*(Mark 12:18), so they present Jesus with an elaborate scenario to "prove" that the resurrection can't be true. *"Jesus said to them, 'Is this not the reason you are wrong, because you know neither the Scriptures nor the power of God?'"*(Mark 12:24). He blasts them because he sees proof of the resurrection in the Old Testament Scriptures.

"And as for the dead being raised, have you not read in the book of Moses, in the passage about the bush, how God spoke to him, saying, 'I am the God of Abraham, and the God of Isaac, and the God of Jacob'?"(Mark 12:26). God says *"I am the God of Abraham"* rather than "I was." God speaks to Moses in present tense about people who are long dead physically. Abraham, Isaac, and Jacob *continue* to have a relationship with God. God remains their God, despite their deaths.

"He is not God of the dead, but of the living. You are quite wrong"(Mark 12:27). He is the God of the living. God gives us life, breath, and all things. Continuing in a relationship with God ensures life because he is its source. The Sadducees have limited God (*"you know neither the Scriptures nor the power of God,"* Mark 12:24) by believing that his power is limited to giving us life *now*. Jesus tells us that if we are God's people, we are *always* God's people. Death cannot sever or terminate that bond.

One Thing to Think About: Do I find it reassuring that death doesn't stop my relationship with God?

One Thing to Pray For: Hope and patience to remain connected to God through life and death

WEEK 21 – THURSDAY

Reading: Mark 12:28-44

The Widow's Two Mites

Jesus has silenced his critics and is sitting with his disciples in the temple, watching people give. It is significant that this scene follows directly after his sharp words against the scribes *"who devour widows' houses"*(Mark 12:40). Even though the scribes are finding ways to abuse their spiritual authority to get at widows' money, Jesus reminds us that even the overlooked and victimized can please God.

"Many rich people put in large sums"(Mark 12:41). These are the ones everyone (perhaps including the disciples) would notice. *"And a poor widow came and put in two small copper coins, which make a penny"*(Mark 12:42). In modern terms, her contribution is about 75 cents. Jesus lauds her: *"Truly, I say to you, this poor widow has put in more than all those who are contributing to the offering box"*(Mark 12:43). He asserts that she has given *more* than the big givers. How? *"For they all contributed out of their abundance, but she out of her poverty has put in everything she had, all she had to live on"*(Mark 12:44). Jesus evaluates giving differently. "More" is based on what she has, not what she gives.

Jesus sees us according to what we have, not what we don't have (2 Cor 8:12). He knows when we do right even though it is a tremendous sacrifice. The amazing part is that by definition, such people and sacrifices go unnoticed by the world—by everyone but Jesus, that is. He encourages us here to quiet acts of faith, piety, and service—not because they will "make a difference" but because we know God sees and appreciates them. We do it for him.

One Thing to Think About: What acts of service do I do that are unnoticed and unappreciated by the world?

One Thing to Pray For: Eyes to see and appreciate sincere service like Jesus does

WEEK 21 – FRIDAY

Reading: Mark 13:1-23

On Guard But Not Alarmed

The disciples comment on the beauty of the temple, prompting a dark and foreboding statement from Jesus. *"Do you see these great buildings? There will not be left here one stone upon another that will not be thrown down"*(Mark 13:2). The remainder of the chapter centers around some of the specifics of how and when this will happen, as well as the expected response of Jesus' disciples.

As Jesus warns what difficulties lie ahead as God works in the world, he outlines general attitudes for disciples. *"But be on your guard"*(Mark 13:9). *"But be on guard"*(Mark 13:23). Jesus wants them to be aware that they are not somehow immune to the circumstances around them. Knowing that Jesus has foretold God acting against Jerusalem, there is a heightened watchfulness and care they must maintain.

Yet Jesus also says *"when you hear of wars and rumors of wars, do not be alarmed. This must take place, but the end is not yet"*(Mark 13:7). *"And when they bring you to trial and deliver you over, do not be anxious beforehand what you are to say, but say whatever is given you in that hour, for it is not you who speak, but the Holy Spirit"*(Mark 13:11). So on the one hand Jesus teaches them to be on guard, while at the same time not being alarmed or anxious. He reassures them of God's presence and help in times of difficulty—as well as the knowledge that God is in control of the whole process.

These thoughts fit our day—a day of international and societal challenges and a day of hostility against Jesus and his people. It is a different context, but assuredly a similar one. As disciples we must be on guard, but not alarmed or anxious. We must maintain faithfulness in the midst of uncertainty.

One Thing to Think About: Do I tend toward anxiety or trust?

One Thing to Pray For: Faithful responses to difficult times

WEEK 22 – MONDAY

Reading: Mark 13:24-37

No One Knows the Day or the Hour

Jesus continues his teaching on the coming destruction of the temple. He is giving markers for the disciples to watch for before this destruction comes—like the presence of the *"abomination of desolation"*(Mark 13:14) and the appearance of false christs and false prophets performing signs (Mark 13:22). He expects them to be able to read these signs and know the general time when his words of doom will be fulfilled (Mark 13:28-31).

But in my reading, Mark 13:32 stands apart. *"But concerning that day or hour, no one knows, not even the angels in heaven, nor the Son, but only the Father."* No one can guess or know—and this remains true whether Jesus is speaking of the exact timing of Jerusalem's desolation or Jesus' ultimate return. The focus is on the limitations of this knowledge. It is a secret—and a secret which has *not* been revealed to us. We would be foolish to guess. Such efforts are by definition a waste of time, regardless of the interpretive scheme or rationale that supports them.

The proper responses to waiting for an uncertain time is to make efforts to be continually prepared. *"Be on guard, keep awake"*(Mark 13:33). *"Stay awake"*(Mark 13:35). *"Stay awake"*(Mark 13:37). It is tempting to find fault with this aspect of Jesus' teaching. Is he really expecting us to be on our guard for 2000 years? Yet it is important to remember the human tendency to take definite timeframes and abuse them, waiting until the last minute. Is that preferable?

We await the return of Jesus, but we know not when. Let's be ready, be awake, and be at work.

One Thing to Think About: How would you respond if you knew exactly when Jesus will return?

One Thing to Pray For: Jesus to come quickly

WEEK 22 – TUESDAY

Reading: Mark 14:1-11

Leave Her Alone!

A woman (John tells us it is Mary, John 12:3) pours expensive ointment on Jesus. Some of the disciples (including Judas, John 12:4) are angered by this. *"Why was the ointment wasted like that? For this ointment could have been sold for more than three hundred denarii and given to the poor"*(Mark 14:4-5). They scold her.

Jesus rushes to Mary's defense. *"Leave her alone. Why do you trouble her? She has done a beautiful thing to me"*(Mark 14:6). Why are you criticizing her? Jesus even sees a deeper meaning in her actions: *"she has anointed my body beforehand for burial"*(Mark 14:8). He assures them all that her act will live on (Mark 14:9).

Jesus takes aim here at the critical spirit that would scold others for acts of service and faith done in a different way than we think they should. Criticism attempts to invalidate good done *and* discourage future acts. It "troubles" people and sees their good negatively, making people feel guilty for doing good in the "wrong way."

Jesus validates her, defends her, and honors her. Will we be the critics—or will we be like Jesus?

One Thing to Think About: Have I ever been discouraged from doing good by someone else's criticism?

One Thing to Pray For: Appreciation for those who do good for Jesus—even if it looks different from what I'd do

WEEK 22 – WEDNESDAY

Reading: Mark 14:12-31

Is It I?

Jesus wants to eat the Passover meal with his disciples. He makes special preparations for a place where they can do this privately. As they begin eating, he drops a bombshell: *"Truly, I say to you, one of you will betray me, one who is eating with me"* (Mark 14:18). This is a new revelation and it is staggering. These men have given three years of their lives to follow and learn from Jesus. They know him and one another so well. How is this possible?

"They began to be sorrowful and to say to him one after another, 'Is it I?'" (Mark 14:19). I read a moment of sad silence as they process this, followed by a desire for more information. And the slow realization dawns on each: could he be talking about me? Is it I? Jesus gives a warning to the betrayer (*"woe to that man,"* Mark 14:21) but doesn't publicly identify him.

"Is it I?" Jesus asks *all* the disciples this to warn Judas while simultaneously prompting this introspection. Judas is not the only one who will have a crisis of faith this night. He is not the only one to be warned. "Is it I?" is a question we must be prepared to ask ourselves at all times. It is the question when we are reading the warnings of scripture, frankly looking at our character flaws, and analyzing the blame in broken relationships. It's not always about others. Is it I? Am I the one?

One Thing to Think About: Do I have difficulty seeing fault in myself? Why (or why not)?

One Thing to Pray For: Honesty to see my own sin and weakness

WEEK 22 – THURSDAY

Reading: Mark 14:32-52

Not What I Will, But What You Will

It is a dark and gloomy night. Jesus has eaten the Passover, but his tone is not joy over God's deliverance of Israel from Egypt. He speaks instead of his betrayer, his blood being poured out, and the disciples falling away tonight. In the garden now, he leaves his disciples behind so he can pray, telling only Peter, James, and John of his inner turmoil (Mark 14:34). This is Jesus' moment of crisis—and in this moment, he prays.

"*And going a little farther, he fell on the ground and prayed that, if it were possible, the hour might pass from him*"(Mark 14:35). This is Jesus' heart. Is there another way to accomplish the Father's will without this suffering? "*And he said, 'Abba, Father, all things are possible for you. Remove this cup from me. Yet not what I will, but what you will'*"(Mark 14:36). Jesus is well aware of God's power ("*all things are possible*"), so he asks his Father for relief from this burden that the whole mission has been leading toward.

Yet even as he expresses his heart, he stresses his submission. "*Not what I will, but what you will.*" It is the Father's will that remains supreme, no matter what. This must be our perspective in prayer—and in life. We ask for God to change things, but we not only acknowledge that God's will is controlling, we also *submit* to it.

Jesus pours out his heart to God and in prayer. He comes to the conclusion that this is God's will and must be done. After this moment, he never again wavers. The battle is won here, in the passionate prayer of Gethsemane.

One Thing to Think About: Do I pray in my moments of crisis?

One Thing to Pray For: Humility to submit to God's will even if I prefer something else

WEEK 22 – FRIDAY

Reading: Mark 14:53-72

Are You the Christ?

Jesus is seized and led to the high priest's house, where the ruling council is illegally assembled in the middle of the night. A sham of a trial ensues. *"Now the chief priests and the whole council were seeking testimony against Jesus to put him to death, but they found none"*(Mark 14:55). Notice that they are looking for testimony of some *capital* offense because they have already decided that he needs to die. Can we imagine a trial where the sentence is determined before the crime is identified?

"For many bore false witness against him, but their testimony did not agree"(Mark 14:56). This is a problem for a trial that's just for show. Even the quite dangerous accusation—that Jesus said he would destroy the temple (Mark 14:58)—is not agreed-upon testimony. Every fact must be established by two or three witnesses (Deut 17:6), a standard they are struggling to meet. Things are getting out of hand here.

Finally, the high priest takes control. *"Are you the Christ, the Son of the Blessed?"*(Mark 14:61). Matthew tells us that Caiaphas puts Jesus under oath here (Matt 26:63). For Jesus, to deny the question is to lie. It is the moment of truth. *"And Jesus said, 'I am, and you will see the Son of Man seated at the right hand of Power, and coming with the clouds of heaven'"*(Mark 14:62). Jesus confesses. The high priest tears his garments (he is probably relieved). Now he can pronounce the sentence they all have come to see: *"And they all condemned him as deserving death"*(Mark 14:64).

If Jesus is not the Christ, why say this and sign his own death warrant? This is about courage. Jesus' silence is not a product of cowardice. He is ready to die. He is unafraid.

One Thing to Think About: Do I have courage to own my identity as a Christian when the stakes are high?

One Thing to Pray For: Trust that God will make all the wrongs right in his time—like Jesus

WEEK 23 – MONDAY

Reading: Mark 15:1-15

Barabbas!

Having condemned Jesus in their own private council, the leaders bring him to Pilate, the Roman governor. After some questioning, Pilate is surprised to find the suspect almost completely silent. He decides to use his custom of releasing a prisoner at the feast to get rid of this odd problem.

"And he answered them, saying, 'Do you want me to release for you the King of the Jews?' For he perceived that it was out of envy that the chief priests had delivered him up" (Mark 15:9-10). Pilate asks the crowd this because he thinks there will be a division between the leaders and the crowd. The crowd loves Jesus while the leaders are envious. What Pilate has not counted on is the leaders stirring up the people to ask for Barabbas' release instead of Jesus'(Mark 14:11). Somehow the people ask for this murderer to be set free and Jesus crucified—even over Pilate's objections.

God's Son is about to be crucified—God's people are asking for his blood—God's leaders are engineering the project—and the only one who objects is the pagan governor. Barabbas' release highlights the remarkable depth of the leaders' hatred for and rejection of Jesus. They will see him dead no matter how it may hurt them.

Barabbas also represents the desire we all have occasionally to do *anything but serve God*. There is no caution, no wisdom, no courage, and no obedience in this crowd. I have been guilty of similar failures in my stubbornness. I have chosen anything but Jesus. And so I too have cried for Barabbas.

One Thing to Think About: What would I have done if I were in the crowd that day?

One Thing to Pray For: Wisdom to see the consequences of my actions *before* I commit them

WEEK 23 – TUESDAY

Reading: Mark 15:16-32

Hail, King of the Jews!

Jesus has been condemned and judged worthy of death twice now, though he is completely innocent. He is scourged (Mark 15:15) and given to the soldiers who will oversee his execution. Rumors of Jesus' royalty have surrounded his ministry and now swirl around his trial: *"Are you the King of the Jews?"*(Mark 15:2). Pilate (with a smirk) calls him this (Mark 15:9, 12). He will put it over his head on the cross (Mark 15:26).

The soldiers, picking up on this, hold a mock coronation of the prisoner. They *"called together the whole battalion"*(Mark 15:16), around 600 men. They clothe him in royal purple. They fashion a crown out of thorns. And in the spirit of honoring the Roman Caesar, they cry, *"Hail, king of the Jews"*(Mark 15:18). They kneel and spit on him and hit him.

It is staggering to see the king of all the earth mocked and shamed as if he is not a king at all. Jesus endures more than pain for us. He goes through shame. He humbles himself so that God will exalt him at the proper time.

One Thing to Think About: Would I be willing to suffer shame for others like Jesus has?

One Thing to Pray For: Trust in God's ultimate exaltation of the humble

WEEK 23 – WEDNESDAY

Reading: Mark 15:33-47

The Torn Temple Curtain

As Jesus hangs dying, the earth responds. There is darkness from noon to 3 PM (Mark 15:33). People continue to mock and watch until finally Jesus gives a loud cry and dies.

"And the curtain of the temple was torn in two, from top to bottom"(Mark 15:38). Matthew and Luke also record this. It is an odd detail and strange occurrence. The darkness could have a natural explanation. Earthquakes can also happen. But how can we account for this giant curtain being torn? *"From top to bottom"* also points to the fact that it is an *unnatural* tearing—one not achievable by human means. It makes me wonder what the Jewish leaders think when they discover it.

The temple curtain is important because it separates the Holy Place in the temple from the Most Holy Place, where God lives. Only once a year can the high priest (and *only* the high priest) enter. The curtain being torn means access to God's presence is now open where it was closed before—as Jesus dies.

This is about new access to God (see Heb 10:19-20). God signals this to us by the tearing of the curtain. Now *we*—Aaronic blood or not—can come to God with confidence through Jesus' blood. Praise God!

One Thing to Think About: Does God *have* to hear my requests or allow me into his presence?

One Thing to Pray For: Gratitude for God opening himself up to us

WEEK 23 – THURSDAY

Reading: Mark 16:1-13

The Women at the Tomb

Jesus is hastily buried before the Sabbath, which begins at sundown Friday night. This is a kindness done by Joseph of Arimathea (Mark 15:43). Joseph buys a shroud, wraps his body, and lays him in the tomb. *"Mary Magdalene and Mary the mother of Joses saw where he was laid"* (Mark 15:47).

It is not surprising that as soon as possible (early Sunday morning), the women head back to the tomb to anoint Jesus' body with oil and spices. Perhaps they feel that Joseph's efforts were insufficient. Though they are concerned about the stone, they find it rolled away. *"And entering the tomb, they saw a young man sitting on the right side, dressed in a white robe, and they were alarmed"* (Mark 16:5). The details—right side, white robe—are notable because they indicate eyewitness testimony. The man tells them that Jesus is not here because he is risen—and that they must tell Peter and the disciples.

"And they went out and fled from the tomb, for trembling and astonishment had seized them, and they said nothing to anyone, for they were afraid" (Mark 16:8). They immediately disobey the angel! Mary Magdalene finally does tell some of the disciples, but they don't believe (Mark 16:9-11).

Women are the first witnesses to Jesus' resurrection. Their story rings true. They are surprised and afraid, for they have only come to anoint his body. They *don't* rush off and tell others—and when they eventually do tell, they are not believed. God chooses women—which their contemporary society would have dismissed or denigrated—to be the first witnesses of the resurrection. What a God!

One Thing to Think About: How would I have responded to the empty tomb?

One Thing to Pray For: Deeper faith in Jesus' power over death

WEEK 23 – FRIDAY

Reading: Mark 16:14-20

The Gospel to the Whole Creation

Jesus finally appears to the apostles as they are eating. Since they have not believed the women, Jesus rebukes them (Mark 16:14). He "commissions" the apostles to something new. They must now "*go into all the world*"(Mark 16:15) to tell others about Jesus.

"*Proclaim the gospel to the whole creation*"(Mark 16:14). The emphasis here is on people of every kind (rather than every single human). This is a contrast to the Limited Commission, when Jesus sends them to preach *only* to the lost sheep of the house of *Israel* (Matt 10:5-6). Jesus now throws the doors of the kingdom wide open.

How do they interpret results of their preaching? "*Whoever believes and is baptized will be saved, but whoever does not believe will be condemned*"(Mark 16:16). Salvation is offered, but only for those willing to believe the gospel and obey it. Signs will also follow the believers (Mark 16:17-18), giving further ways for the disciples to see the results of their work.

The gospel is a universal message. It is not just for people like me. Everyone needs to hear. I cannot disqualify anyone or assume that I know how they will respond. While this word is given to the apostles, in some small way we help fulfill this commission as we teach those around us.

One Thing to Think About: How would I view the gospel differently if it were intended for only one racial group?

One Thing to Pray For: A heart to share the gospel with all people

WEEK 24 – MONDAY

Reading: John 1:1-18

The Word Became Flesh

John introduces Jesus in a different way than other gospel writers. He takes us back to the beginning of all things. At the beginning, *"the Word was with God, and the Word was God"*(John 1:1). He was there, making all things. John shows us the Word as an eternal being, both with God and God himself. Next comes John the Baptist, a witness to what is shortly to happen regarding this Word (John 1:6-8).

"And the Word became flesh and dwelt among us"(John 1:14). This is the great radical truth of Christianity: God has become a man. He looks like a man, lives among men, yet is still God. This explains John the Baptist's enigmatic statement *"He who comes after me ranks before me, because he was before me"*(John 1:15).

"No one has ever seen God; the only God, who is at the Father's side, he has made him known"(John 1:18). This great Bible fact—that no one has seen God and lived—is mitigated by Jesus showing and explaining the Father. In Jesus, we see God and understand him anew.

God has revealed himself in the most shocking way by becoming his creation and subjecting himself to its limitations. He has not stood aloof—which would have been his right in both power and holiness—but has approached us by invading history and *becoming* us. Jesus is more than a man—but definitely a man—who brings grace, truth, and knowledge of God.

One Thing to Think About: Is it hard for me to believe that God could become a man?

One Thing to Pray For: Deeper appreciation for the great mystery of the incarnation

WEEK 24 – TUESDAY

Reading: John 1:19-34

Behold, the Lamb of God!

As John the Baptist gains a following, the leaders want to know what he is claiming about himself. He confesses that he is not the Christ (John 1:20) and that he is not Elijah or the Prophet (John 1:21). His denial of being Elijah could be because many in this time believe in the literal return of Elijah or because John himself does not know he is the fulfillment of Elijah (cf. Matt 17:10-13). John insists he is just the herald and the preparer (John 1:23).

"*The next day he saw Jesus coming toward him, and said, 'Behold, the Lamb of God, who takes away the sin of the world!'*"(John 1:29). John identifies Jesus as the Christ. He is also aware of the essence of the work of Jesus. He has come not just to be a king, but to remove sin. John explains that even though he knew Jesus before, he did not know that he was the Lamb of God (John 1:33). As John bears witness, many of his disciples begin to follow Jesus as a result of this emphatic endorsement.

John the Baptist's words point toward the idea of sacrifice (lamb) that removes sin. His appearance is not just good news because he reveals the Father (John 1:18), but because he himself will take away sin. If we do not feel the great need for the sins of the world to be removed, purified, and restored to order, we may struggle feeling that Jesus and his mission are important and worthwhile.

One Thing to Think About: Why was John the Baptist needed?

One Thing to Pray For: Forgiveness of my sins by the blood of the Lamb

WEEK 24 – WEDNESDAY

Reading: John 1:35-51

How Do You Know Me?

John the Baptist has identified Jesus as the Lamb of God. Some of John's disciples start following Jesus (John 1:37). They begin to spread the word. Andrew finds Peter: *"We have found the Messiah"*(John 1:41). Philip finds Nathanael: *"We have found him of whom Moses in the Law and also the prophets wrote, Jesus of Nazareth, the son of Joseph"*(John 1:45).

Nathanael's lip curls. Nazareth? *"Can anything good come out of Nazareth?"*(John 1:46). Jesus identifies Nathanael as *"an Israelite indeed, in whom there is no deceit"*(John 1:47). He is an honest and sincere man. This description is so accurate that Nathanael is surprised. *"How do you know me?"*(John 1:48). Jesus is ready for him. *"Before Philip called you, when you were under the fig tree, I saw you"*(John 1:48). Presumably Nathanael was all alone before, but now Jesus says he saw him there.

"Rabbi, you are the Son of God! You are the King of Israel!"(John 1:49). Philip was right about you! I picture Jesus chuckling at this point. *"You will see greater things than these"*(John 1:50). There will be stronger proofs than this!

This story reminds us that Jesus knows us intimately—where and how we live, what we are like, what we do—and that nothing escapes his notice. Knowing how he knows me, do I hear him? Do I trust that his words are just what *I* need?

One Thing to Think About: What would Jesus say about me?

One Thing to Pray For: The faith of Nathanael—to know Jesus because of how he knows me

WEEK 24 – THURSDAY

Reading: John 2:1-12

Water to Wine

Jesus attends a wedding with his disciples and his mother. There is interesting interplay between Jesus and Mary. *"When the wine ran out, the mother of Jesus said to him, 'They have no wine.' And Jesus said to her, 'Woman, what does this have to do with me? My hour has not yet come.' His mother said to the servants, 'Do whatever he tells you'"*(John 2:3-5). Mary is convinced he is going to do something about the wine problem, but Jesus seems to resist initially. We can't do much more than speculate about what they are thinking.

Jesus tells the servants to fill the jars with water, then draw some out to take to the master of the feast. His method leaves no room for accusing him of tampering or shenanigans. The master marvels: *"Everyone serves the good wine first, and when people have drunk freely, then the poor wine. But you have kept the good wine until now"*(John 2:10). The replacement wine is better! Its origin is unknown to the broader crowd, yet *"his disciples believed in him"*(John 2:11).

Water doesn't become wine naturally. This just can't happen. Jesus created water and wine and now demonstrates his complete mastery over both. I have lived my whole life at the mercy of nature. Jesus controls it completely. Such power is unheard of.

The goal of the miracle is to produce faith in Jesus. Who can do things like this?

One Thing to Think About: Is there anything in my life—relationships, circumstances, personality—that Jesus cannot change?

One Thing to Pray For: The power of Jesus to change my heart

WEEK 24 – FRIDAY

Reading: John 2:13-25

The Greatest Sign

Jesus goes to Jerusalem at the Passover. He is vexed over the sellers and moneychangers in the temple, so he makes a whip of cords and drives them out, turning over their tables. His voice rings out in the courtyard: *"Take these things away; do not make my Father's house a house of trade"*(John 2:16). This is my Father's house! Jesus has a zeal for his Father and his house (John 2:17).

Afterward (when Jesus has calmed down a bit), the Jewish leaders confront him. *"What sign do you show us for doing these things?"*(John 2:18). His answer is odd. *"Destroy this temple, and in three days I will raise it up"*(John 2:19). They misunderstand, but Jesus is speaking of his body (John 2:20-21). When asked for a sign to authenticate him, Jesus speaks of his resurrection.

The resurrection of Jesus is his greatest sign. What could prove his authority more dramatically? He also calls this the sign of the prophet Jonah (Matt 12:39) and declares it the only sign to be given. The demands for proof keep coming, but how can there be anything greater than this? They destroy his temple and in three days he raises it again.

One Thing to Think About: Why does Jesus insist on cleansing the temple?

One Thing to Pray For: Zeal for God like Jesus has

WEEK 25 – MONDAY

Reading: John 3:1-8

Born Again

Nicodemus is a ruler, a member of the Sanhedrin, a Pharisee, and a teacher. He comes to Jesus to make this bold affirmation: *"Rabbi, we know that you are a teacher come from God, for no one can do these signs that you do unless God is with him"*(John 3:2). He appears sincere in this, especially in light of his later service after Jesus' death (John 19:39). He is convinced that Jesus is from God.

Jesus replies to his faith statement with a challenge. *"Truly, truly, I say to you, unless one is born again he cannot see the kingdom of God"*(John 3:3). Something is required before one can see the kingdom—a new birth. Nicodemus is confused, taking the physical application and approach. By mentioning re-entering his mother's womb, is he expecting Jesus to perform another sign? Jesus repeats, *"Truly, truly, I say to you, unless one is born of water and the Spirit, he cannot enter the kingdom of God"*(John 3:5). Water and *Spirit* emphasize that this is not physical, as Nicodemus thinks. He goes on to describe the birth of the Spirit as like the wind, known more by effects than sight (John 3:6-8).

Jesus teaches here that <u>a complete change in life is required to enter the kingdom</u>. A new birth must occur—not bodily, but spiritual. This is a challenge for Nicodemus because it means he must *change* to see the kingdom. It is not automatic simply because he is a Jew or a religious leader.

Jesus shows us that kingdom people are made new—converted—reborn—by God's Spirit. Baptism (*"water,"* John 3:5) is a part of this, but it is something that is seen by *effects* more than any physical manifestation (John 3:8).

One Thing to Think About: Has my rebirth/new birth made an obvious difference in my life?

One Thing to Pray For: God to continue to change and work on my heart (Phil 2:12-13)

WEEK 25 – TUESDAY

Reading: John 3:9-21

Why We Love Darkness

Nicodemus is still stumped by Jesus' "new birth" idea. Jesus adds another image that is likely more familiar to him: *"And as Moses lifted up the serpent in the wilderness, so must the Son of Man be lifted up, that whoever believes in him may have eternal life"*(John 3:14-15). When Israel suffered deadly snakebites, God instructed Moses to make a bronze serpent that would heal everyone who looked at it. Now, through Jesus, God is providing a means by which his people can escape the threat of imminent death.

"Whoever believes in him is not condemned, but whoever does not believe is condemned already, because he has not believed in the name of the only Son of God"(John 3:18). Unbelievers are already condemned. Why? They have refused the light (Jesus). *"And this is the judgment: the light has come into the world, and people loved the darkness rather than the light because their works were evil"*(John 3:19). Jesus uses the term "darkness" to describe ignorance, shame, and hatred. Why would we love this? *"Because their works were evil."*

"For everyone who does wicked things hates the light and does not come to the light, lest his works should be exposed"(John 3:20). We don't want our evil to be exposed. But if we do right, we are unafraid of light and unafraid of whether others know what we do (John 3:21). Jesus is explaining that those who reject him do so because the process of exposure and conviction is too painful for them. They refuse to go through it.

We love darkness because of our shame. Jesus has come to draw us to him so that when we come to the light, we are cleansed and liberated to do works we can be proud of.

One Thing to Think About: Do I tend to hide wrong things I do? Why?

One Thing to Pray For: A heart that always comes to the light

WEEK 25 – WEDNESDAY

Reading: John 3:22-36

He Must Increase, But I Must Decrease

John the Baptist has continued his work, bearing witness and preparing people for Jesus. Now word comes to him that Jesus is having tremendous success baptizing disciples (even more than John, John 4:1). John's disciples feel threatened on behalf of their master. The scene reminds me of young Joshua, jealous on Moses' behalf because others are prophesying, only to be rebuked by Moses (Numbers 11:26-29).

John's disciples are worried that he is losing importance, but he is unconcerned. "*John answered, 'A person cannot receive even one thing unless it is given him from heaven'*"(John 3:27). This is tremendous perspective on fame and influence. He continues: "*The one who has the bride is the bridegroom. The friend of the bridegroom, who stands and hears him, rejoices greatly at the bridegroom's voice. Therefore this joy of mine is now complete*"(John 3:29). John rejoices because this is what his mission has all been about.

But the pinnacle of John's reply is this: "*He must increase, but I must decrease*"(John 3:30). Jesus will grow but John will weaken—and this is good. John is comfortable with a diminishing role as Jesus' role expands. John's spirit is admirable. He has a work promoting another. The better job he does, the less notice he gets. Yet God is pleased and Jesus honors him highly.

This is the Christian spirit. I promote you, not myself. It's about the kingdom, not about me. God deserves praise, not me. I serve instead of being served. I look forward to the next generation and the work of God advancing. Jesus must increase, but I must decrease.

One Thing to Think About: Do I have a hard time letting others shine?

One Thing to Pray For: The humility of John

WEEK 25 – THURSDAY

Reading: John 4:1-15

Never Thirsty Again

Jesus *"had to pass through Samaria"*(John 4:4). Maybe he knows whom he will meet there. As he rests alone by a well near Sychar, he engages a woman who is shocked that he even speaks to her. Jesus has no patience for prejudices here. He's after her heart.

"If you knew the gift of God, and who it is that is saying to you, 'Give me a drink,' you would have asked him, and he would have given you living water"(John 4:10). Jesus offers her "living water." The woman, taking the physical angle, asks where he would get it (John 4:11). *"Everyone who drinks of this water will be thirsty again, but whoever drinks of the water that I will give him will never be thirsty again. The water that I will give him will become in him a spring of water welling up to eternal life"*(John 4:13-14). Jesus' living water will make her *never thirsty again*. The woman follows Nicodemus' pattern of thinking Jesus is speaking physically (John 4:15).

Jesus compares our great spiritual need to thirst and promises a way that we can forever quench it. We each possess deep needs—the need to matter, the need to belong, the need to be loved. We satsify them briefly, like taking sips of water, but inevitably we thirst again. The people around us, the short-lived pleasure of pleasure, and the fleeting peace of possessions do not truly fill the hole within us. Only Jesus can promise that we will never be thirsty again.

One Thing to Think About: Would I have understood what Jesus means by living water?

One Thing to Pray For: The deep satisfaction that only Jesus provides

WEEK 25 – FRIDAY

Reading: John 4:16-38

A Question about Worship

Jesus is still speaking with the woman at the well. He changes tactics here, bringing up her husband and family situation. She is evasive (*"I have no husband,"* John 4:17) and when Jesus surprises her by knowing the facts, she is impressed but quickly changes the subject. *"Our fathers worshiped on this mountain, but you say that in Jerusalem is the place where people ought to worship"*(John 4:20). Where should we worship?

She is alluding to a long-standing debate between Samaritans and Jews: is worship appropriate on Mount Gerizim or Jerusalem? While Jesus briefly answers her question (Jerusalem, John 4:22), he informs her that there is a deeper worship question: *How* should we worship? This is more important than where.

Jesus says that an *"hour is coming"*(John 4:21) and *"the hour is coming, and is now here"*(John 4:23) where things are changing in God's expectations about worship. Very soon *"neither on this mountain nor in Jerusalem will you worship the Father"*(John 4:21). The time is coming when the place won't matter anymore. Jesus is foreshadowing a major shift away from Jerusalem as the center of worship.

God is seeking people who will worship him in spirit and truth (John 4:23-24). The *how* of worship means honoring God with my *spirit* in addition to seeking the *truth* of his word regarding worship. Worship in spirit and truth is possible anywhere.

One Thing to Think About: What do I find challenging about worship?

One Thing to Pray For: Sincerity to worship God in spirit and truth

WEEK 26 – MONDAY

Reading: John 4:39-54

From Secondhand to Firsthand

After her talk with Jesus, the woman at the well leaves her water jar to go tell the townsfolk about him. She shares how he knows her so well: *"Come, see a man who told me all that I ever did. Can this be the Christ?"*(John 4:29). She leads some of the Samaritans to believe in Jesus (John 4:39) and they ask him to stay.

But something happens as these Samaritans see and hear Jesus for themselves. *"And many more believed because of his word. They said to the woman, 'It is no longer because of what you said that we believe, for we have heard for ourselves, and we know that this is indeed the Savior of the world'"*(John 4:41-42). Many more believe in Jesus because of his own word. Now *"we have heard for ourselves."* There is a sense of a deeper, firmer faith in these words. We are no longer just trusting this woman. We have heard him for ourselves and now we *know*.

Our experience with Jesus begins *secondhand*. Like these Samaritans, we are *told* about Jesus by others. We believe their testimony—whether we're talking about the apostles or our fellow Christians who introduce us to him. But we have a need to move to this firsthand relationship—where *I* know Jesus, *I* hear his words, *I* believe in him, *I* study his word for myself, and *I* pray through him. When we experience Jesus for ourselves, faith comes alive, certainty emerges, and maturity begins.

One Thing to Think About: Is my faith based on what others say about Jesus or what I think/know/have seen myself?

One Thing to Pray For: A firsthand relationship with Jesus

WEEK 26 – TUESDAY

Reading: John 5:1-18

God Doesn't Take Saturdays Off

Jesus approaches a lame man at the pool of Bethesda. *"Do you want to be healed?"*(John 5:6). Not everyone who is sick wants to get better. Jesus seeks to draw the man out about his desire for healing. As he heals him, Jesus tells him to take up his bed and walk (John 5:8-9). When the Jews accost the man for carrying his bed on the Sabbath, he refers them (eventually) to Jesus (John 5:15).

The Jews are unhappy with Jesus' perspective on the Sabbath. He heals and commands people to carry things on the Sabbath. He explains: *"My Father is working until now, and I am working"*(John 5:17). Jesus discusses *"working"*—the specific action that violates the Sabbath. The Father keeps on working on the Sabbath—God doesn't take Saturdays off—and therefore Jesus is working. He takes his cues from the Father and does his work.

The Sabbath has never been a rule that just must be kept for its own sake. It has always been for the benefit of man. So when a pressing need of man can be met on the Sabbath, *God* always meets it. Even on Saturdays, he continues to give to all life, breath, and all things (Acts 17:25). Jesus refuses to apologize for doing a kindness to a man in need simply because he is in need on the wrong day.

There is never a wrong time to do God's work.

One Thing to Think About: Can I honor God's expectation that I rest AND his expectation that I do good for others?

One Thing to Pray For: Diligence to work God's will like Jesus

WEEK 26 – WEDNESDAY

Reading: John 5:19-29

An Hour Is Coming

On the heels of healing the lame man and the Jews' hostile reaction, Jesus explains his relationship with the Father. He emphasizes both his unity with the Father and his dependence on him (John 5:19). The Father gives life and the Son does too (John 5:21). The Father gives the task of judgment to the Son so that all may honor Son and Father (John 5:22-23). Honoring Jesus means honoring God.

But as Jesus describes his role as judge, he adds this: *"Truly, truly, I say to you, whoever hears my word and believes him who sent me has eternal life. He does not come into judgment, but has passed from death to life"*(John 5:24). Hearing and believing means *avoiding* judgment and passing from death to life. As in John 4:21, Jesus here gives truth that is both predictive and informative: *"Truly, truly, I say to you, an hour is coming, and is now here, when the dead will hear the voice of the Son of God, and those who hear will live"*(John 5:25). An hour is coming. As it connects back to John 5:24, the reference to death and resurrection looks spiritual here. Those who hear Jesus will *live* (eternally and spiritually).

But this shouldn't surprise us because Jesus has power over *physical* life and death too. *"Do not marvel at this, for an hour is coming when all who are in the tombs will hear his voice and come out, those who have done good to the resurrection of life, and those who have done evil to the resurrection of judgment"*(John 5:28-29). An hour is coming in which everyone *will* hear his voice and come out of their graves to their own fate. So it makes sense that those who *now* hear his voice can pass from death to life.

This text is important because it teaches that all people will be resurrected bodily, but some will go to the *"resurrection of judgment."* It shows that Jesus has power over life and death that validates his spiritual teaching. It teaches us to await the "coming hour" with anticipation of the *"resurrection of life."*

One Thing to Think About: Why does Jesus take such pains to give honor to the Father when he is also God?

One Thing to Pray For: The arrival of the "coming hour" and its resurrection

WEEK 26 – THURSDAY

Reading: John 5:30-47

Witnesses of Jesus

The problem in this text is that Jesus can talk about himself, but his testimony on its own is unreliable and inadmissible (John 5:31). In response, he presents validating witnesses. *"You sent to John, and he has borne witness to the truth"*(John 5:33). John has proclaimed Jesus the Lamb of God and sent his followers to him.

There are greater witnesses (because John is just a man). *"For the works that the Father has given me to accomplish, the very works that I am doing, bear witness about me that the Father has sent me"*(John 5:36). The signs Jesus keeps doing testify that he is from God (see John 3:2). Jesus also refers to the Father as a witness (John 5:37) but it is unclear if this is in addition to the works (John 5:36) and word (John 5:39).

He goes further. *"You search the Scriptures because you think that in them you have eternal life; and it is they that bear witness about me"*(John 5:39). Look to your law! Moses *"wrote of me"*(John 5:46). What more can God do than work, teach, validate, and send servants?

Jesus' speech highlights the fact that <u>what appears to be an evidence problem is often a motive problem</u>. He points out that they do not have the love of God within them (John 5:42), seek the praise of men (John 5:44) and do not believe Moses (John 5:47). When our hearts are corrupt, no amount of evidence will tip the scales. We will find the "truth" that supports what we already want to do.

One Thing to Think About: How is God's patience illustrated in this section?

One Thing to Pray For: A heart to seek God's glory and not man's (John 5:44)

WEEK 26 – FRIDAY

Reading: John 6:1-15

The Withdrawing King

Jesus is out by the seaside with the multitude, healing and presumably teaching. Food becomes an issue. Jesus challenges Philip (John 6:5) "*to test him*"(John 6:6). He then ends up taking a boy's five loaves and two fish to feed the crowd. This is right up their alley. It is not just a sign, but a sign they can all feel and taste. It is a sign which will soon gain him the wrong kind of following.

"*When the people saw the sign that he had done, they said, 'This is indeed the Prophet who is to come into the world!' Perceiving then that they were about to come and take him by force to make him king, Jesus withdrew again to the mountain by himself*"(John 6:14-15). Jesus knows what is about to happen. They are going to rally behind him in a fit of passion and excitement. They are going to try to install him as king and "make" him the Messiah. This is not God's plan. So Jesus withdraws.

Jesus sees the offer of tremendous popularity—of earthly power a Galilean carpenter could scarcely dream of—and he runs the other way. There is character here. There is self-denial. There is devotion to the Father's will here that will not allow shortcuts. There is wisdom here that refuses heat-of-the-moment decisions.

We are followers of the withdrawing king.

One Thing to Think About: Would I have the strength to withdraw from a crowd chanting my name like this?

One Thing to Pray For: Courage to quiet tempting voices and make righteous choices

WEEK 27 – MONDAY

Reading: John 6:16-40

The True Bread of Heaven

This section can be difficult if we miss the disconnect between Jesus and his audience. Jesus has made bread for the crowds and so they follow him to the other side of the Sea of Galilee. *"Truly, truly, I say to you, you are seeking me, not because you saw signs, but because you ate your fill of the loaves. Do not work for the food that perishes, but for the food that endures to eternal life, which the Son of Man will give to you"* (John 6:26-27). They are only seeking him because he fed them and they want another free meal. Jesus pushes them to higher priorities.

They ask him for a sign. If you want us to believe, give us bread like Moses (John 6:30-31)! Jesus replies, *"Truly, truly, I say to you, it was not Moses who gave you the bread from heaven, but my Father gives you the true bread from heaven. For the bread of God is he who comes down from heaven and gives life to the world"* (John 6:32-33). Jesus himself is the bread. When we believe in and come to him, we have no more spiritual hunger or thirst (John 6:35).

Like Nicodemus and the woman at the well, this crowd is focused on the physical while Jesus pushes them to think spiritually. The result is that they miss him entirely. Jesus' primary appeal is spiritual—satisfying hunger and thirst (John 6:35) and offering eternal life (John 6:40). He criticizes their lesser focus (John 6:27).

This passage offers the essence of *"seek first the kingdom of God and his righteousness, and all these things will be added to you"* (Matt 6:33). Jesus is what we *truly* need and is more integral to real life than food. Do I feel that way about him?

One Thing to Think About: In what ways do I tend to give physical things priority over spiritual?

One Thing to Pray For: A deeper appreciation for what Jesus offers

WEEK 27 – TUESDAY

Reading: John 6:41-59

Drawn by the Father

As some in the crowd object to Jesus' statement about coming down from heaven (John 6:38, 42), he explains their reaction. *"No one can come to me unless the Father who sent me draws him. And I will raise him up on the last day. It is written in the Prophets, 'And they will all be taught by God.' Everyone who has heard and learned from the Father comes to me"* (John 6:44-45). This has led some to conclude that God puts unbelief in the hearts of some and faith in others. This is a misunderstanding.

The method of drawing here is hearing and learning (John 6:45), which presupposes willingness. In John, Jesus repeatedly describes unbelievers as *unwilling*: they won't do God's works (especially faith) (John 6:28-29), they refuse to come (John 5:40), they love the praise of men (John 5:44), they hate exposing their evil (John 3:19-21), they judge by appearances (John 7:24), and they long to do the devil's work (John 8:44). They are not drawn by the Father because they will not hear and learn from him (see John 8:47).

What Jesus is addressing here is our need to listen submissively to the voice of God. Only those who have *"heard and learned from the Father"* will come to Jesus. God's voice must overrule our shame, our physical desires, appearances, and our desires to do evil. God is pulling us to him, but we must choose him over all else.

One Thing to Think About: What desires do I have that rival my desire to do God's will?

One Thing to Pray For: God's will to be done above my own—and for my will to *become* his

WEEK 27 – WEDNESDAY

Reading: John 6:60-71

Do You Want to Go Away as Well?

This sad chapter ends tragically. Jesus has given the crowd a deliberately challenging saying as they reason together. *"Truly, truly, I say to you, unless you eat the flesh of the Son of Man and drink his blood, you have no life in you"*(John 6:53). Even his disciples bristle at this. *"When many of his disciples heard it, they said, 'This is a hard saying; who can listen to it?'"*(John 6:60). Surprisingly, Jesus doesn't apologize or soften the teaching. He lets his audience squirm.

"After this many of his disciples turned back and no longer walked with him"(John 6:66). They give up being disciples because they do not understand this teaching. *"So Jesus said to the twelve, 'Do you want to go away as well?'"*(John 6:67). Jesus' tone reveals sadness and irritation. Others are abandoning him. Will the apostles join them?

"Simon Peter answered him, 'Lord, to whom shall we go? You have the words of eternal life, and we have believed, and have come to know, that you are the Holy One of God'"(John 6:68-69). Peter reaffirms his commitment. There's nowhere else to go! You are the one with the answers!

Even today Jesus' followers sometimes "go away" and turn back from following him. Often that happens for the same reasons—questions we can't answer or an aspect of his teaching we can't fully grasp. It helps to remember—especially when we are tempted to give up on Jesus—this sense that he takes such desertion personally. We may paint it as frustration with a certain group of his disciples or something within us, but it is a rejection of him.

Do you want to go away as well?

One Thing to Think About: How do I react when Jesus says or does something I don't understand?

One Thing to Pray For: Loyalty to remain with Jesus because he has the words of eternal life

WEEK 27 – THURSDAY

Reading: John 7:1-13

Not Even His Brothers Believed

John 7 highlights different reactions to Jesus. The question of his identity rivets the people. It is time for the Feast of Booths, commemorating Israel's time in the desert. His brothers mockingly encourage him to go up to Jerusalem for the feast. "*Leave here and go to Judea, that your disciples also may see the works you are doing. For no one works in secret if he seeks to be known openly. If you do these things, show yourself to the world*"(John 7:3-4). Go "*show yourself to the world!*" If you're so great, go hit the big time! John's comment—"*for not even his brothers believed in him*"(John 7:5)—makes their tone clear. They are mocking him.

"*Jesus said to them, 'My time has not yet come, but your time is always here'*"(John 7:6). Jesus pushes back. This is not his goal or the time and place to pursue it. He further points out their connection to the world (John 7:7). Though he does eventually go up, it is private (John 7:10) rather than to draw attention. Just as when the crowd wants to make him king by force (John 6:15), Jesus' character and mission are again misunderstood.

This story reminds us of the rejection Jesus endures, even from his own family. Though it occasionally appears to frustrate him, he is never discouraged to the point of giving up his mission. He will do the Father's will at the appropriate time—even when those he loves mock him.

One Thing to Think About: How do I respond when I'm disappointed in those close to me?

One Thing to Pray For: Determination to persevere in doing right, regardless of the reaction of others

WEEK 27 – FRIDAY

Reading: John 7:14-36

Judge Righteous Judgment

Jesus is now in Jerusalem for the Feast of Booths. There is a lot of chatter about him. People are unsure what to make of him, especially since he has done an incredible miracle in healing the lame man (John 5:9) but he healed on the Sabbath. Jesus teaches and they marvel: *"How is it that this man has learning, when he has never studied?"*(John 7:15). Where does this come from (see Mark 6:2)?

Jesus insists that his teaching comes from God (John 7:16) and that those who sincerely want to do the will of God will realize this. *"If anyone's will is to do God's will, he will know whether the teaching is from God or whether I am speaking on my own authority"*(John 7:17). Jesus is concerned that the crowd is clouded in judgment. Because they are not all truly seeking the Father's will, confusion (rather than certainty) reigns.

"I did one work, and you all marvel at it...If on the Sabbath a man receives circumcision, so that the law of Moses may not be broken, are you angry with me because on the Sabbath I made a man's whole body well? Do not judge by appearances, but judge with right judgment"(John 7:21, 23-24). When we *"judge by appearances,"* we think in a shallow way. We don't consider consistency. We don't think through implications. Righteous judgment demands careful thought, honesty, and pure motives. Only this leads to truth.

One Thing to Think About: Do I tend to make snap judgments about people, situations, or issues?

One Thing to Pray For: My will to be to do God's will (John 7:17)

WEEK 28 – MONDAY

Reading: John 7:37-52

Spiritual Bullying

Jesus makes an incredible statement that harkens back to his conversation with the woman at the well—out of the heart of the believer will flow rivers of living water (John 7:38). John connects this to the indwelling Spirit given after Jesus' death (John 7:39). It is a promise of continual sustenance and satisfaction from God. Not only will believers be satisfied, but they will in turn bless others ("*out of his heart will flow rivers of living water*").

John records some responses to Jesus' speech. Some are convinced while others have legitimate questions about his bona fides (John 7:40-42). The Pharisees send officers to arrest him, but they come back emptyhanded: "*No one ever spoke like this man!*"(John 7:46). The Pharisees respond with a string of bitter accusations: "*Have you also been deceived? Have any of the authorities or the Pharisees believed in him? But this crowd that does not know the law is accursed*"(John 7:47-49). Nicodemus raises a legitimate point about the fairness of the process, but he too is shouted down (John 7:50-52).

This section reminds us that none of our spiritual decisions are made in a vacuum. Others influence us. Particularly concerning are those who would attempt to affect our spiritual decisions by strong language, personal attacks, insults, and peer pressure. They feel that if others are left alone to make their own calls, they may decide wrong. They seek control. They are spiritual bullies.

Do I know spiritual bullies? Is it possible for me to be one?

One Thing to Think About: Is there a line between being a strong encourager and a spiritual bully?

One Thing to Pray For: Strength to follow Jesus regardless of what those around me think

WEEK 28 – TUESDAY

Reading: John 8:3-24

Missing the Real Threat

The story of the woman caught in adultery (John 7:53-8:11) is missing from some early manuscripts. It certainly resonates thematically with what follows—Jesus saying he judges no one (John 8:15) and speaking frankly about the sin of his audience (John 8:7, 21). He convicts his audience by turning their attention away from the sin of others and toward their own (*"let him who is without sin..."*).

Jesus can barely mention that he is the light of the world (John 8:12) before the Pharisees jump on him for uncorroborated testimony. He points them to his Father (John 8:16) and now they want to interrogate the Father too (John 8:19). Twice Jesus tells them that without him they will die in their sins (John 8:21, 24).

What is bewildering here is that Jesus speaks of life and death—*eternal* life and death—and they can't see past a minor procedural point. They are convinced that the threat in this situation is Jesus and his lone wolf testimony, but they are missing the real threat. The real threat *comes from within them*. Sin is the real threat. Only Jesus can help us deal with sin and avoid the death it brings. Jesus keeps warning: *"Unless you believe that I am he you will die in your sins"* and *"Let him who is without sin among you be first to throw a stone at her."* Meanwhile, they keep shooting at the wrong target.

We tend to think that *others* are the problem—and that we must try to correct *them*. The real threat is much closer to home, harder to acknowledge, and harder to correct.

One Thing to Think About: What tends to distract me from the real issue in my spiritual life?

One Thing to Pray For: The light of life (John 8:12)

WEEK 28 – WEDNESDAY

Reading: John 8:25-38

The Truth Will Set You Free

Despite the very vocal opposition of some Pharisees, *"many believed in him"*(John 8:30). Jesus encourages these: *"If you abide in my word, you are truly my disciples, and you will know the truth, and the truth will set you free"*(John 8:31-32). To truly, really, and authentically be Jesus' disciples, we must abide in his word. When we do this, Jesus will give us truth through that word that will liberate us.

This confuses his audience. *"We are offspring of Abraham and have never been enslaved to anyone. How is it that you say, 'You will become free'?"*(John 8:33). This is, of course, not true. The Jews were often enslaved prior to this—and even now are under Roman rule. But the point is that they don't know what Jesus is promising. *"Truly, truly, I say to you, everyone who practices sin is a slave to sin"*(John 8:34). Sin makes slaves. But *"if the Son sets you free, you will be free indeed"*(John 8:36). It is striking how differently these religious Jews see their sin than Jesus does.

Truth liberates. It breaks sin's hold. It reveals a better way. It teaches us of God's love, grace, and higher path. True discipleship in Jesus breeds freedom. We need only to abide in his word. When we follow him, we are truly his disciples. When the Son sets us free, we are truly free.

One Thing to Think About: In what ways have I been set free from my past sin? Are there sins I still need to be set free from?

One Thing to Pray For: Endurance to abide in Jesus' words

WEEK 28 – THURSDAY

Reading: John 8:39-59

Who Is Your Father?

In this escalating discussion with the Jews, Jesus introduces a new meaning for the word and idea of "father." *"They answered him, 'Abraham is our father.' Jesus said to them, 'If you were Abraham's children, you would be doing the works that Abraham did'"*(John 8:39). They assert that Abraham is their father and shockingly, Jesus argues with them! He introduces a different idea—that the father/child relationship is about *similarity*, not just physical ancestry. They are not *like* Abraham, so claiming him as father doesn't fit.

Jesus goes further. He hints that they have a different father and they loudly protest, arguing that God is their Father (John 8:41). Some have thought that their jab about fornication (John 8:41) might be casting aspersions on Jesus' birth to parents not officially wed.

"If God were your Father, you would love me, for I came from God and I am here"(John 8:42). *"Whoever is of God hears the words of God. The reason why you do not hear them is that you are not of God"*(John 8:47). *"You are of your father the devil, and your will is to do your father's desires. He was a murderer from the beginning, and does not stand in the truth, because there is no truth in him"*(John 8:44). In Jesus' language, I am the son (or daughter) of the one I choose to follow and emulate. My actions determine my parentage.

Who is my Father? What do my actions show about the one I am like and listen to? Far more important than my heritage and ethnicity is my allegiance.

One Thing to Think About: Are there areas of my life—my friends, job, money, recreation, self-evaluation—that do not reflect God as my Father?

One Thing to Pray For: Willingness to hear God's word always

WEEK 28 – FRIDAY

Reading: John 9:1-17

Rabbi, Who Sinned?

"*As he passed by, he saw a man blind from birth. And his disciples asked him, 'Rabbi, who sinned, this man or his parents, that he was born blind?'*"(John 9:1-2). Encountering a man *born* blind raises a theological question. It assumes that such conditions are punishment for sin. But congenital defects raise the question of whose sin caused it: the parents or the child (in the future)? The Pharisees certainly share in this mentality (John 9:34).

"*Jesus answered, 'It was not that this man sinned, or his parents, but that the works of God might be displayed in him'*"(John 9:3). Neither the man nor his parents have sinned. Jesus rejects this explanation. This is not a punishment for anyone's personal sin. Jesus is not arguing that the man and his parents never sinned, just that their sin is not the cause of his blindness.

It is very interesting that Jesus does not spend much time musing on the origins and philosophical reasons for the man's blindness. He is just ready to heal him and display God's works in him (John 9:3). There is an urgency to this (John 9:4-5). Much like Luke 13:1-5, there is no real discussion of why bad things happen. The stress is instead on how God can help now and my responsibility now.

Our energy and time are better spent in seeking God in the state we are in than in exploring all the "why"s of the world. This man is blessed by receiving his sight, but the greater gift is his spiritual vision and seeing the Messiah—not in plumbing the question of the cause of his ailment.

One Thing to Think About: Could this apply to my curiosity about the causes of suffering I have experienced?

One Thing to Pray For: The works of God to be displayed in me

WEEK 29 – MONDAY

Reading: John 9:18-34

The Closed Mind

The Pharisees decide to make an "investigation" of Jesus' healing of the blind man on the Sabbath. They question him, then (not believing him) they question his parents just to confirm he had been born blind. *"But how he now sees we do not know, nor do we know who opened his eyes. Ask him; he is of age. He will speak for himself"* (John 9:21). They are terrified.

John adds that they speak this way because *"they feared the Jews, for the Jews had already agreed that if anyone should confess Jesus to be Christ, he was to be put out of the synagogue"* (John 9:22). Their minds are closed. It is not possible that he is the Christ. Now let's massage the facts to match our conclusion.

They call the blind man in for a second interview. They call Jesus a sinner (John 9:24) and that they don't know where he is from (John 9:29). The blind man shows tremendous guts by lecturing them about the ridiculousness of their position (John 9:33). Unable to answer, they attack him: weren't you born blind (John 9:34)?

The story shows powerfully that when our minds are closed, we cannot possibly find truth. We decide conclusions before we look at evidence. As Christians, we have been convinced because at some point our minds were open. Our task is to continue to maintain an open mind (1 Thess 5:21).

One Thing to Think About: What actions contribute to an environment like this where people are afraid to speak openly?

One Thing to Pray For: A heart to *always* seek truth—even if it means I was wrong before

WEEK 29 – TUESDAY

Reading: John 9:35-10:6

Sight and Blindness

The aftermath of Jesus healing the blind man continues in this section. He has been cast out of the synagogue. Jesus finds him again and the man puts his faith in Jesus as the Son of Man/Son of God (John 9:38). Jesus then spiritualizes the concept of blindness and teaches us something about what has happened here.

"For judgment I came into this world, that those who do not see may see, and those who see may become blind" (John 9:39). Jesus has come to make the blind see and to make the seeing blind. The Pharisees bristle. *"Are we also blind?"* (John 9:40). *"Jesus said to them, 'If you were blind, you would have no guilt; but now that you say, "We see," your guilt remains'"* (John 9:41). The blind—those aware of their need—can be healed, but those already think they see are beyond help. Their guilt remains.

The one thing that never seems to occur to the Pharisees in this exchange is that Jesus may truly be from God. They are blind. There is also a blindness to their own sin and need. They are quick to doubt Jesus, quick to doubt the blind man's testimony, and quick to ignore his well-reasoned argument—yet remarkably slow to examine themselves. They are blind but they think they can see.

The religion of Jesus will not allow us to simply look at *others* and *their* flaws or the holes in *their* arguments. He insists we look at ourselves first—or else remain blind.

One Thing to Think About: Do I know I am blind—or do I think I see?

One Thing to Pray For: The vision that can only come from God

WEEK 29 – WEDNESDAY

Reading: John 10:7-18

Why Jesus Is the Good Shepherd

Immediately after the discussion over the blind man, Jesus launches into an extended metaphor describing his relationship with his followers as a shepherd with his sheep. His sheep follow him because they know and trust him (John 10:3, 5). But why do they trust him?

Jesus contrasts himself with other "leaders"—those who "*(climb) in by another way*"(John 10:1), "*are thieves and robbers*"(John 10:8), seek their own gain (John 10:10) and flee at the first sign of difficulty (John 10:12-13). Jesus calls them "hired hands" because they are not worthy of being called shepherds. Some people in positions of leadership are only there to enrich and empower themselves. They cannot be trusted.

Jesus is the good shepherd—the leader we are all truly seeking. He provides for his sheep: "*If anyone enters by me, he will be saved and will go in and out and find pasture*"(John 10:9). He protects his sheep, keeping them in the fold (John 10:1, 9) and laying down his life when danger approaches (John 10:15). Jesus has come for *us*, not for himself: "*The thief comes only to steal and kill and destroy. I came that they may have life and have it abundantly*"(John 10:10).

We can trust Jesus. His entire mission has been for our benefit. In him we hear the voice and goodwill of the Father. His teachings are for our good. His sacrifice is for our salvation. His blessings help us. And so we follow.

One Thing to Think About: How am I like a sheep? Is this a flattering comparison?

One Thing to Pray For: Discernment to only hear and follow the voice of the Good Shepherd

WEEK 29 – THURSDAY

Reading: John 10:19-30

No One Will Snatch Them

Jesus continues his extended metaphor about shepherds and sheep. John keeps reminding us of the people's responses to him: "*they did not understand*"(John 10:6), refuse to listen because they believe "*he has a demon, and is insane*"(John 10:20), and seek plainer declarations (John 10:24). Jesus says simply, "*You do not believe because you are not among my sheep*"(John 10:26).

Jesus' sheep know him, are known by him, and choose to submit to him. "*My sheep hear my voice, and I know them, and they follow me*"(John 10:27). Because of this, "*I give them eternal life*"(John 10:28). Eternal life is true knowledge of and relationship with God, continuing through this life and perfected in the life to come. "*And they will never perish*"(John 10:28) is not a promise of avoiding physical death, but something just as universal and far worse: God's judgment.

"*And no one will snatch them out of my hand*"(John 10:28). Jesus' sheep need not fear external forces or the ill will of those around them. Jesus is stronger than those who would try to harm them. Perhaps Jesus is still thinking about that blind man—the only honest person in the whole situation, yet the one treated the worst. In spite of it all, he is *Jesus'* sheep and therefore is secure, though all the world protest.

As if to further reassure, he insists that his power and will are the same as the Father's (John 10:29-30). There is security here. When I choose to follow Jesus, I need fear no man.

One Thing to Think About: Do I feel secure as a follower of Jesus?

One Thing to Pray For: The peace of knowing the protective power of Christ

WEEK 29 – FRIDAY

Reading: John 10:31-42

Another Almost Stoning

Jesus has explained that his protection and the Father's are the same. "*I and the Father are one*"(John 10:30). This makes the Jews take up stones (John 10:31)—a remarkable escalation of tensions, but one we've seen previously in John (8:59). Jesus calmly asks for the charges on which stoning is justified. They assert that he has blasphemed by making himself God (John 8:33). He refutes their charge by challenging their definition of blasphemy.

"*Is it not written in your Law, 'I said, you are gods'? If he called them gods to whom the word of God came—and the Scripture cannot be broken—do you say of him whom the Father consecrated and sent into the world, 'You are blaspheming,' because I said, 'I am the Son of God'*"(John 10:34-36). If Scripture can say "you are gods" and not be blaspheming, am I blaspheming because I say I'm God's Son? How can I say something tamer than Scripture and be blaspheming?

Then he addresses what they are ignoring—the proof. "*If I am not doing the works of my Father, then do not believe me; but if I do them, even though you do not believe me, believe the works, that you may know and understand that the Father is in me and I am in the Father*"(John 10:37-38). If I back it up, at least believe *that*! At least believe God is at work, even if you don't believe in me!

I am struck here by Jesus' *patience* to carefully explain himself, even though they won't hear. It is also notable that Jesus moves on and immediately finds more fruitful ground among former disciples of John (John 10:40-42). There is a time when both safety and common sense tell us to seek more receptive audiences.

One Thing to Think About: Does it concern me to know I can be absolutely convinced I'm right—to the point of stoning someone—and be completely wrong?

One Thing to Pray For: A heart to seek truth—even if it challenges my preconceptions

WEEK 30 – MONDAY

Reading: John 11:1-16

For the Glory of God

Having been threatened again in Jerusalem, Jesus and his disciples retreat beyond the Jordan. Mary and Martha, sisters who are clearly dear to Jesus, send word that their brother is seriously ill. *"But when Jesus heard it he said, 'This illness does not lead to death. It is for the glory of God, so that the Son of God may be glorified through it'"*(John 11:4). This is odd and somewhat offensive. Jesus declares that it is good that Lazarus is sick. His sickness is about God's glory.

His next step is also strange. *"So, when he heard that Lazarus was ill, he stayed two days longer in the place where he was"*(John 11:6). How is Lazarus' sickness going to glorify God if it does not lead to death and Jesus makes no move to heal him? When he does decide to return to Jerusalem, his disciples are afraid and repeatedly try to talk him out of it (John 11:8, 12) before resigning themselves to death (John 11:16).

Finally he breaks the bad news. *"Lazarus has died, and for your sake I am glad that I was not there, so that you may believe"*(John 11:14-15). I am glad because it means that you will believe. This is about the glory of God (see also John 11:40). Only after Lazarus is raised will they begin to see the faith-building power and wonder that springs out of Lazarus' premature death.

Difficult things can ultimately bring God glory. Scary things can bring God glory. Hard-to-understand things can bring God glory. Do I have anything difficult, scary, or hard to understand in my life?

One Thing to Think About: Do I give glory to God when adverse circumstances show his goodness?

One Thing to Pray For: God to work in my life in a way that brings glory to him, not me

WEEK 30 – TUESDAY

Reading: John 11:17-37

Jesus Wept

When Jesus arrives in Bethany, Martha and Mary both reproach him with the same words: *"Lord, if you had been here, my brother would not have died"* (John 11:21, 32). They have faith that Jesus could have healed their brother, but the path forward now is unclear.

Martha still believes—*"even now I know that whatever you ask from God, God will give you"* (John 11:22)—but seems reluctant (John 11:24). Mary breaks down at her brother's tomb. Seeing these ebbs and flows of grief, Jesus is affected. *"When Jesus saw her weeping, and the Jews who had come with her also weeping, he was deeply moved in his spirit and greatly troubled"* (John 11:33). His emotions overcome him. *"Jesus wept"* (John 11:35). *"Then Jesus, deeply moved again, came to the tomb"* (John 11:38).

It is easy for us to overlook this detail because we know what happens next in the story: Lazarus is going to live again. John highlights that Jesus is touched deeply and moved to the point of tears. This is particularly amazing because <u>Jesus knows that Lazarus will soon be raised, but it still affects him to watch people grieve</u>.

I don't have to wonder if Jesus cares when I hurt and grieve. Even though there is hope of resurrection, grief and sadness are a part of the life Jesus experiences in the flesh. They are part of our lives too.

One Thing to Think About: Do I weep with others the way Jesus does?

One Thing to Pray For: Deeper awareness of Jesus' compassion for me

WEEK 30 – WEDNESDAY

Reading: John 11:38-57

Lazarus, Come Out!

Lingering near the tomb with the grieving family, Jesus makes a faux pas. *"Jesus said, 'Take away the stone.' Martha, the sister of the dead man, said to him, 'Lord, by this time there will be an odor, for he has been dead four days'"*(John 11:39). Seeing the tomb would have been possible a couple of days earlier, but now Martha reproaches him, revealing that she is not seriously thinking he will raise Lazarus.

Jesus prays aloud (John 11:41-42) so that others know that what he is about to do is not for his own glory. He always points people to the Father. *"When he had said these things, he cried out with a loud voice, 'Lazarus, come out.' The man who had died came out, his hands and feet bound with linen strips, and his face wrapped with a cloth"*(John 11:43-44). Lazarus, come out! The same voice that commands waves and wind, demons and sicknesses, now orders a human back from the grave. *This* is power. Jesus doesn't need to touch him or see him. He only speaks the word.

"Unbind him, and let him go"(John 11:44). Set him free. This is not just a show. He really intends for Lazarus to be raised from the dead. Many believe in Jesus because of this miracle (John 11:45) while others don't and squeal to the Pharisees (John 11:46). They plot to kill him (John 11:53) and to re-kill Lazarus (John 12:10-11).

We come face to face here with the breathtaking power of Jesus. No force—even death itself—is too great for him. If I have any hope in the face of death, it is only through him.

One Thing to Think About: Why would some choose not to believe even after seeing this?

One Thing to Pray For: Deeper hope in Jesus' power over death

WEEK 30 – THURSDAY

Reading: John 12:1-19

Judas and the Moneybag

After the raising of Lazarus, Jesus and the disciples eat with the newly reunited family. Interestingly, we find (just as in Luke's account) Martha serving while Mary attends to Jesus. This time she anoints his feet with ointment and wipes them with her hair (John 12:3).

"But Judas Iscariot, one of his disciples (he who was about to betray him), said, 'Why was this ointment not sold for three hundred denarii and given to the poor?'"(John 12:4-5). Judas objects to Mary's act of service, claiming to be a defender of the poor. Yet *"he said this, not because he cared about the poor, but because he was a thief, and having charge of the moneybag he used to help himself to what was put into it"*(John 12:6). Judas has eyes for the money this ointment would have brought into his reach. Jesus corrects him (John 12:7).

I am intrigued by the detail that Jesus allows Judas to be in charge of the moneybag despite the fact that he knows he is a thief. Is he testing Judas? Does he hope he'll change? Are all the sermons Jesus preaches about money primarily directed at him?

This situation reminds us that every temptation is also a *test*—will we obey or not? What are we made of? If God removes all temptation, we have no way to prove ourselves, no test to pass, and no way of knowing whether we have real faith.

One Thing to Think About: Does it help to think of adverse circumstances and temptations as tests? Why or why not?

One Thing to Pray For: God's help to remain steadfast through temptation

WEEK 30 – FRIDAY

Reading: John 12:20-36

Dying to Live

As some Greeks approach Jesus, he breaks into a soliloquy about his mission and goals. Perhaps he is thinking particularly about how his crucifixion will be the ultimate outreach to foreign people (John 12:32). The specifics aren't clear, but Jesus focuses on the fact that his hour has come (John 12:23). It is time to die. He expresses his thoughts by a series of paradoxes. *"Truly, truly, I say to you, unless a grain of wheat falls into the earth and dies, it remains alone; but if it dies, it bears much fruit. Whoever loves his life loses it, and whoever hates his life in this world will keep it for eternal life"* (John 12:24-25). Wheat dies to live. Loving your life means you lose it. Hating your life means you find it. Death means judgment for the world, but not for Jesus (John 12:31). For Jesus, death means success (John 12:32).

All of this seems obscure and frightening. The point that Jesus is teaching is that there are higher purposes than just staying alive. If we become convinced that our *survival* is the most important thing, we'll sacrifice truth, justice, love, and service for ourselves. Then we begin to add other things—I want to survive comfortably, happily, peacefully, etc. But when we are willing to sacrifice ourselves for our God (*"hates his life,"* John 12:25), we can then truly live. It is then that we achieve his purposes and find meaning whether we live or die. This is Jesus' perspective.

There are more important things than our physical survival. How we treat others, honor God, control ourselves, do good in the world, place hope and faith in Jesus, and model Christian perspectives on life matters more than whether we survive a few more years. Jesus knows he is facing death and approaches it unafraid. He will behave the same way whether he lives or dies. Disciples know that—unless Jesus returns first—they will die. With that constant awareness, we should focus attention on *how* we are living rather than simply on prolonging our lives. None of this means that we should be reckless with our lives or cold to those who are suffering. Rather, we serve, help, and mourn without fear—like Jesus.

One Thing to Think About: Do I care more about my life than God's purposes?

One Thing to Pray For: A heart of sacrifice and self-denial

WEEK 31 – MONDAY

Reading: John 12:37-50

Judged by Jesus' Words

In John's gospel, this marks the end of the public ministry of Jesus. John summarizes the response of the people: *"Though he had done so many signs before them, they still did not believe in him"*(John 12:37). Though it is not a complete rejection, John's words still hold as essentially true: *"He came to his own, and his own people did not receive him"*(John 1:11). Some have faith in him but are too afraid to confess it, revealing corruption within (John 12:42-43).

Jesus has one last word for the crowd. *"Whoever believes in me, believes not in me but in him who sent me. And whoever sees me sees him who sent me"*(John 12:44-45). Their reaction to him is equal to their reaction to God. *"The one who rejects me and does not receive my words has a judge; the word that I have spoken will judge him on the last day"*(John 12:48). Rejection will be judged by Jesus' words. The reason is that his words come from the Father, the source of eternal life (John 12:49-50). God's words cannot be rejected without consequence.

Each teaching and command is not merely advice or suggestion. We can scarcely afford to merely have an opinion about Jesus' teaching. It will *judge* us.

We do not know Jesus physically, but these words speak to us as well. Jesus' words will judge *me* at the last day. Have I been born again? Do I believe? Do I hear his correction about money—pride—family? What will his words say about me on the last day?

One Thing to Think About: Is my life truly shaped by Jesus' words?

One Thing to Pray For: The light of Jesus' wisdom, truth, and goodness

WEEK 31 – TUESDAY

Reading: John 13:1-20

A Servant Is Not Greater Than His Master

John does not share some of the details of the Passover meal that we find in the other gospels. We do not see Jesus investing the bread and fruit of the vine with special significance regarding his crucifixion here. Instead, John focuses on an interruption during the meal.

Jesus "*rose from supper. He laid aside his outer garments, and taking a towel, tied it around his waist. Then he poured water into a basin and began to wash the disciples' feet and wipe them with the towel that was wrapped around him*"(John 13:4-5). The emphasis in foot-washing is that it is a menial task that doesn't fit with Jesus' status. It is an act of humiliating service. This is the basis for Peter's shocked objection: "*Lord, do you wash my feet?*"(John 13:6). It is hard to overstate how startling this picture would be to an ancient Jew. So Jesus works his way around the room, methodically handling and cleaning their feet.

Jesus interprets his actions. "*You call me Teacher and Lord, and you are right, for so I am. If I then, your Lord and Teacher, have washed your feet, you also ought to wash one another's feet*"(John 13:13-14). This is about status vs. service. I am your Lord, yet I have served you; you must treat one another this way. "*Truly, truly, I say to you, a servant is not greater than his master*"(John 13:16). If the master lowers himself, how can we think we are too good to do it?

Jesus reminds us that every humiliating, difficult, sacrificial act he performs is also a challenge to his followers. Do I think I'm better than my master?

One Thing to Think About: Do I resent having to give up time, money, or my own plans to serve others?

One Thing to Pray For: A servant's heart

WEEK 31 – WEDNESDAY

Reading: John 13:21-38

By This All Will Know

Jesus' attention turns to his betrayer and he is upset. *"After saying these things, Jesus was troubled in his spirit, and testified, 'Truly, truly, I say to you, one of you will betray me'"*(John 13:21). He mentions the betrayal, gives bread to Judas, and Judas exits to do his work—yet most of the apostles don't catch on yet (John 13:28).

Jesus now has some last words for the eleven, knowing that the wheels are in motion for his death and that the time is short (John 12:33). *"A new commandment I give to you, that you love one another; just as I have loved you, you also are to love one another"*(John 13:34). Jesus has loved them to the end (John 13:1) and has now loved them by lowering himself to wash their feet. His love is at times tough, patient, compassionate, and honest. His love draws people to him wherever he is. Now he commands: *"as I have loved you, you also are to love one another."*

"By this all people will know that you are my disciples, if you have love for one another"(John 13:35). This is how people identify *you* with *me*—when you love like I have loved you. Jesus is saying that the primary recognition others have of our association with him is relational, not doctrinal. This is not to denigrate doctrine, but to affirm that others identify the character of Jesus much more readily than his words.

People are not only listening to what we say. They are watching how we love. If they see us claim connection to Jesus, yet treat others poorly and harshly, they are turned off. But consider the power of disciples who share a heart of service, compassion, and sacrifice like Jesus. Who could we draw to him?

One Thing to Think About: Do people see me loving like Jesus?

One Thing to Pray For: The patient, compassionate, honest love of Jesus

WEEK 31 – THURSDAY

Reading: John 14:1-11

I Will Come Again

The Passover meal has taken on an ominous tone. Jesus has spoken of a betrayer. "*Yet a little while I am with you*"(John 13:33). He has foretold Peter's denial (John 13:38). In this section, he gives comfort about ultimate outcomes, when the events of this dark night are long in the past.

"*In my Father's house are many rooms. If it were not so, would I have told you that I go to prepare a place for you?*"(John 14:2). Jesus is going to the Father (John 14:5-6) for the purpose of preparing a place for them. "*And if I go and prepare a place for you, I will come again and will take you to myself, that where I am you may be also*"(John 14:3). If I go, I will come again. My leaving is not permanent. When Jesus returns, he will take them to himself so that they can be together (presumably "in my Father's house," John 14:2).

Jesus also asserts that he is the only way to this communion with the Father. "*I am the way, and the truth, and the life. No one comes to the Father except through me*"(John 14:6). It is a startlingly exclusive claim.

When Jesus says "*I will come again*," he promises his disciples something that remains unfulfilled. He will return to "*take you to myself*"(John 14:3). Until then, he is preparing a place for us (John 14:2). So disciples hold vigil for their master.

One Thing to Think About: Do I think often about the time when Jesus will come again so that we may always be together?

One Thing to Pray For: Jesus to return quickly

WEEK 31 – FRIDAY

Reading: John 14:12-21

Another Helper

Jesus is breaking the news to the disciples that he is leaving them to go to the Father (John 14:28). John 14-17 serves as an extended "last words" speech to them. These are things he wants them to remember and words to prepare them for the next steps in his absence. Much of his focus is on their need to continue to obey him after his departure (John 14:15, 21, 24).

"And I will ask the Father, and he will give you another Helper, to be with you forever" (John 14:16). Jesus promises a helper and comforter, the Holy Spirit. They will not be on their own. Christians receive the Holy Spirit, who is a guarantee of our inheritance (Eph 1:13-14), the agent of our resurrection (Rom 8:11), and the one who works within us to refine us into the character of Jesus (Gal 5:22-25).

Jesus also promises *truth* to the apostles through the Spirit (John 14:26; 15:26; 16:13). This probably relates to their role as authoritative spokesmen for him (Acts 2:42, 1 Cor 14:37, 1 Thess 2:13). Just as Jesus did when physically present, the Spirit now brings truth to his disciples.

Don't overlook the point: God has made provision for his people in this "in-between time"—the time between Jesus' comings. We have help. We have truth revealed by God. We have God living within us. Praise God for his Spirit!

One Thing to Think About: Why is Jesus so concerned about the comfort of his people?

One Thing to Pray For: Proper understanding of—and appreciation for—God's Holy Spirit

WEEK 32 – MONDAY

Reading: John 14:22-31

My Peace I Give to You

As Jesus prepares the apostles for his departure, he is concerned about their emotional state. *"Let not your hearts be troubled"*(John 14:1). *"Let not your hearts be troubled, neither let them be afraid"*(John 14:27). He has promised to return to take them (John 14:3) and to send another comforter (John 14:16) to help them. All of this is intended to reassure.

"Peace I leave with you; my peace I give to you. Not as the world gives do I give to you. Let not your hearts be troubled, neither let them be afraid"(John 14:27). Jesus wants them to have the peace that comes from trusting God (see John 14:1). He wants them to have the peace that persists through undesired circumstances. He wants them to have peace that is unbowed by the hatred of others (see John 16:2). He wants them to have the peace that waits for him with endurance.

There is no peace like the peace that comes from reconciliation with God. My emotions are no longer subject to the whims of people or the volatility of my circumstances. Peace with God gives proper context to everything that happens in my world: it cannot change the most important thing. If we have resolved the great conflict of our lives, all else pales in comparison. This is the peace Jesus gives.

One Thing to Think About: Does the peace of Jesus reign in my heart?

One Thing to Pray For: Comfort for my troubled and fearful heart

WEEK 32 – TUESDAY

Reading: John 15:1-17

Disciples Are Dependent

Jesus is continuing to speak to the apostles the night before his death. The imminence of the cross gives his words added weight and urgency. Here he gives an extended metaphor to describe his relationship with them.

"*I am the true vine, and my Father is the vinedresser. Every branch in me that does not bear fruit he takes away, and every branch that does bear fruit he prunes, that it may bear more fruit*"(John 15:1-2). Jesus is the vine; disciples are the branches; the Father is the vinedresser. The goal is fruit: actions, words, and relationships that achieve God's purposes. The Father takes away unfruitful branches (Jesus later says their lack of fruit is due to not abiding in the vine, John 15:6). The Father prunes fruitful branches—the painful process of cutting back to promote further fruit-bearing and growth.

"*Abide in me, and I in you. As the branch cannot bear fruit by itself, unless it abides in the vine, neither can you, unless you abide in me. I am the vine; you are the branches. Whoever abides in me and I in him, he it is that bears much fruit, for apart from me you can do nothing*"(John 15:4-5). The thrust of this picture is that <u>disciples are dependent</u>. Just like branches can't bear fruit on their own, neither can we. In case we miss it, Jesus spells it out: "*apart from me you can do nothing.*"

Many in our world—especially in Eastern religions—encourage us to look *within* ourselves for truth and meaning. To them, spirituality is self-exploration. Jesus is stressing that the source of truth, life, and purpose is not within us. It is in him. I must stay connected to him or I wither, stagnate, and die.

One Thing to Think About: Is it hard for me to accept that I am not complete in myself?

One Thing to Pray For: The fruit that springs from my connection to Jesus

WEEK 32 – WEDNESDAY

Reading: John 15:18-27

Why the World Hates Us

Jesus is preparing his disciples for life without him. He has spoken to them of the comfort and help of the Spirit, the promise of his return, and the dependent nature of their ongoing relationship with Jesus after his departure. But he also must prepare them—and by extension, us—for the opposition they can expect from the unbelievers around them.

"If the world hates you, know that it has hated me before it hated you" (John 15:18). The "world" here is not every person, but those who have an allegiance to sin and darkness. They will hate us because they hate Jesus (John 15:18, 20). Particularly they hate that Jesus reveals that they are guilty of sin. *"If I had not come and spoken to them, they would not have been guilty of sin, but now they have no excuse for their sin"* (John 15:22).

The world also hates Jesus' disciples because we are not like them. *"If you were of the world, the world would love you as its own; but because you are not of the world, but I chose you out of the world, therefore the world hates you"* (John 15:19). They will hate us because they do not know the Father (John 16:3).

All of this is to say that Jesus' disciples should expect to experience hostility, rejection, and harm because of what we believe and practice. We do not seek this out, yet it is a part of being called out of the world. A further question: should we hate others? Doesn't hating others (even when they "deserve" it) make us more like the world than the Father?

One Thing to Think About: Is it hard for me to accept that the world may hate me?

One Thing to Pray For: Endurance when we experience opposition for our faith

WEEK 32 – THURSDAY

Reading: John 16:1-11

The Spirit Will Convict the World

In this discourse, Jesus has had a lot to say about the coming Comforter/Helper, the Holy Spirit. He will be with the apostles forever (John 14:16), teach them all things and bring to their remembrance Jesus' words (John 14:26), and bear witness along with the apostles (John 15:26-27). Here Jesus stresses that his departure is actually a blessing because of what the Spirit will do through them (John 16:7).

"And when he comes, he will convict the world concerning sin and righteousness and judgment"(John 16:8). He will convict the world. Conviction means pointing out to someone their sin and summoning them to repentance. *"concerning sin, because they do not believe in me"*(John 16:9). They have rejected the way of escape from sin (John 8:24, 31-32). *"concerning righteousness, because I go to the Father, and you will see me no longer"*(John 16:10). True righteousness has come and will soon depart the world, revealing the ideal. Our attempts at righteousness are revealed to be inadequate next to his. *"concerning judgment, because the ruler of this world is judged"*(John 16:111). The Spirit will expose false judgments (John 7:24) and condemn the father of all false judgments, Satan.

What does the Spirit's conviction look like? It looks like the preaching of the Spirit-inspired gospel by these same apostles. The result of that preaching is people being *"cut to the heart"* by the message (Acts 2:37, 7:54). This is conviction. The Spirit will bear witness, guide them in all truth, bring to their remembrance—and through them convict the world and summon it to repentance. This process continues today as the Spirit's and apostles' witness (John 15:26-27) lives on.

One Thing to Think About: Why is it so important that the world be convicted?

One Thing to Pray For: The conviction of the Spirit—even if it is unpleasant

WEEK 32 – FRIDAY

Reading: John 16:12-24

Sorrow to Joy

Jesus gives his disciples an enigmatic statement that puzzles them: "*A little while, and you will see me no longer; and again a little while, and you will see me*"(John 16:16). They begin to whisper to one another about what this could mean (John 16:17-19). Jesus explains: "*Truly, truly, I say to you, you will weep and lament, but the world will rejoice. You will be sorrowful, but your sorrow will turn to joy*"(John 16:20). In the moment, you will be sad while the world rejoices, but sorrow will turn into joy.

To explain, he calls to mind the vivid picture of a woman in labor. "*When a woman is giving birth, she has sorrow because her hour has come, but when she has delivered the baby, she no longer remembers that anguish, for joy that a human being has been born into the world*"(John 16:21). The joy overwhelms the sorrow so that it is only a different memory. In fact, we are thankful for such sorrow because it produces such joy.

"*So also you have sorrow now, but I will see you again, and your hearts will rejoice, and no one will take your joy from you*"(John 16:22). Jesus is more specific: you have sorrow now (because he is going away) but *I will see you again*. Is he speaking of his resurrection or his ultimate return? Both fit the metaphor.

We don't experience precisely what the first disciples did, but we have a similar pattern. We feel sorrow as we are distant from the one we love, then joy as we discover he has found a way to return to us. We have sorrow as we see him die that turns to joy as we see he lives again. We feel sorrow over our sin, which turns to joy over his forgiveness. Jesus turns our sorrow into joy.

One Thing to Think About: Am I living a life of joy?

One Thing to Pray For: Courage to pray in confidence

WEEK 33 – MONDAY

Reading: John 16:25-33

Take Heart; I Have Overcome the World

In this last part of his long sermon and exhortation, Jesus addresses an undercurrent of thought among the disciples. They are frustrated with his obscure style of speaking. "*I have said these things to you in figures of speech. The hour is coming when I will no longer speak to you in figures of speech but will tell you plainly about the Father*"(John 16:25). Jesus acknowledges that he has been speaking in figures but will soon stop.

"*I came from the Father and have come into the world, and now I am leaving the world and going to the Father*"(John 16:28). He tells them plainly what is about to happen and the disciples breathe a sigh of relief (John 16:29-30), even stating that they now believe.

"*I have said these things to you, that in me you may have peace. In the world you will have tribulation. But take heart; I have overcome the world*"(John 16:33). All of Jesus' words are intended to give peace despite hard circumstances: let not your hearts be troubled, I will come again, I will send a Helper, abide in me, the world hated me too, sorrow to joy, no more figures. The world brings trouble, but I have overcome it!

The greatest encouragement imaginable is that Jesus is victorious over the world and its ruler. The world will never have the last word. And because Jesus has overcome, I can overcome through him. When we relate to Jesus—when the world seems to oppose us and we find little room for hope—he tells us to take heart!

One Thing to Think About: How does Jesus' victory give me hope?

One Thing to Pray For: Confidence in Jesus' victory

WEEK 33 – TUESDAY

Reading: John 17:1-5

Glorify Your Son

After giving this lengthy speech to his disciples, Jesus prays. This part of his prayer focuses on his relationship with the Father and the next steps for him. "*Father, the hour has come*"(John 17:1). "*I glorified you on earth, having accomplished the work that you gave me to do*"(John 17:4). It is clear that Jesus' relationship with the Father extends back far before his birth (John 17:5), yet has reached a new stage with Jesus completing his earthly mission.

He has only one request in this section: "*glorify your Son*"(John 17:1, 5). Jesus asks for a return to the glory he had previous to this mission (John 17:5). He has lowered himself and taken on human flesh for a while due to his great love for us and allegiance to the Father and his will. He speaks to his desire to glorify the Father through *his* glorification (John 17:1). This prayer has been answered. Truly the Father appears greater in our time because of the work of Jesus.

This section underscores the great sacrifice Jesus has made for us *just in coming* to earth and revealing God to us. Jesus has been humiliated for us. He has emptied himself (Phil 2:7). There are details of this—the strain of the relationship between Jesus and the Father or the nature of Jesus as God and man—that we don't fully understand, yet we grasp the principle. Are we willing to sacrifice for others? To seek God's glory? To be humbled now so that God will exalt us?

One Thing to Think About: Do I want God to glorify me? Why?

One Thing to Pray For: Humility now so that God will exalt me later

WEEK 33 – WEDNESDAY

Reading: John 17:6-19

Guard Them and Sanctify Them

Jesus continues his prayer to the Father, transitioning here from praying about himself to praying for the people whom he is soon to leave behind. He seems especially concerned about the continuation of what he has begun in them after he has gone. *"And I am no longer in the world, but they are in the world, and I am coming to you"*(John 17:11). A crisis point is coming in which the Father's help is desperately needed.

The disciples have received God's word from Jesus (John 17:8) and have been given to Jesus (John 17:9). Now they need to be guarded: *"Holy Father, keep them in your name"*(John 17:11). They are no longer of the world (John 17:16) but they must continue to interact with the world (John 17:18). Now they need to be sanctified: *"Sanctify them in the truth; your word is truth"*(John 17:17). Jesus asks that the Father preserve them holy and special and different in a worldly world.

It is notable the role *words* play in this. Words cause the separation between disciples and the world (John 17:6-8) and words continue to sanctify them (John 17:17, 19). Words are the means by which God has called his people—and the means by which he continues to call them to purity.

Guarding and sanctifying mean that our greatest needs are continually met by our God, even while our Savior is not present with us.

One Thing to Think About: Do I see being guarded from Satan as a priority the way Jesus does?

One Thing to Pray For: The Father to keep and sanctify me through his truth

WEEK 33 – THURSDAY

Reading: John 17:20-26

The Testimony of Unity

Having prayed for himself and his disciples, Jesus now turns his attention to the future—"*those who <u>will</u> believe in me through their word*"(John 17:20). He prays for unity: "*that they may all be one, just as you, Father, are in me, and I in you, that they also may be in us*"(John 17:21). The model for this unity is Jesus' oneness with the Father (John 17:21, 22, 23a).

When separate people and personalities are made one, it is a work of God. This is true in marriage, where God joins two people together (Matt 19:4-6). It is also true of a local church where we have the "*unity of the Spirit*"(Eph 4:3) despite very diverse backgrounds and opinions. There is a testimony given when followers of Jesus are one with each other (as Jesus is one with the Father).

"*I in them and you in me, that they may become perfectly one, so that the world may know that you sent me and loved them even as you loved me*"(John 17:23). Jesus asks this of the Father "*so that the world may know.*" He has already encouraged them to love one another and bear witness to the world (John 13:34-35). Here it is their oneness—that singularity of purpose (John 17:26) and refusal to separate from one another (which Judas lacked, John 17:12)—that teaches the world.

Our unity does not demonstrate everything about Jesus, but it emphatically declares his reality among us. The challenge for us is to pursue unity—singularity of purpose and refusal to separate—when challenged by adversity, selfishness, and hurt.

One Thing to Think About: Am I committed to maintaining unity with other disciples?

One Thing to Pray For: The unity Jesus prayed for—so the world would receive his testimony through us

WEEK 33 – FRIDAY

Reading: John 18:1-14

Shall I Not Drink the Cup?

After Jesus has spoken at length to the disciples, they retreat to the garden. John does not record the scene where Jesus prays for the cup to pass, but jumps straight into Judas leading the arresting party to him. John shows us Jesus as decisive and certain without focusing on the struggle of his prayers.

"*So Judas, having procured a band of soldiers and some officers from the chief priests and the Pharisees, went there with lanterns and torches and weapons*"(John 18:3). This is scary! But Jesus is not scared. "*When Jesus said to them, 'I am he,' they drew back and fell to the ground*"(John 18:6). Peter lashes out to defend Jesus (John 18:10) but Jesus rebukes him. "*Shall I not drink the cup that the Father has given me?*"(John 18:11). Peter's effort is misguided because it is not tuned in to the Father's will and mission.

Jesus marches to a different beat than his apostles. They are scared of opposition when he is not (John 11:8). They are resistant to him serving while he insists on it (John 13:6-9). They are sad that he is leaving while he says it is to their advantage (John 16:6). The reason for this difference is Jesus' absolute commitment to the Father's will. Now the Father's will leads Jesus to an unpleasant place, but his question ("*Shall I not drink the cup that the Father has given me?*") shows that disobedience is in no way an option for him.

While there is much to say here about bravery and self-restraint, the most noteworthy feature of this story is how Jesus unflinchingly chooses the Father's will over his own comfort.

One Thing to Think About: Will I respond like Jesus when my obedience costs me my comfort?

One Thing to Pray For: Deeper allegiance to the will of my good God

WEEK 34 – MONDAY

Reading: John 18:15-27

Why Do You Strike Me?

Jesus is arrested and brought to both of the High Priests (John 18:19, 24). The reason for this oddity is that Annas is Caiaphas' father-in-law and the former high priest. He appears to be the one with real power and hence he sees Jesus first. Annas interrogates Jesus *"about his disciples and his teaching"*(John 18:19). Jesus bristles at this. *"I have spoken openly to the world"*(John 18:20).

He goes further. *"Why do you ask me? Ask those who have heard me what I said to them; they know what I said"*(John 18:21). Jesus suggests that there are other motives at play here. Annas is trying to get Jesus to incriminate himself. *"Why do you ask me?"* means that Jesus is challenging the injustice of arresting a rabbi only to fish for crimes for which to kill him.

One of the officers strikes Jesus. He challenges this injustice too: *"If what I said is wrong, bear witness about the wrong; but if what I said is right, why do you strike me?"*(John 18:23). He does not object to being struck if he has done wrong, but again asks for reasons.

Jesus' "why"s intrigue me. They speak to motives. They are attempts to expose the deeper motivation problems in these men and what they are doing. His "why"s are powerful. Why do I do what I do? Why do I sin? Why do I cater to certain people? Why do I fear? There is cause for self-examination here.

One Thing to Think About: What does Jesus see when he examines my motives?

One Thing to Pray For: A pure heart

WEEK 34 – TUESDAY

Reading: John 18:28-40

A Kingdom Not of This World

Jesus is now shuffled from Annas to Caiaphas (where we learn from other accounts that he is condemned by the Jewish governing council, the Sanhedrin) and on to Pilate, the Roman governor. This is the meeting that will determine his fate. *"So Pilate entered his headquarters again and called Jesus and said to him, 'Are you the King of the Jews?'"*(John 18:33). This rumor has followed Jesus throughout his ministry. This is the important question to Pilate, although I suspect he asks with a bemused smirk— *this guy* the king? It is important to remember that contemporary messianic conceptions center around a God-approved king acting as a new David. Pilate is asking him if he is the Christ.

"My kingdom is not of this world. If my kingdom were of this world, my servants would have been fighting, that I might not be delivered over to the Jews. But my kingdom is not from the world"(John 18:36). Jesus works to correct Pilate's misconception. He is a king, but his kingdom is *"not of this world"*—not a kingdom in the way Pilate uses that word. It is a statement about *origins*—divine rather than worldly—and about *nature*—it is not physical, like the kingdom/republic/empire of Rome. His evidence is that his servants refuse to fight, which is suicide for any earthly kingdom.

"Then Pilate said to him, 'So you are a king?' Jesus answered, 'You say that I am a king. For this purpose I was born and for this purpose I have come into the world—to bear witness to the truth. Everyone who is of the truth listens to my voice"(John 18:37). Pilate tries a backdoor trap—*"So you are a king?"*—but Jesus focuses on his purpose of testifying to the truth, not simply reigning.

Jesus remains a different kind of king reigning over a different kind of kingdom. We must see this in a different way than Pilate, noticing God's imprint on Jesus' work and kingdom.

One Thing to Think About: Is it difficult for me to believe Jesus is enthroned and reigning now?

One Thing to Pray For: Faith to see and appreciate a kingdom not of this world

WEEK 34 – WEDNESDAY

Reading: John 19:1-11

The Greater Sin

The scene of Jesus' trial is full of remarkable reverses and paradoxes. The Son of God is treated like a criminal while sinful men decide his fate. The real king is mocked by those who serve the lesser king. Perhaps none is as surprising or tragic as the contrast between Pilate and the Jewish leaders.

Pilate declares Jesus innocent (John 19:4, 6) but the chief priests cry, "*Crucify him, crucify him!*"(John 19:6). Pilate is afraid when he hears that Jesus claims to be the Son of God (John 19:7) but the Jews are ready to kill him. Jesus tells Pilate, "*Therefore he who delivered me to you has the greater sin*"(John 19:11). This refers to Caiaphas, the high priest. The great failure here is his, not Pilate's. Caiaphas does not render God's judgments or appropriately administer the justice Moses' law requires. A religious man with an educated conscience has an opportunity to do the right thing and fails spectacularly.

The failure of the Jewish people here has been used to justify anti-Semitism, which is utterly wrong and completely unfair. These people fail in their moment of crisis just as we all do. All of us are equally guilty before God for our own sins. In fact, there remains a strong possibility that we will look down on their failure without considering our own.

We are blessed—like the Jews of Jesus' day—to know God's word and will. The question is: Do we do what we know?

One Thing to Think About: What is expected of me based on what God has given me?

One Thing to Pray For: Courage to do what's right—even when it's unpopular

WEEK 34 – THURSDAY

Reading: John 19:12-22

What I Have Written I Have Written

Pilate is anxious to release Jesus and relieve himself of the problem, but the Jews pressure him by invoking Caesar's name. *"But the Jews cried out, 'If you release this man, you are not Caesar's friend. Everyone who makes myself a king opposes Caesar'"*(John 19:12). This is a thinly-veiled threat.

Pilate sits on his judgment seat and again mocks the idea of Jesus as king. *"Behold your king!"*(John 19:14). *"Shall I crucify your king?"*(John 19:15). The reply of the people—*"we have no king but Caesar"*(John 19:15)—shows that the people have come full circle from the events of John 6:15. Pilate blinks first and delivers him up to be crucified. Jesus bears his cross out to Golgotha and *"there they crucified him"*(John 19:18).

"Pilate also wrote an inscription and put it on the cross. It read, 'Jesus of Nazareth, the King of the Jews'"(John 19:19). The Jews protest that this is merely his *claim*, not the truth. They deny him as their king. *"Pilate answered, 'What I have written I have written'"*(John 19:22). What's done is done.

This little exchange underscores how a vital theological idea is transformed into a political issue. The Jews don't want to be associated with Jesus as king. Pilate is laughing at the idea yet wanting to do justice. Yet through it all Jesus remains king. Though he clearly doesn't intend to, Pilate gives Jesus the most fitting epitaph of all.

One Thing to Think About: In what ways have I seen God work through people who didn't realize it?

One Thing to Pray For: Stronger trust in God to work in ways I don't perceive

WEEK 34 – FRIDAY

Reading: John 19:23-30

Woman, Behold Your Son!

We watch Jesus on the cross as soldiers gamble for his clothes. He has nothing left physically—no possessions and nothing left to take away. Some of the women are watching him, including his mother (who must be devastated). John is also there.

"*When Jesus saw his mother and the disciple whom he loved standing nearby, he said to his mother, 'Woman, behold your son!'*"(John 19:26). He is not referring to himself here but is entrusting her care to John. John is now her "son." "*Then he said to the disciple, 'Behold, your mother!' And from that hour the disciple took her to his own home*"(John 19:27). Mary is now John's "mother"—an expression that John understands because he takes care of her from this point forward.

Jesus has more things on his to-do list on the cross—like fulfilling prophecy (John 19:28). Finally he cries "*It is finished*"(John 19:30)—the hour, the task, his life—and dies.

This touching moment of concern for Mary shows us Jesus thoughtful for others to the very end. He takes care of his mom as he bears shame and pain. He has not forgotten his obligations or his love for her. In death he is exactly what he has been in life—compassionate and selfless.

One Thing to Think About: How often do I do legitimately selfless acts?

One Thing to Pray For: Compassion to see the needs of others and work to meet them

WEEK 35 – MONDAY

Reading: John 19:31-42

What John Saw

Jesus has given up his spirit but his body is still hanging on the cross. The Jews go to Pilate to ask for the soldiers to break the legs of the condemned and hasten their deaths. They break the legs of the thieves, but as they approach Jesus, they see he is already dead and do not break his (John 19:33). Instead they pierce his side and blood and water come out.

John calls attention to himself as witness. *"He who saw it has borne witness—his testimony is true, and he knows that he is telling the truth—that you also may believe"*(John 19:35). John records his own testimony to help his readers come to faith. John confesses that he saw blood and water and that he saw that Jesus was already dead. Two prophecies are fulfilled in this: *"Not one of his bones will be broken"*(John 19:36) and *"They will look on him whom they have pierced"*(John 19:37). In Jesus' crucifixion, God is doing exactly what he said he would do.

John shows us several witnesses that all attest to the same thing. The Roman soldiers admit Jesus really died. John himself sees Jesus die. The Scriptures predicted that Jesus would die. These witnesses are vital because they mean that Jesus really died—and therefore really has been raised from the dead. We can base our faith on reliable testimony.

One Thing to Think About: What makes someone a credible witness? Does John meet this description?

One Thing to Pray For: Confidence in Scripture like John has

WEEK 35 – TUESDAY

Reading: John 20:1-10

The Grave Clothes

After Joseph and Nicodemus bury Jesus, the disciples wait until Sunday to visit the tomb. Mary Magdalene goes early (John 20:1). She sees the large stone taken away from the front of the tomb and rushes to tell John and Peter. *"They have taken the Lord out of the tomb, and we do not know where they have laid him"*(John 20:2). She assumes *"they"* have taken him and that someone has *"laid him"* somewhere—revealing that Mary still believes he is dead.

John and Peter race to the tomb; John wins the race but waits for Peter to catch up before entering the tomb. *"Then Simon Peter came, following him, and went into the tomb. He saw the linen cloths lying there, and the face cloth, which had been on Jesus' head, not lying with the linen cloths but folded up in a place by itself"*(John 20:6-7) With great detail John explains the positions of the grave clothes. Linen cloths are lying in one place with the *"face cloth"* folded and by itself. Either someone has stripped Jesus, then carried away his naked body (why?) or Jesus has risen and no longer needs them. John says he *"saw and believed"*(John 20:8).

The level of eyewitness detail here is remarkable. It is clear that he is meticulously explaining what he saw. John's witness is intended *"that you also may believe"*(John 19:35; 20:31). When he speaks so precisely, he is not embellishing or creating a legend. These are matters too important to fabricate.

One Thing to Think About: Is there any reasonable way to account for the empty tomb—other than the resurrection?

One Thing to Pray For: Praise to God for the empty tomb!

WEEK 35 – WEDNESDAY

Reading: John 20:11-23

I Am Sending You

Mary Magdalene has a unique experience near the tomb. She doesn't yet think that he might be risen (John 20:2). She sees angels inside Jesus' tomb and complains to them that someone has taken Jesus' body (John 20:13). Jesus is there, but she mistakes him for the gardener until he says her name. After she identifies him, they talk together. She rushes off to tell the other disciples.

The scene switches to the apostles meeting that same evening when Jesus appears to them. In one of the great understatements in all of Scripture, John informs us that "*the disciples were glad when they saw the Lord*"(John 20:20). "*Jesus said to them again, 'Peace be with you. As the Father has sent me, even so I am sending you'*"(John 20:21). Throughout this gospel, Jesus has continually repeated the fact that he has been sent from the Father. Now he sends his disciples as he has been sent. Their mission is just beginning.

"*Receive the Holy Spirit. If you forgive the sins of any, they are forgiven them; if you withhold forgiveness from any, it is withheld*"(John 20:22-23). They will need the Holy Spirit for this work, and with the Holy Spirit comes authority. The Spirit does not come upon them at this time (that occurs after Jesus' ascension, Acts 2) nor is the forgiveness statement a carte blanche giving them authority to change God's law. He is assuring them that though he will ascend, they will be equipped by God for their vital mission.

When Jesus gives us a work, he equips us to do it.

One Thing to Think About: How would I feel if I was there when Jesus appeared?

One Thing to Pray For: A sense of the importance of the mission of spreading the good news about Jesus

WEEK 35 – THURSDAY

Reading: John 20:24-31

Believing Thomas

We have given Thomas a bad rap. Because he misses Jesus' initial visit when he shows them his hands and side (John 20:20), he confesses that he won't believe until he sees what the others have seen (John 20:25). It is the ultimatum in Thomas' language that turns us off: *"Unless I see...I will never believe"*(John 20:25).

Yet the focus of this text is Thomas' faith, not his doubt. *"Then he said to Thomas, 'Put your finger here, and see my hands; and put out your hand, and place it in my side. Do not disbelieve, but believe.' Thomas answered him, 'My Lord and my God!'"*(John 20:27-28). My Lord and my God! It does not take long for Thomas to come to his conclusion and take it to its logical end.

Jesus responds to him, *"Have you believed because you have seen me? Blessed are those who have not seen and yet have believed"*(John 20:29). He blesses those who reach this kind of faith *without* sight. This is not a criticism of Thomas, but an acknowledgement of the difficulty of faith without sight. John writes all this *"so that you may believe that Jesus is the Christ, the Son of God, and that by believing you may have life in his name"*(John 20:31). This gospel is intended for us, the readers, to come to this kind of faith and so have this kind of life.

Faith is the goal of the message. By hearing these words, we can come to believe in Jesus ourselves and entrust our spiritual lives and hopes for salvation in him. John wants us to believe like Thomas.

One Thing to Think About: Can I believe in Jesus without seeing him?

One Thing to Pray For: The blessing and life Jesus has promised to believers

WEEK 35 – FRIDAY

Reading: John 21:1-14

It Is the Lord!

The disciples have returned home to Galilee. It isn't clear yet what their next steps are. *"Simon Peter said to them, 'I am going fishing'"*(John 21:3). Is he returning to his business? Unlike modern times, their style of fishing is probably not done for relaxation. They have no luck. Jesus appears on the shore: *"Cast the net on the right side of the boat, and you will find some"*(John 21:6). Once they obey Jesus, they bring in a tremendous quantity of fish.

Peter's mind must go back to the other time Jesus told him where to fish (Luke 5:4). *"It is the Lord!"*(John 21:7). Never one to wait, Peter jumps into the water and swims to Jesus, who has prepared breakfast for them by the sea. *"Now none of the disciples dared ask him, 'Who are you?' They knew it was the Lord"*(John 21:12). Jesus still appears to be in a veiled form that is not immediately recognizable but it becomes clear to them who he is. This is the third appearance after his resurrection (John 21:14).

Peter recognizes Jesus because of his characteristic power and knowledge. There is discernment involved in being certain that it is the Lord, but Peter soon has no doubt. His impulsive dive out of the boat testifies to his certainty. Like Peter, we see events and people that hint at the Lord behind them. Do we have the discernment to see where Jesus is at work?

One Thing to Think About: Would I be tempted to be frustrated with Jesus (for not revealing himself more clearly or telling me about the next steps) if I were Peter?

One Thing to Pray For: Discernment to see the Lord

WEEK 36 – MONDAY

Reading: John 21:15-25

What about Him?

After breakfast, Jesus challenges Peter. *"Do you love me?"*(John 21:15). Three times Jesus asks, Peter answers affirmatively, and Jesus tells him to *"feed my lambs"* or *"tend my sheep"*(John 21:15, 16, 17). Often we focus on the Greek words for love and miss the point. Jesus wants Peter's love for him to translate to loving his people.

"Truly, truly, I say to you, when you were young, you used to dress yourself and walk wherever you wanted, but when you are old, you will stretch out your hands, and another will dress you and carry you where you do not want to go"(John 21:18). Peter is going to be martyred for his connection to Jesus (John 21:19). *"Follow me"*(John 21:19) reminds Peter that Jesus has already suffered this fate.

Receiving this bad news, Peter turns to John. *"Lord, what about this man?"*(John 21:21). The implied question is "Shouldn't he have to die too?". Jesus responds, *"If it is my will that he remain until I come, what is that to you? You follow me"*(John 21:22). If I want John to live forever physically, what difference does that make to you? You follow me.

Peter here represents our tendency to look around at others and judge their lives as unfairly easy. Unhappy with our gifts, our money, our problems, or our suffering, we lock onto others who seem to have it better in these areas. We imply that God is unfair. What about him, God? Jesus' response helps us: What is that to you? You follow me!

One Thing to Think About: Do I ever get frustrated because others have more or better than I do?

One Thing to Pray For: A heart to follow Jesus no matter what

WEEK 36 – TUESDAY

Reading: Matthew 1:1-17

The Bruised Lineage

Five women are mentioned in Jesus' genealogy. Each name holds the whiff of scandal. Tamar (Matt 1:3) has children with her father-in-law by dressing as a prostitute, seducing him, and shaming him into acknowledging his deed. Rahab (Matt 1:5) is a non-Jew and a prostitute. Ruth (Matt 1:5), David's great-grandmother, is another foreigner. Bathsheba is not even named; she is simply *"the wife of Uriah"* (Matt 1:6), highlighting David's adultery. Mary (Matt 1:16) will also deal with the whispers of scandal (Matt 1:19-20).

Matthew seems to go out of his way to show just how human Jesus' family is. Generation after generation contains people who sully the family name. Since Jesus is born to human parents, he comes from a lineage marred by sin. At times we lament losing our "good name"—yet we never truly *redeem* our heritage. Despite our best efforts, we only add sin to sin.

That is where Jesus is different. Jesus comes from a bruised lineage, but he redeems it. He comes *from* flawed people *to* flawed people and redeems the families of the earth, including his own.

There is also a bit of grace here. If Jesus' family involves foreigners, sinners, and cautionary tales, then he is unafraid to associate with sinners like us. Soon enough, he will show God's willingness to receive all kinds of people.

One Thing to Think About: How does Jesus' flawed heritage help me relate to him?

One Thing to Pray For: God's help in redeeming our families

WEEK 36 – WEDNESDAY

Reading: Matthew 1:18-25

Being a Just Man

Unlike Luke, who details the angel appearing to Mary, Matthew states the divine conception of Jesus very matter-of-factly: *"When his mother Mary had been betrothed to Joseph, before they came together she was found to be with child from the Holy Spirit"* (Matt 1:18). But he informs us of the very delicate predicament this puts Joseph in. It is obvious to Joseph that she has been unfaithful. Betrothal is a binding commitment but without intimate relations. Since she has broken this commitment, what can he do?

"And her husband Joseph, being a just man and unwilling to put her to shame, resolved to divorce her quietly" (Matt 1:19). *"Being a just man"* here means Joseph does not want to shame the woman he loves. It is hard to imagine a husband thinking so clearly and compassionately while feeling betrayed. He decides to *"divorce her quietly"*—as opposed to drawing public attention to her and her act. But an angel appears to warn him away from this course: *"do not fear to take Mary as your wife, for that which is conceived in her is from the Holy Spirit"* (Matt 1:20).

Joseph listens to his dream (Matt 1:24), which would be remarkably difficult because it seems like avoiding "reality." Joseph reveals his character by staying with Mary despite having serious doubts about her. He shows his willingness to believe an angel in a dream, no matter how unlikely his message. He refuses to allow his hurt and anger to overrule his faith.

Joseph is commended to us here for his compassion in a difficult and hurtful situation. Am I this concerned for those who hurt me?

One Thing to Think About: Am I unwilling to put people to shame?

One Thing to Pray For: The vision to see what is right—even when I am hurt

WEEK 36 – THURSDAY

Reading: Matthew 2:1-12

Wise Men from the East

Jesus, conceived by the Holy Spirit, is born in Bethlehem. *"Now after Jesus was born in Bethlehem of Judea in the days of Herod the king, behold, wise men from the east came to Jerusalem, saying, 'Where is he who has been born king of the Jews? For we saw his star when it rose and have come to worship him'"* (Matt 2:1-2). The first in Matthew's gospel who are aware of this event are wise men from the East—possibly Babylon or points further.

By reading the stars, these men are convinced someone has been *born* and that this baby is a *king* and that he is to be king of the *Jews*. Believing he deserves worship, they come to honor him. They come to Herod in Jerusalem (Matt 2:1), assuming that a new prince would reside in the palace. But the newborn king is not there. On they go to Bethlehem, following the advice of the scribes (Matt 2:5) and the star that goes before them (Matt 2:9). After they offer gifts to him (Matt 2:11) and return home another way after a divine warning (Matt 2:12).

The universe itself is giving signs of Jesus' birth—signs that everyone seems to understand except the Jews. The Jews know the where, but do not respond to this good news—except Herod, who responds in an awful way. Meanwhile the wise men humbly and quietly travel a great distance to honor this child.

One Thing to Think About: Are my eyes open to what God is doing in my time?

One Thing to Pray For: The heart of the wise men: "we have come to worship him"

WEEK 36 – FRIDAY

Reading: Matthew 2:13-23

Angels, Dreams, and Prophecies

The facts of what happens in this section are rather straightforward. Jesus' family spends some time in Egypt, Herod kills all the male children in Bethlehem, and Jesus' family eventually settles in Nazareth. Reading this one way, we see the ordinary events of life—political unrest causing some to flee, a tragic act of political violence, and a decision to hunker down in a quiet hamlet like Nazareth.

But Matthew's details show frenzied divine activity beneath the surface. After Joseph has taken Mary as wife due to the angel's appearance in a dream, it happens again (Matt 2:13) and again (Matt 2:19) and again (Matt 2:22). The sojourn in Egypt fulfills a prophecy (Matt 2:15), as does Herod's slaughter of the innocents (Matt 2:17-18)—which comes after the wise men are warned in a dream (Matt 2:12). Even Jesus growing up in Nazareth fulfills a (admittedly unclear) prophecy (Matt 2:23).

The effect of all this is powerful. God is extremely concerned about this child and deeply involved in his circumstances. All of heaven seems to be on call for Jesus' mission. This will continue (Matt 4:11). As hard as it can be to believe, the ups and downs of Jesus' life are exactly what God wants them to be.

In the absence of revelation from God, the events of life often feel ordinary and undirected. Can we trust that underneath the surface of life, God is hard at work?

One Thing to Think About: Is this how I would have acted if I were God?

One Thing to Pray For: Deeper understanding of God's control and influence in the affairs of life

WEEK 37 – MONDAY

Reading: Matthew 3:1-10

Prepare the Way of the Lord!

Matthew breaks from the story of Jesus' youth to tell us about John the Baptist. John preaches in the wilderness and embodies Isaiah's prophecy: *"The voice of one crying in the wilderness: 'Prepare the way of the Lord; make his paths straight'"*(Matt 3:3). John is the herald who goes before Jesus to announce his coming. The Lord is coming behind him and all must be ready for his appearing.

John's preaching work always redirects his audience away from himself to the Lord. *"Repent, for the kingdom of heaven is at hand"*(Matt 3:2). *"He who is coming after me is mightier than I, whose sandals I am not worthy to carry"*(Matt 3:11). The essence of his message is summed up in one word: repent. The idea is that the Coming One is so great that our lives must be found ready for him.

John prepares the way for Jesus by rekindling the people's spiritual fervor. When Jesus comes, there will be a people trying to please God and ready for the next chapter. They will be putting away sin and living in expectation, with their hearts turned toward God.

The unspoken reality here is that we tend to allow time to dull our spiritual intensity and we must be freshly awoken to God's presence and work. Now we await not the coming of Jesus, but his return. Am I prepared?

One Thing to Think About: Am I awakening others to the pressing reality of spiritual things?

One Thing to Pray For: A prepared heart

WEEK 37 – TUESDAY

Reading: Matthew 3:11-17

To Fulfill All Righteousness

As John the Baptist's ministry continues to thrive, Jesus comes to the Jordan to receive baptism as well. There is a problem here. John's message centers around repentance (Matt 3:2), which implies sin. Many confess their sins at baptism (v. 6). The other gospel writers call John's baptism "*a baptism of repentance for the forgiveness of sins*"(Mark 1:4, Luke 3:3). The problem is that Jesus has no sin, and therefore no need for baptism.

John recognizes this incongruity. "*John would have prevented him, saying, 'I need to be baptized by you, and do you come to me?'*"(Matt 3:14). John's message that one greater is coming after him is not mere talk; he really believes it. "*But Jesus answered him, 'Let it be so now, for thus it is fitting for us to fulfill all righteousness.' Then he consented*"(Matt 3:15). Jesus insists on baptism "*to fulfill all righteousness.*" What could this mean?

Jesus is certainly an example to us, showing that baptism is not too lowly or degrading for us. If he is willing, how could we not be? Perhaps the thought is linked to what follows directly—the descent of the Spirit and voice from heaven, signaling God's favor and the beginning of his ministry, begun by baptism. Jesus pleases God by submitting to his expectations for righteousness (including baptism). I tend toward the idea that Jesus wants to endorse John as a servant of God in the strongest possible way. How could he take John's disciples as his own (which he does, John 1:40ff) if he doesn't submit to John? How could he later challenge the Pharisees on rejecting John (Matt 20:25) if he practically rejects him too?

Jesus speaks to higher purposes and plans than we can fully know, but no matter what the exact reason, we see Jesus fully submissive to the Father's will, regardless of the cost.

One Thing to Think About: If I were John, would I be tempted to feel flattered or proud that Jesus had come to me (rather than humble)?

One Thing to Pray For: An ever-present desire to "fulfill all righteousness" in my part of God's plan

WEEK 37 – WEDNESDAY

Reading: Matthew 4:1-11

Competing Voices

The Spirit leads Jesus into the wilderness to be tempted. This seems to be a necessary precursor to beginning his work. Satan will challenge Jesus throughout his ministry, but we have a preliminary showdown here. The temptations follow a pattern: a short statement offering or proposing something to Jesus, followed by Jesus pointing to Scripture.

"If you are the Son of God, command these stones to become loaves of bread." "If you are the Son of God, throw yourself down..." "All these I will give you, if you will fall down and worship me"(Matt 4:3, 6, 9). The voice of the tempter proposes, offers, and challenges. There is menace behind his words. He is attempting to provoke Jesus. Three times Jesus replies *"it is written"*(Matt 4:4, 7, 10) and quotes Scripture.

Some mystery attends Jesus' temptation—turning stones to bread is not a common temptation for us—yet there is a strong similarity to our experience. Like us, Jesus hears competing voices: the challenge and offer of Satan and then the voice of a holy God calling (through Scripture) for him to trust. We live in this same world of competing voices—the voice enticing us and the one calling us to faithfulness. Which voice will we hear? Will we have the courage of Jesus?

One Thing to Think About: Why is it hard to remember God's words and expectations when we are being tempted?

One Thing to Pray For: Courage to hear and obey God's voice

WEEK 37 – THURSDAY

Reading: Matthew 4:12-25

They Left Their Nets

Jesus has been baptized by John and successfully jousted with Satan in the wilderness. He now moves to Capernaum and begins to preach a message of repentance and the imminence of God's kingdom (Matt 4:17). As he does, he begins to call disciples—men who probably have had prior contact with him.

"And he said to them, 'Follow me, and I will make you fishers of men'"(Matt 4:19). *"He called them"*(Matt 4:21). They understand that this is a call to more than an afternoon walk with Jesus. He is calling them to be disciples and follow his teaching. *"Immediately they left their nets and followed him"*(Matt 4:20). *"Immediately they left the boat and their father and followed him"*(Matt 4:22). There is no hesitation because they want what Jesus is offering them.

These men must sacrifice physical concerns for higher spiritual priorities. Leaving their nets, boats, and parents means forfeiting normal life and gainful employment. They choose to trust Jesus and walk by faith without any certainty about how they will provide for themselves. These men opt for all those awkward conversations with wives and dads and all those nagging doubts. They hear the call of Jesus and they drop everything to follow. Their respect for Jesus, desire for his transformation, and willingness to obey God gets them moving.

Do I feel the same way about the words of Jesus?

One Thing to Think About: What have I left to follow Jesus?

One Thing to Pray For: Jesus to have priority and supremacy in my life

WEEK 37 – FRIDAY

Reading: Matthew 5:1-12

Jesus Hands Out Blessings

Our text begins the Sermon on the Mount, the best-known and most influential of Jesus' sermons. He begins by handing out blessings, telling us what types of dispositions will be blessed by God.

Jesus blesses those we would count *unfortunate*. The poor in spirit, the mourners, the hungry, and the persecuted are those Jesus says are blessed by God. He turns worldly values upside down. When unpleasant states stress our need for God and drive us to him, we are blessed.

Many of Jesus' blessings are for those who are *intense*. This list contains people who feel themselves utterly spiritually destitute, mourning over sin, hungering for righteousness, pure and undistracted in heart. Jesus wants us to become a people of passion who have turned that passion fully toward our Father.

Jesus blesses those who *treat others well*—the merciful, peacemakers, and those who do not respond to evil. At times we are tempted to believe that our religion can be separated from our treatment of our fellow-man. Jesus teaches us emphatically that loving God means loving people.

Where do we stand in the beatitude test? Will we answer Jesus' call?

One Thing to Think About: Am I hungering and thirsting for righteousness—or just fine the way things are?

One Thing to Pray For: Wisdom to see where I am lacking—courage to face the problem—diligence to continue to work on it through grace

WEEK 38 – MONDAY

Reading: Matthew 5:13-26

Anger Management

Jesus begins to interpret certain items in the Law of Moses that his contemporaries misunderstand and misapply. *"You have heard that it was said to those of old, 'You shall not murder; and whoever murders will be liable to judgment'"*(Matt 5:21). The Law can be misconstrued to give the impression that God is only concerned with murder.

"But I say to you that everyone who is angry with his brother will liable to judgment; whoever insults his brother will be liable to the council; and whoever says, 'You fool!' will be liable to the hell of fire"(Matt 5:22). Jesus says differently. Anger, insults, and ugly names are just as troublesome to God and worthy of punishment. To take God seriously, we must look deeper into our motivations. Murder springs from anger. Anger unregulated causes all kinds of problems. Jesus wants to cure the murder problem by purifying the *hearts* of his people so that they can manage anger.

What does proper handling of anger look like? *"So if you are offering your gift at the altar and there remember that your brother has something against you, leave your gift there before the altar and go. First be reconciled to your brother and then come and offer your gift"*(Matt 5:23-24). There is a priority on fixing problems *now* (quickly, v. 25). I don't allow my anger to fester. I work to swiftly restore relationships. My anger does not lead to ugly words and outbursts. It does not fester into resentment and vendetta. I keep short accounts and close them. *This* is God's intent.

One Thing to Think About: Are there relationships in which I need to be reconciled to my brother (v. 24)?

One Thing to Pray For: Discipline to control my mouth and body when angry

WEEK 38 – TUESDAY

Reading: Matthew 5:27-37

Adultery in the Heart

Jesus comments on the Mosaic command: "*You have heard that it was said, 'You shall not commit adultery'*"(Matt 5:27). As with murder, this can be understood to mean that God is only concerned about adultery rather than other problems on the sexual spectrum. "*But I say to you that everyone who looks at a woman with lustful intent has already committed adultery with her in his heart*"(Matt 5:28). As with murder and anger, it is foolish for us to separate adultery from lust.

Lust is the inordinate desire that leads us toward actions that are wrong. Jesus teaches that not only is the *act* of adultery forbidden, but so is the *look* intended to incite lust. When we look at others this way, we have already committed adultery in our hearts. We *want* to do it, are *thinking* about doing it, and we lack only the opportunity.

This is a powerful rebuke for our sexually saturated society, which promotes products through sex appeal. It is a powerful rebuke for the growing pornography industry, which assures us (against all reason and evidence) that looking is harmless. It is a powerful rebuke for individual disciples, who by looking and thinking in impure ways inflame lusts they have a hard time controlling.

Radical action may be required (Matt 5:29-30)—not the literal loss of body parts, but the elimination of the conduits of sin—to restore and ensure our purity. Sexual compromise has consequences—and victims.

One Thing to Think About: Do I struggle to believe that the things that I *think* are as serious as the things I *do*?

One Thing to Pray For: Purity of look and thought

WEEK 38 – WEDNESDAY

Reading: Matthew 5:38-48

Turn the Other Cheek

Jesus takes time to correct these last two misconceptions about the Law of Moses. They are united by the topic of people wronging us. *"You have heard that it was said, 'An eye for an eye and a tooth for a tooth'"*(Matt 5:38). This part of the Law was intended to speak about *judicial* punishment, not personal revenge. That context seems to have been lost or blurred by Jesus' time.

"But I say to you, Do not resist the one who is evil. But if anyone slaps you on the right cheek, turn to him the other also"(Matt 5:39). Don't resist evil people (who work to harm you). Turn the other cheek. In case we are tempted to ignore this principle, Jesus gives several more illustrations—clothes, miles, and giving (Matt 5:40-42). We respond kindly—without resistance—to those who work to harm us. He seems to be speaking about the ordinary harms of life rather than matters of life and death.

Why? Jesus' disciples treat their enemies and friends the same because that's what God does. *"so that you may be sons of your Father who is in heaven. For he makes his sun rise on the evil and on the good, and sends rain on the just and on the unjust"*(Matt 5:45). Jesus sees it as unvirtuous to love people just because they love us (Matt 5:46). Do you have to be nice to me for me to be kind? Christians follow a higher standard.

None of this is easy. It means fighting urges for revenge and self-defense. It means acting out of higher motives than what we *feel*.

One Thing to Think About: Are there certain people I have trouble loving?

One Thing to Pray For: A wider, more open heart—like my Father's (v. 44-45)

WEEK 38 – THURSDAY

Reading: Matthew 6:1-6

You Are Not My Audience

Jesus warns his disciples about doing righteous acts to impress others. This is an insidious danger because we may do the same things, but for problematic reasons: impressing and receiving praise from people. While we can be an influence for good when others see our good works (Matt 5:16), here Jesus insists that we take a long look at our motivations.

Jesus warns about those who give "*that they may be praised by others*"(Matt 6:2) or pray "*that they may be seen by others*"(Matt 6:5). When we have these motives, we are playing to an audience. We want others to know, to see, to praise, and to respect us. "*Truly, I say to you, they have received their reward*"(Matt 6:2, 5). We will receive no blessing for God in this. In fact, God is scarcely involved.

You are not my audience. God did not make me so that I could try to take pride and value from my popularity or the respect of others. Jesus did not come to earth and offer himself so that we would all be impressed with each other. God is the audience that matters, the reward we seek, and the one we want to see our hearts and actions.

One Thing to Think About: How concerned am I about what people—especially certain people—think of my life?

One Thing to Pray For: Stronger allegiance to God, not others

WEEK 38 – FRIDAY

Reading: Matthew 6:7-18

Toward Deeper Praying

Jesus teaches a new type of prayer, driven by short statements of priority. He wants his disciples to focus on the *important* aspects of their relationships with God.

"Our Father in heaven, hallowed be your name"(Matt 6:9). Prayer must come from the proper perspective, where we show respect for him and acknowledge our smallness. God deserves praise and he deserves it from *me*.

"Your kingdom come, your will be done, on earth as it is in heaven"(Matt 6:10). This is a prayer for God's purposes in saving his people to be fulfilled. To Jesus and his disciples it is a prayer for God to act in a new way in bringing the kingdom. In our time we look for the expansion of that kingdom.

"Give us this day our daily bread"(Matt 6:11). We ask God for the physical necessities *for the day*, as the Israelites gathered only enough manna for each day.

"and forgive us our debts, as we also have forgiven our debtors"(Matt 6:12). What we seek from God we extend to others. Jesus teaches us to evaluate our relationships as we pray.

"And lead us not into temptation, but deliver us from evil"(Matt 6:13). We ask God for guidance and help for the trials of that day.

These items are not all the wants we have. They are deeply connected to our need and the heart of God. Jesus wants us to pray deeper.

One Thing to Think About: How does my praying change my thinking to be more like God's?

One Thing to Pray For: Deeper prayer driven by God's honor and God's priorities rather than my own

WEEK 39 – MONDAY

Reading: Matthew 6:19-34

Birds and Flowers

Jesus warns about money and acquisition impairing our spiritual lives. If our treasures are in earthly things, they can be taken from us (Matt 6:19-21). If we serve money, we cannot serve God (Matt 6:24). But money and acquisition also tend to breed anxiety as we worry about whether we will have what we need.

"Therefore I tell you, do not be anxious about your life, what you will eat or what you will drink, nor about your body, what you will put on"(Matt 6:25). Don't be anxious about the necessities of life. Why? *"Look at the birds of the air: they neither sow nor reap nor gather into barns, and yet your heavenly Father feeds them. Are you not of more value than they?"*(Matt 6:26). The birds don't work, but God feeds them! Look at the birds! *"Consider the lilies of the field, how they grow: they neither toil nor spin, yet I tell you, even Solomon in all his glory was not arrayed like one of these"*(Matt 6:28). The lilies don't work, but God clothes them!

The lesson here is not "Don't work" but "Don't worry." If we see the birds and flowers cared for by God, we can be certain that we will be too. *"Are you not of more value than they?"*(Matt 6:26). *"Will he not much more clothe you?"*(Matt 6:30).

Birds and flowers are proof of God's constant care for his creation, which includes us. Rather than being distracted by our stuff and bank accounts, we must be about the real business of life: *"But seek first the kingdom of God and his righteousness, and all these things will be added to you"*(Matt 6:33).

One Thing to Think About: Do I really believe God will always take care of me?

One Thing to Pray For: The heart to always seek kingdom first

WEEK 39 – TUESDAY

Reading: Matthew 7:1-11

The Log Test

Jesus addresses our tendency to judge others by harsher standards than we use to judge ourselves. *"Judge not, that you be not judged. For with the judgment you use it will be measured to you"*(Matt 7:1-2). Others don't merely exist for us to judge them. This kind of evaluation—a desire to condemn others—says more about us than them.

"Why do you see the speck that is in your brother's eye, but do not notice the log that is in your own eye?"(Matt 7:3). Why do we fixate on others' flaws when we have so many of our own to tend to? Centuries later, it remains a powerful and probing question. Jesus tells us that we are only distracting ourselves from unpleasant aspects of our own character. We use others to feel better about ourselves. *"You hypocrite, first take the log out of your own eye, and then you will see clearly to take the speck out of your brother's eye"*(Matt 7:5). Address your issues first and the tone changes.

At times we look at others with a desperate need to feel better about ourselves. Our hunger for validation, our aching consciences, and our deep insecurities drive us to criticize instead of complimenting. We condemn and condescend and for a moment feel better about our own sinking ship.

Jesus gives us the log test: What is *my* flaw? How am I addressing this in myself? Am I only looking to condemn? Am I trying to help? Have I taken out my log? Only then am I ready to help others with their specks—and then only with much greater humility.

One Thing to Think About: How do I use others as a pretext to avoid self-examination?

One Thing to Pray For: The humility to look at myself *first*—before I look at others

WEEK 39 – WEDNESDAY

Reading: Matthew 7:12-20

Fruit Inspection

Not everything is as it appears. Jesus warns us about people who appear to be something they are not. *"Beware of false prophets, who come to you in sheep's clothing but inwardly are ravenous wolves"*(Matt 7:15). They are false prophets posturing as real prophets. They are *"ravenous"* wolves who use their docile appearance to harm and take advantage of the unsuspecting.

Knowing this danger, how can we protect ourselves? *"You will recognize them by their fruits"*(Matt 7:16). *"Thus you will recognize them by their fruits"*(Matt 7:20). Fruit inspection is necessary. The principle Jesus is teaching is one we still rely on. No matter what the leaves or trunk look like, we identify trees by their fruits. If it produces apples, it's an apple tree. Period.

"So, every healthy tree bears good fruit, but the diseased tree bears bad fruit. A healthy tree cannot bear bad fruit, nor can a diseased tree bear good fruit"(Matt 7:17-18). If we bear bad fruit, the tree is bad, regardless of the window dressing. A person who does evil is evil, despite appearances to the contrary. You can't fake fruit.

Our job is to see if the fruit—the way of life, treatment of others, and piety—matches the teaching. We inspect the fruit to be certain that those among us—especially teachers—are not wolves in sheep's clothing. We show concern about the *lives* of those we allow to influence us. You can't fake fruit.

One Thing to Think About: What do my relationships—words—tough choices—say about *my* heart?

One Thing to Pray For: Discernment to recognize good fruit—and bad

WEEK 39 – THURSDAY

Reading: Matthew 7:21-29

Follow Through

This last section of the Sermon on the Mount deals with the danger of responding favorably to Jesus without follow-through. *"Not everyone who says to me, 'Lord, Lord,' will enter the kingdom of heaven, but the one who does the will of my Father who is in heaven"*(Matt 7:21). Calling Jesus "Lord" is not sufficient to enter the kingdom if not accompanied by real obedience. Jesus foresees some even taking his name and doing good deeds (Matt 7:22-23) but not doing the will of the Father. The truly frightening part of this passage is that they think they are fine while failing to obey. They most certainly are not fine and Jesus promises to tell them he never knew them.

"Everyone then who hears these words of mine and does them will be like a wise man who built his house on the rock"(Matt 7:24). Jesus' famous parable about the two builders is about the difference between hearing and doing and hearing and *not* doing. Jesus knows many of his listeners will agree with what he says. He also knows that few will start to live differently because of it. The wise person is the one who chooses to rearrange his life based on the truth Jesus has taught.

It is not enough to claim Jesus as Lord or to like his teaching. We must do the Father's will instead of our own. We must do what we know. It is not enough to *like* Jesus' teaching on peacemaking, love, and anger. Will we follow through? Will we build our lives on it?

One Thing to Think About: Do I ever try to avoid the force of Jesus' words?

One Thing to Pray For: Jesus to say he knows me "on that day"

WEEK 39 – FRIDAY

Reading: Matthew 8:1-13

Jesus Marvels

A centurion, a man of some authority in the Roman army, approaches Jesus. He is a good man. We know this because he comes on behalf of a sick servant and because many Jews praise him and vouch for him, an extraordinarily rare thing (see Luke 7:3-5). Jesus agrees to come heal him, but the centurion stops him.

"Lord, I am not worthy to have you come under my roof, but only say the word, and my servant will be healed. For I too am a man under authority, with soldiers under me. And I say to one, 'Go,' and he goes, and to another, 'Come,' and he comes, and to my servant, 'Do this,' and he does it"(Matt 8:8-9). The man first shows honor to Jesus ("I am not worthy"). But there is more. He understands the nature of Jesus' authority. The centurion is a middle manager in the army. He is both "under authority"(answering to higher-ups) and "with soldiers under me"(in charge of others). This is precisely Jesus' position—following the Father's will but with authority. Thus the man knows that Jesus has power to speak and it be done.

"When Jesus heard this, he marveled and said to those who followed him, 'Truly, I tell you, with no one in Israel have I found such faith'"(Matt 8:10). Jesus marvels. No one in Israel has faith like this! This level of understanding of his power and trust in his authority is even more shocking in the mouth of a Gentile.

Jesus goes on to describe the believing Gentiles sitting at table in the kingdom while unbelieving Jews are thrown out. Jesus encourages and celebrates faith, even when it is found in unlikely places.

One Thing to Think About: Would I have had the faith to trust that this man could heal without even being present?

One Thing to Pray For: The kind of faith that pleases Jesus

WEEK 40 – MONDAY

Reading: Matthew 8:14-22

Hurdles for Disciples

The more Jesus heals, the bigger his crowds grow. "*Now when Jesus saw a crowd around him, he gave orders to go over to the other side*"(Matt 8:18). He seems to be taking steps to avoid the crowd, which can be an impediment to his purposes.

"*And a scribe came up and said to him, 'Teacher, I will follow you wherever you go'*"(Matt 8:19). This scribe has a good spirit about him—he promises to follow Jesus anywhere. But there is something Jesus sees that he does not. "*Foxes have holes, and birds of the air have nests, but the son of Man has nowhere to lay his head*"(Matt 8:20). Following Jesus is not as glamorous as it might sound. Jesus is more homeless than an animal and this man will be too. Jesus seems to be aware of the man's love of comfort and exposes this as a hurdle to the man's enthusiastic desire to follow.

"*Another of the disciples said to him, 'Lord, let me first go and bury my father.' And Jesus said to him, 'Follow me, and leave the dead to bury their own dead'*"(Matt 8:21-22). He wants to fulfill his family responsibilities but Jesus insists that he must be first. The dead will take care of themselves.

There is more to this section (and its parallel, Luke 9:57-62) than Jesus just being ugly or negative. These are real hurdles for disciples—things that prevent us from truly following Jesus. His goal is to get us to address these thing and sort out our priorities *beforehand*. As people who are trying to follow Jesus, we must be aware that it will very often be uncomfortable. We will be commonly forced to choose between Jesus and family, Jesus and comfort, Jesus and fun. As challenging as those choices are, we can't say he didn't warn us.

One Thing to Think About: What are the hurdles to *my* discipleship?

One Thing to Pray For: Jesus' supremacy in my life

WEEK 40 – TUESDAY

Reading: Matthew 8:23-34

O You of Little Faith

As they travel across the Sea of Galilee, a great storm arises. The boat is filling with water. Jesus is sleeping. The apostles, old hands at navigating these waters, are convinced this is the end. *"And they went and woke him, saying, 'Save us, Lord; we are perishing'"*(Matt 8:25). Their panic level rises to such a degree that they rush to wake Jesus. *"And he said to them, 'Why are you afraid, O you of little faith?'"*(Matt 8:26). The storm is still going on. Jesus reproaches their "little faith" because they are afraid. Then he rebukes the winds and sea. The disciples are left marveling at Jesus: *"What sort of man is this, that even winds and sea obey him?"*(Matt 8:27).

A few verses earlier, Jesus applauds the centurion for having "such faith" as is not found in Israel (Matt 8:10). Here instead of applause, he calls the apostles "little faiths." Faith is not simply an intellectual exercise (I now think this where I once thought that). For Jesus, faith is about the reality of God changing my decisions and my life. It is the difference between begging for his blessing from afar (centurion) and panicking when things are out of my control (disciples). This storm has exposed the disciples' lack of faith.

When I have little faith, I am afraid easily. I feel I am on my own. I worry about how I'm going to take care of myself. Jesus challenges us to allow our faith to affect more of our lives. Our daily provision and physical safety are in his hands. When he gives teaching, it will bless us to keep it—even if we are afraid it will be difficult.

One Thing to Think About: Would Jesus say I have "little faith" based on my actions?

One Thing to Pray For: Increase my faith!

WEEK 40 – WEDNESDAY

Reading: Matthew 9:1-13

Mercy and Not Sacrifice

Jesus calls Matthew from his work at the tax office. He follows, possibly resigning his position. "*And as Jesus reclined at table in the house, behold, many tax collectors and sinners came and were reclining with Jesus and his disciples. And when the Pharisees saw this, they said to his disciples, 'Why does your teacher eat with tax collectors and sinners'*"(Matt 9:10-11). The Pharisees complain because Jesus eating with tax collectors does not square with their sense of rabbinic propriety.

"*But when he heard it, he said, 'Those who are well have no need of a physician, but those who are sick. Go and learn what this means, "I desire mercy, and not sacrifice." For I came not to call the righteous, but sinners'*"(Matt 9:12-13). Jesus has come to help the sick. He tells the Pharisees to "*go and learn*" what this prophecy from Hosea means. They know the passage—they probably know the context and interpretations—yet his assignment is to "*go and learn what this means.*" It is possible for us to know a passage backward and forward yet not live by it—and so miss God.

"Mercy and not sacrifice" means that we see that God's priority is *people*. We cannot think we are on God's wavelength if we follow all the rules but have no heart for people—have no compassion—are only concerned with whether they will defile us. This is not how God feels. Jesus protests.

One Thing to Think About: Am I focused on mercy like Jesus?

One Thing to Pray For: A heart for the lost

WEEK 40 – THURSDAY

Reading: Matthew 9:14-26

Weddings, Patches, and Wineskins

The disciples of John the Baptist are confused by Jesus' practice. *"Why do we and the Pharisees fast, but your disciples do not fast?"*(Matt 9:14). Jesus uses several different images to explain why fasting is not appropriate for the moment.

"Can the wedding guests mourn as long as the bridegroom is with them? The days will come when the bridegroom is taken away from them, and then they will fast"(Matt 9:15). You don't mourn at a wedding. Only when the groom leaves is anyone sad. *"No one puts a piece of unshrunk cloth on an old garment, for the patch tears away from the garment, and a worse tear is made"*(Matt 9:16). You don't put a new patch on old clothes or it will shrink and tear again. *"Neither is new wine put into old wineskins. If it is, the skins burst and the wine is spilled and the skins are destroyed. But new wine is put into fresh wineskins, and so both are preserved"*(Matt 9:17). You don't put new wine into old wineskins. The new wine will ferment and expand, while the rigid wineskin will burst.

Fasting is associated with mourning—something inappropriate while Jesus is present. The *tone* is all wrong. Jesus gives us a series of ill-fitting things to help us grasp it. He expects his disciples to be aware of the times and react appropriately. When he has left his disciples, *"then they will fast"*(Matt 9:15). This places modern disciples in a time when sadness and mourning is appropriate while waiting for our Savior.

Fasting is appropriate today while we wait for the return of the groom. Disciples are fixated on the return of their teacher.

One Thing to Think About: What kinds of behaviors, attitudes, and teachings are most appropriate to our time?

One Thing to Pray For: Wisdom to be aware of the times

WEEK 40 – FRIDAY

Reading: Matthew 9:27-38

The Harvest Is Plentiful but the Laborers Are Few

As Jesus engages people, he is touched by their need. *"When he saw the crowds, he had compassion for them, because they were harassed and helpless, like sheep without a shepherd"*(Matt 9:36). Seeing the crowd prompts compassion in him as he considers their plight. Without a shepherd, sheep are easy prey. These people need leadership, protection, and direction.

"Then he said to his disciples, 'The harvest is plentiful, but the laborers are few'"(Matt 9:37). Changing metaphors, he speaks of a field of crops ready to be brought in. He sees potential in the crowds (*"the harvest is plentiful"*), but also urgency (lest the crop spoil). *"The laborers are few"* is Jesus' acknowledgement that the work is too much for any of them to do as they are. When we catch a glimpse of the immensity of the need of our world, it is overwhelming.

"Therefore pray earnestly to the Lord of the harvest to send out laborers into his harvest"(Matt 9:38). Pray. Even though Jesus is himself on the ground, he urges his followers to *couple their work with prayer*. Prayer means we take the need seriously (instead of becoming jaded). Prayer drives us to trust that God can do what we cannot. Prayer gives perspective to our work.

We live today in the same world—sheep without a shepherd, harvest plentiful, laborers few. Are we praying?

One Thing to Think About: Is it overwhelming for me to think about how many needy people (physically and spiritually) there are in the world?

One Thing to Pray For: More laborers!

WEEK 41 – MONDAY

Reading: Matthew 10:1-15

Shake Off the Dust

Jesus sends the twelve out to preach and heal. It is a mission focused solely on Israel (Matt 10:6). This entire chapter is Jesus' speech preparing them for what they will find as they more directly engage the world. Looming in the background of his message is the likelihood of rejection (Matt 10:13, 16, 17, 25). It comes with the territory of bringing a message from God—and always has.

"And if anyone will not receive you or listen to your words, shake off the dust from your feet when you leave that house or town. Truly, I say to you, it will be more bearable on the day of judgment for the land of Sodom and Gomorrah than for that town" (Matt 10:14-15). Shaking the dust from the feet is the practice of Jews who, upon returning from Gentile territory, want no association with that place to cling to them. It is the ancient equivalent of returning to our home state and immediately going to the car wash to remove any trace of where we've been. It is an act of protest. Jesus teaches his people to do this to testify to the rejection of their message (Luke 9:5). The rejecters are unclean, like the Gentiles.

There is more here. Jesus is teaching his disciples the need they will have to move on in their teaching efforts. We cannot allow the rejection and evil attitudes of some to cling to us and continue to discourage us. We must brush it off. There is always more teaching to do and we can't let the rejecters discourage us.

One Thing to Think About: Do I sometimes allow the fear of rejection to keep me from teaching others?

One Thing to Pray For: Courage to keep telling others about Jesus—even when some have rejected

WEEK 41 – TUESDAY

Reading: Matthew 10:16-33

Fear, Hair, and Sparrows

Jesus is still preparing his disciples for their preaching tour. Here he is even more direct about the reality of persecution. *"If they have called the master of the house Beelzebul, how much more will they malign those of his household?"*(Matt 10:25). At least the disciples—then and now—can take comfort in the fact that Jesus has been treated similarly.

Jesus wants them not to fear. *"Have no fear of them"*(Matt 10:26). *"Do not fear those who kill the body but cannot kill the soul"*(Matt 10:28). *"Fear not"*(Matt 11:31). Why shouldn't we fear? The evil done to us will come to light—*"for nothing is covered that will not be revealed, or hidden that will not be known"*(Matt 10:26). They cannot touch the part of us that matters, but can only kill the body (Matt 10:28). God watches sparrows (Matt 10:29) and *"you are of more value than many sparrows"*(Matt 10:31). *"But even the hairs of your head are all numbered"*(Matt 10:30). God knows me intimately and is aware of the smallest injury or evil done to me.

There is something greater than what we fear. The God who knows us so well is with us. But there is also a threat here. *"Rather fear him who can destroy both body and soul in hell...whoever denies me before me, I will also deny before my Father who is in heaven"*(Matt 10:28, 33). God is the one to fear, not man.

Men have power. Some of them have political influence, others are physically superior, and some are intimidating in other ways. Meanwhile Jesus warns us to fear God over man. Whose power will we let influence our behavior?

One Thing to Think About: Why do we tend to fear men more than God?

One Thing to Pray For: The fear of God to be greater in my heart than the fear of men

WEEK 41 – WEDNESDAY

Reading: Matthew 10:34-42

Not Peace, But a Sword

Just before he sends out his disciples to preach, Jesus wants to correct a misconception about him and his purpose. *"Do not think that I have come to bring peace to the earth. I have not come to bring peace, but a sword"*(Matt 10:34). He doesn't want his followers to think that he has come to bring peace on earth, then be disappointed when they see conflict. Instead, Jesus has come to bring *"a sword."* Jesus does not bring violence. He is saying that his coming will be a source of division, separation, contention, and conflict. He speaks more to the *effect* of his coming than his *purpose*.

"For I have come to set a man against his father, and a daughter against her mother, and a daughter-in-law against her mother-in-law. And a person's enemies will be those of his own household"(Matt 10:35-36). Families will be set at odds. Why? *"Whoever loves father or mother more than me I not worthy of me, and whoever loves son or daughter more than me is not worthy of me"*(Matt 10:37). Jesus will demand priority *even over family*. Not everyone will hear this call and accept it. It will tear up families and make enemies. I suspect the apostles are about to see this in living color as they go out preaching.

Jesus creates inconvenience. He redraws relational lines. He shakes up our lives. He brings a sword. If we are not interested in this, we are "not worthy." It is a call to tear down idols we have made in our hearts—even if those idols are our own families.

One Thing to Think About: Have I seen the divisive impact of Jesus in my own life?

One Thing to Pray For: A love for Jesus that is greater than my love for anything else

WEEK 41 – THURSDAY

Reading: Matthew 11:1-19

Are You the Coming One?

As Jesus' fame spreads, it reaches John the Baptist, who is imprisoned by Herod. *"Now when John heard in prison about the deeds of the Christ, he sent word by his disciples and said to him, 'Are you the one who is to come, or shall we look for another?'"* (Matt 11:2-3). To fully understand John's purpose here takes some conjecture, which puts us on dangerous ground.

Is John asking Jesus for a demonstration for the benefit of his disciples? This would make sense if he wants them to become Jesus' disciples, but there is no hint to this in the text and after they receive Jesus' answer, they leave him (Matt 11:7). Has John begun to doubt? His question (*"shall we look for another?"*) certainly has a harsh tone to it.

Are you the Christ? Jesus does not answer directly. A simple "yes" would not really satisfy. Jesus does not stop and perform some great miracle or teaching. *"Go and tell John what you hear and see"* (Matt 11:4). Many of these miracles are stated signs of the Messiah's work (Isa 35:5-6, 61:1). It's really happening and they are allowed to see it. *"And blessed is the one who is not offended by me"* (Matt 11:6). This statement seems out of place with the others. Is it addressing the undertone of John's question (Matt 11:3)? Perhaps Jesus is concerned that in his imprisonment, John has gotten frustrated and Jesus wants to speak to that.

Messiah is more than a claim for Jesus. His actions show that he has unleashed a new hour of the LORD's favor. Jesus wants John's faith to be rooted in the facts about his work and fulfillment of prophecy, not mere words.

One Thing to Think About: Am I ever tempted to be "offended"—caused to stumble or doubt—by Jesus?

One Thing to Pray For: Deeper faith in Jesus as God's Christ

WEEK 41 – FRIDAY

Reading: Matthew 11:20-30

A New Yoke

Jesus praises God for his genius in hiding his wisdom from the wise and revealing them to the humble (Matt 11:25). There is more: we can only know the Father if Jesus chooses to reveal him (Matt 11:27). It is in this context that Jesus offers his invitation to come learn the secrets of heaven.

"Come to me, all who labor and are heavy laden, and I will give you rest" (Matt 11:28). We are about to have two stories about the Sabbath and its abuses by the elaborate system of regulations the Pharisees have devised. Jesus offers true rest from the burdens and laboring under the heavy yoke of when the rules become the master.

"Take my yoke upon you, and learn from me, for I am gentle and lowly in heart, and you will find rest for your souls. For my yoke is easy, and my burden is light" (Matt 11:29-30). Take *my* yoke and learn from *me*. Jesus is something different, new, and light. He gives rest. He adds that he is *"gentle and lowly in heart"* — someone we want to lead us and someone we want to be like. He will teach us truths about God that will make our lives happier, deeper, and more peaceful. He will transform us from the inside out — a promise that we could never realize under the heavy yoke of sin.

We find our way hard — even our own self-driven attempts at religion — and Jesus offers for us to simply follow and find rest. It is a new yoke.

One Thing to Think About: Do I relate to the idea of laboring and being heavy laden?

One Thing to Pray For: The rest and knowledge Jesus promises

WEEK 42 – MONDAY

Reading: Matthew 12:1-21

Mercy and Not Sacrifice—Again

It is another Sabbath showdown. "*At that time Jesus went through the grainfields on the Sabbath. His disciples were hungry, and they began to pluck heads of grain and to eat. But when the Pharisees saw it, they said to him, 'Look, your disciples are doing what is not lawful to do on the Sabbath'"*(Matt 12:1-2). They are hungry and doing nothing wrong to grab food that is hanging all around them. The Pharisees contend that they have spotted yet another violation and chide Jesus over it.

Jesus lists several other seeming violations: David eating the showbread while running for his life (Matt 12:3-4) or the priests, who *work* on the Sabbath (in the temple no less) (Matt 12:5). His point is that we understand that these are justifiable exceptions to the Sabbath rule—and so is hungry people grabbing grain.

"*And if you had known what this means, 'I desire mercy, and not sacrifice,' you would not have condemned the guiltless*"(Matt 12:7). Jesus has already given them a homework assignment (Matt 9:13) to go learn what this passage means. Evidently they haven't done it. He critiques the way the Pharisees ignore people and their needs in favor of their rules. They have sacrifice down, but God says he desires mercy (treating others compassionately) *more* than sacrifice. God is concerned with people and when we are out of step with God on this, we can "*condemn the guiltless*"(Matt 12:7).

Our zeal for the law of God never excuses us for treating people poorly.

One Thing to Think About: Are there way or situations where I am more concerned about rules than people?

One Thing to Pray For: A heart of mercy, not just sacrifice

WEEK 42 – TUESDAY

Reading: Matthew 12:22-37

The Mouth and the Heart

The Pharisees criticize Jesus' power of exorcism, accusing him of employing Satan's power. Jesus lashes out at this, warning that they are blaspheming the Holy Spirit. But he goes further: these words don't come from nowhere.

"*Either make the tree good and its fruit good, or make the tree bad and its fruit bad, for the tree is known by its fruit. You brood of vipers! How can you speak good, when you are evil? For out of the abundance of the heart the mouth speaks*"(Matt 12:33-34). Jesus uses his aphorism of knowing a tree by its fruit and applies it to speech. Our speech isn't pulled out of the air. It emanates from our hearts. Our mouths reveal our hearts—whether they are full of negativity, jealousy, and hate or full of positivity, peace, encouragement, and love. The mouth is the measure of the heart.

"*I tell you, on the day of judgment people will give account for every careless word they speak, for by your words you will be justified, and by your words you will be condemned*"(Matt 12:36-37). Words matter too. God has blessed us with the power of speech and assures us that we will answer for how we have used it. Careless, evil, destructive words will condemn; godly, true, wise words will justify.

These thoughts are sobering. Fixing my speech is truly about correcting my heart. What is my mouth telling others about my heart? Am I using my mouth for good? Is God glad he gave *me* the power to speak?

One Thing to Think About: Do I tend to think that words aren't a big deal?

One Thing to Pray For: "Good treasure" within that leads to good words

WEEK 42 - WEDNESDAY

Reading: Matthew 12:38-50

The Story of a Demon

Tensions are escalating. The Pharisees have challenged Jesus over the Sabbath and accused him of casting out demons by Beelzebub. Now comes the request for a sign (Matt 12:38) which is met by more harsh words from Jesus: *"An evil and adulterous generation seeks for a sign, but no sign will be given to it except the sign of the prophet Jonah"*(Matt 12:39). Especially does Jesus take aim at *"this generation"*(v. 39, 45)—the people of his day who reject all of God's overtures.

He tells an odd story. *"When the unclean spirit has gone out of a person, it passes through waterless places seeking rest, but finds none"*(Matt 12:43). A demon is cast out. It should be a moment of great joy! But the demon has nowhere to go, so he decides to go back to the man. *"Then it says, 'I will return to my house from which I came.' And when it comes, it finds the house empty, swept, and put in order. Then it goes and brings with it seven other spirits more evil than itself, and they enter and dwell there, and the last state of that person is worse than the first. So also will it be with this evil generation"*(Matt 12:44-45). When he returns, he finds his former home *"empty, swept, and put in order"*—perfect for demon habitation. He brings seven friends and the last state is worse than the first. *"So it will be with this evil generation."*

Jesus has come to earth—God in the flesh—and has graced these people with his presence. He has taught in their synagogues and healed their diseases. He has shown God to them and had compassion on them. They have had their "demon" cast out. Yet this is not the end of their story. They will soon have all their problems return—and worse problems. The last state will be worse than the first because *none of Jesus' blessing has produced any change.* Evil will find a ready home in them.

Will God's blessings prompt us to change?

One Thing to Think About: Is it possible for God's blessings to convince us we don't need to repent?

One Thing to Pray For: The true life-change Jesus intends

WEEK 42 – THURSDAY

Reading: Matthew 13:1-23

The Purpose of Parables

This chapter contains a collection of many of Jesus' parables about the kingdom of God. Parables are a unique kind of extended illustration that usually involves a story. *"Then the disciples came and said to him, 'Why do you speak to them in parables?'"*(Matt 13:10). This question follows the story of the sower, where Jesus describes how crops grow in different kinds of soil—without any clear point or explanation. We can understand the strangeness of this and the confusion it would cause.

"And he answered them, 'To you it has been given to know the secrets of the kingdom of heaven, but to them it has not been given'"(Matt 13:11). His use of parables hinges on the presence of two different groups—those who understand and those who don't. *"This is why I speak to them in parables, because seeing they do not see, and hearing they do not hear, nor do they understand"*(Matt 13:13). Parables are a way of communicating the secrets of the kingdom of heaven to some while obscuring them from those who have closed their eyes (Matt 13:15).

Parables have power to reveal God's truth, but only if we are willing to try to understand them—only if we are willing to hear Jesus' explanation—only if we trust that there is deep truth here. But to those who are not interested enough to seek, they become pointless and shallow stories. In this way, parables reveal the genius and glory of God.

One Thing to Think About: Am I interested enough in God and his word to *seek* answers that are not immediately apparent?

One Thing to Pray For: The knowledge God offers (Matt 13:17)

WEEK 42 – FRIDAY

Reading: Matthew 13:24-43

Wheat among Weeds

Jesus explains the kingdom: a man sows wheat but when the plants grow up, there are weeds among the wheat. The crisis of the story is what to do with this field now. "*Then do you want us to go and gather them?*"(Matt 13:28). Should they uproot the weeds? "*But he said, 'No, lest in gathering the weeds you root up the wheat along with them. Let both grow together until the harvest'*"(Matt 13:29-30). Instead of uprooting, the master wants both wheat and weeds to grow together until the harvest.

Jesus then explains his parable. "*The field is the world*"(Matt 13:38), which contains God's people (wheat) and Satan's (weeds). They will grow together until the end (Matt 13:40).

This parable teaches us something essential about God's kingdom and our relationship with him: we will live like wheat among weeds until Jesus returns. We will exist in close proximity to evil people until the end. I repeat: the parable is specifically designed to tell us that God will not remove his people from the world until the time is right.

This proximity of wheat and weeds doesn't have to be bad. Jesus talks about the growth of the kingdom as a mustard seed and leaven (Matt 13:31-33) that grow and spread. We can influence others for good, using our proximity to them to shine as lights to the world (Matt 5:14-16). Jesus emphasizes that our present state is God's will; we should not feel that something has gone wrong just because we live among evil people.

One Thing to Think About: How does the coming judgment give reassurance and urgency to our actions?

One Thing to Pray For: Patience with—and opportunities to influence—those around us

WEEK 43 – MONDAY

Reading: Matthew 13:44-58

Treasure and Pearls

"*The kingdom of heaven is like treasure hidden in a field, which a man found and covered up. Then in his joy he goes and sells all that he has and buys that field*"(Matt 13:44). Treasure! It is exciting—the stuff of pirate stories and fairy tales! But to really find treasure, we would do whatever is required to get it. "*In his joy*" means that we wouldn't even calculate that long because of our excitement.

"*Again, the kingdom of heaven is like a merchant in search of fine pearls, who, on finding one pearl of great value, went and sold all that he had and bought it*"(Matt 13:45-46). The merchant is on a mission. He has something particular he wants and values. When he finds that pearl, he does whatever it takes, selling all else.

Treasure and pearls are fitting images because they translate priority into terms we understand—money. The question "how bad do you want it?" is easily measured when it is reworded "how much would you pay for it?". Jesus is teaching that the kingdom must have the highest value to us.

These stories are not about the ethics of finding a treasure in a field and whether we should tell the owner. They are about putting God's kingdom before everything else, so that it is our treasure and pearl. When this happens, money, time, family, and pleasure take a backseat.

One Thing to Think About: Are there things that I am unwilling to give up for the kingdom?

One Thing to Pray For: The proper value for the kingdom

WEEK 43 – TUESDAY

Reading: Matthew 14:1-12

Herod's Guilty Conscience

The word about Jesus is getting around and it strikes fear in the heart of one man. *"At that time Herod the tetrarch heard about the fame of Jesus, and he said to his servants, 'This is John the Baptist. He has been raised from the dead; that is why these miraculous powers are at work in him'"*(Matt 14:1-2). As Herod hears about Jesus, his thoughts immediately turn to John the Baptist. There is a reason. Herod has done something awful to John. After arresting him, Herod made a rash promise to his stepdaughter, who asked for John's head. *"And the king was sorry, but because of his oaths and his guests he commanded it to be given"*(Matt 14:9). Even when the opportunity came to back down, he was too embarrassed to change his vow and compounded his foolish promise by murder.

Now as Jesus gains popularity, Herod concludes (against all reason) that John has been raised from the dead and now has miraculous powers. Herod is afraid. Herod is guilty. His tortured logic here shows how terribly his deed still haunts him. The first time he hears about a famous preacher, he assumes John has come back to get him. Worse, he fears that John now has *"miraculous powers"* that he will use to torment Herod for his unjust death.

The guilty conscience brings our sin into *every* situation. How many family problems, on-the-job crises, and sicknesses have led Herod to wonder, "Is this because of what I've done?"? When we feel guilty, we see our sin everywhere.

One Thing to Think About: Do I have a guilty conscience?

One Thing to Pray For: The cleansing of heart and conscience Jesus provides

WEEK 43 – WEDNESDAY

Reading: Matthew 14:13-21

You Give Them Something to Eat

A crowd follows Jesus as he tries to withdraw. *"When he went ashore he saw a great crowd, and he had compassion on them and healed their sick"*(Matt 14:14). The disciples urge him to send them away to get food (Matt 14:15). Jesus objects. *"They need not go away; you give them something to eat"*(Matt 14:16). Jesus lays the food problem in the disciples' lap.

On one level, Jesus is feeding and dealing with the crowd while on another level he is training his disciples. John records Jesus at this stage questioning Philip about the problem, adding that *"he said this to test him"*(John 6:6). Philip answers that they need at least 200 denarii just to buy enough bread to feed everyone (John 6:7).

By forcing the disciples to solve the problem, Jesus makes them feel the full weight of it. 200 days' wages! They begin to ask around and find only a boy's small lunch (John 6:9)—five loaves and two fish (Matt 14:17). *"And they took up twelve baskets full of the broken pieces left over"*(Matt 14:20). This probably means that the disciples themselves are picking up the scraps—one basket each—knowing full well that all of this came from a little boy's lunch. This story is in all four gospels, suggesting that it makes a deep impression on all the apostles. When they have experienced the difficulty of the problem firsthand, they are all the more impressed at Jesus' solution.

Now, as then, Jesus tests, challenges, and builds faith in his disciples.

One Thing to Think About: What kind of track record does Jesus have in helping his disciples grow?

One Thing to Pray For: Perseverance and growth in my walk with Jesus

WEEK 43 – THURSDAY

Reading: Matthew 14:22-36

Faith, Doubt, and Water-Walking

Jesus sends his apostles across the sea while he prays, then decides to catch up with them on the sea by walking on the surface of the water. "*But when the disciples saw him walking on the sea, they were terrified, and said, 'It is a ghost!' and they cried out in fear*"(Matt 14:26). They are afraid, but Jesus reassures (Matt 14:27).

Impulsive Peter takes the opportunity: "*Lord, if it is you, command me to come to you on the water*"(Matt 14:28). He expresses here the desire we all have when we observe power—to have that power applied to ourselves and to participate in it. Jesus obliges his request, which seems odd because he usually seems to deny requests like these (Matt 20:22, Luke 9:55). Peter walks toward Jesus but sees the wind and begins to sink. Jesus links Peter's sinking with his doubt. "*O you of little faith, why did you doubt?*"(Matt 14:31). Here Peter literally walks by faith.

Jesus is deeply interested in *cultivating faith* in those he encounters. When Peter—in his fear—begins to doubt, his connection to God weakens and he does what he would do were he on his own (sink). All that we do is done by our connection to an empowering God. Questioning or doubting is not wrong in itself. The danger is in threatening our connection to a life-giving God.

Jesus is sometimes painted (in our culture) as a mere moral teacher, yet he is constantly fixated on faith-building because he wants us to do more than live right. He wants us to believe in God and live by that faith. On our own—without him—we only sink.

One Thing to Think About: Would I have had the courage to take that first step out of the boat?

One Thing to Pray For: Courage to keep my faith fixated on Jesus

WEEK 43 – FRIDAY

Reading: Matthew 15:1-20

Commands and Traditions

The Pharisees challenge Jesus about hand-washing because it breaks the tradition of the elders (Matt 15:2). *"He answered them, 'And why do you break the commandment of God for the sake of your tradition?'"*(Matt 15:3). Jesus makes a distinction between commands and traditions. Commands originate with God (v. 4) while traditions are manmade (v. 5). The Pharisees' zeal for their tradition—which has led them to challenge Jesus—is so strong that they value it over God's commands.

Jesus gives an example—the tradition of Corban, which dedicates certain money to God and leads to people not having money left to honor their parents. God says "honor" while they say "Corban"—keeping their tradition over God's rule. And so their loyalty is proven to be to traditions over commands.

"This people honors me with their lips, but their heart is far from me; in vain do they worship me, teaching as doctrines the commandments of men"(Matt 15:8-9). This is the issue. Traditions are fine in themselves, but they often tend to draw our allegiance *over* God and his word. Traditions can lead us to condemn others over things God never said (Matt 15:2). They can lead us to feel righteous while ignoring God. They can lead us to have a heart far from God and vain worship.

Are we sure that our thoughts, practices, and priorities really come from God's word?

One Thing to Think About: Do I ever have things that seem right or wrong to me that don't come from the Bible?

One Thing to Pray For: A heart close to God that seeks to do *his* will

WEEK 44 – MONDAY

Reading: Matthew 15:21-28

The Humility of Desperation

Jesus briefly departs from the land of Israel to Tyre and Sidon. He is approached by *"a Canaanite woman"*(Matt 15:21)—a description with strongly negative connotations to students of the Old Testament. *"Have mercy on me, O Lord, Son of David; my daughter is severely oppressed by a demon"*(Matt 15:22). The woman is in deep need because of her daughter's condition. Jesus is surprisingly silent. Finally he responds: *"I was sent only to the lost sheep of the house of Israel"*(Matt 15:24). This is getting uncomfortable.

She kneels and begs Jesus. Again he answers brusquely: *"It is not right to take the children's bread and throw it to the dogs"*(Matt 15:26). She answers, *"Yes, Lord, yet even the dogs eat the crumbs that fall from their masters' table"*(Matt 15:27). She is willing to accept being called a dog if Jesus will help. Jesus blesses her great faith.

The focus of this story is how desperation leads us to humility. This woman does not balk at being ignored, insulted, or summarily dismissed. Where most of us would have been offended and hurt (or walked away feeling rejected), she persists. Her desperation is so great that she will endure any kind of insult to get what she needs.

Often our pride stands in the way of us getting what we need. We serve Jesus as long as we don't have to do anything too drastic. We confess sin as long as it's not too specific or embarrassing. We serve others as long as we have time to do what we like (and are appropriately thanked). This woman shows us that our struggle with pride may be about taking ourselves too seriously—and not taking our need seriously enough.

One Thing to Think About: Am I desperate for Jesus' help and healing?

One Thing to Pray For: The humility to seek Jesus no matter what

WEEK 44 – TUESDAY

Reading: Matthew 15:29-39

Jesus Gives Thanks

Matthew records Jesus feeding the 4000 on a different occasion from feeding the 5000 (Matt 14:15-21). Some of the details are different—the number of fish and baskets—but the basic need of people who have come out to hear the word is the same. "*He took the seven loaves and the fish, and having given thanks he broke them*"(Matt 15:36). Giving thanks is a habit Jesus has. "*he looked up to heaven and said a blessing*"(Matt 14:19). It happens at the Last Supper—twice. "*Jesus took bread, and after blessing it broke it*"(Matt 26:26). "*And he took a cup, and when he had given thanks he gave it to them*"(Matt 26:27).

These meals all have special spiritual significance, but Jesus has a practice of thanking God before eating. Even when Jesus is investing these meals with special meaning, he still gives thanks to God. Eating is a way we receive strength to continue life. By acknowledging God as we eat, we remember that it is by his power and grace that we continue to live. We are dependent on food for life—and God for food. We work to provide for ourselves, but we acknowledge that God is the source of our daily bread (Matt 611).

By regularly practicing gratitude, we learn to notice all the ways ordinary life is infused with God and his kindness to us. Giving thanks is more than a ritual. It is a sincere expression of appreciation for God's constant provision.

One Thing to Think About: Am I thankful to God for the way he sustains my life?

One Thing to Pray For: A grateful disposition

WEEK 44 – WEDNESDAY

Reading: Matthew 16:1-12

Beware Leaven

The Pharisees and Sadducees test Jesus by seeking a sign (Matt 16:1). Jesus refuses but seems affected by the spirit demonstrated by this request. He mentions it to his disciples: *"Watch and beware of the leaven of the Pharisees and Sadducees"*(Matt 16:6). Beware. Jesus is concerned that the kind of scene they have just witnessed may not register with the apostles as dreadfully wrong. *"Beware"* implies danger—but what does he mean by *"leaven"*?

The disciples are embarrassed that they have forgotten to bring bread, so they assume this is Jesus' meaning (Matt 16:7). He insists that he is not at all concerned about bread (v. 8-11). *"How is it that you fail to understand that I did not speak about bread? Beware of the leaven of the Pharisees and Sadducees"*(Matt 16:11). Beware of the *leaven*! *"Then they understood that he did not tell them to beware of the leaven of bread, but of the teaching of the Pharisees and Sadducees"*(Matt 16:12). It is teaching that Jesus is addressing. Luke further records Jesus saying that their leaven is hypocrisy (Luke 12:1).

People influence us. Teaching does not happen in a vacuum. Words and actions have an impact. We will be influenced by someone. Jesus' warning here is that we pay attention (*"watch and beware"*) and be certain that our influences are taking us toward Jesus and not away from him. Sometimes we naively think that this will not happen to us because we are so mature or because our influences are not so bad. Jesus challenges us.

One Thing to Think About: Whose leaven is affecting me? Whose must I beware?

One Thing to Pray For: Clarity of vision to see how others affect me

WEEK 44 – THURSDAY

Reading: Matthew 16:13-20

I Will Build My Church

Jesus questions his apostles about his identity—meaning his role more than just his name. *"Who do people say that the Son of Man is?"* (Matt 16:13). Receiving a surprising variety of wrong answers, he asks them their opinion. *"Simon Peter replied, 'You are the Christ, the Son of the living God'"* (Matt 16:16). Jesus praises Peter because this is the right answer: *"Blessed are you, Simon Bar-Jonah! For flesh and blood has not revealed this to you, but my Father who is in heaven"* (Matt 16:17).

But this confession seems to cue Jesus to tell them more about the next step. *"And I tell you, you are Peter, and on this rock I will build my church, and the gates of hell shall not prevail against it"* (Matt 16:18). Much attention is given to *"on this rock"* here. The next steps will certainly hinge on what Peter has confessed (v. 16) and also on Peter himself (v. 18), although without any hint of him being in the role of pope. The emphasis of the verse, though, is *"I will build my church."* Jesus declares his aim of gathering a people who will belong to him and live forever, conquering death. Peter and the other apostles will be instrumental in this (Matt 16:19).

Jesus has built his church—his people—and they exist today all over the world, awaiting his return. They have no fear of death, whose gates cannot prevail against them.

One Thing to Think About: Do I value Jesus' people as much as he does?

One Thing to Pray For: Deeper faith and confidence in Jesus and his power over death

WEEK 44 – FRIDAY

Reading: Matthew 16:21-28

Get Behind Me, Satan!

Peter's confession that Jesus is the Christ has prompted Jesus to reveal the next steps of his work to the apostles—building his church and giving the keys to the kingdom. There is also a shift in tone as Jesus begins to address what will happen in Jerusalem. *"From that time Jesus began to show his disciples that he must go to Jerusalem and suffer many things from the elders and chief priests and scribes, and be killed, and on the third day be raised"*(Matt 16:21). Instead of a mountaintop moment, Jesus casts a pall over the scene.

"And Peter took him aside and began to rebuke him, saying, 'Far be it from you, Lord! This shall never happen to you'"(Matt 16:22). Peter's view of Jesus is so high that he can't even entertain this thought. It is the same spirit that prompts him to later tell Jesus *"you will never wash my feet"*(John 13:8).

"But he turned and said to Peter, 'Get behind me, Satan! You are a hindrance to me. For you are not setting your mind on the things of God, but on the things of man'"(Matt 16:23). Jesus hears Satan's voice in Peter's rebuke. It is the same voice that calls to him in his temptations *"if you are the Son of God..."*. It is the voice that would argue that suffering is so inappropriate for Jesus that it cannot possibly be right. Peter is tempting Jesus and becoming a hindrance. He is speaking from a worldly perspective rather than a spiritual one—which is striking because he was moments earlier complimented by Jesus for doing the opposite (Matt 16:17).

Jesus teaches us here our need to discern the voice of Satan. When we hear it—even when it comes through those closest to us—we must declare with Jesus, "Get behind me, Satan!"

One Thing to Think About: What attacks of Satan's would be most effective on me?

One Thing to Pray For: Courage to discern and resist temptation

WEEK 45 – MONDAY

Reading: Matthew 17:1-13

Listen to Him!

Having warned the disciples that he is going to Jerusalem to his death, Jesus takes Peter, James, and John with him on the mountain. He is *"transfigured before them, and his face shone like the sun, and his clothes became white as light"*(Matt 17:2). As if this is not amazing enough, *"there appeared to them Moses and Elijah, talking with him"*(Matt 17:3). Peter, James, and John are given a remarkable opportunity to see Jesus in his glorified state and two of the greatest men to ever live.

Peter is unsure what to say, so he makes a proposal. *"Lord, it is good that we are here. If you wish, I will make three tents here, one for you and one for Moses and one for Elijah"*(Matt 17:4). Peter's object seems to be to honor all three men. *"He was still speaking when, behold, a bright cloud overshadowed them, and a voice from the cloud said, 'This is my beloved Son, with whom I am well pleased; listen to him"*(Matt 17:5). When Peter wants to honor Moses, Elijah, and Jesus, God speaks declaratively: This is my *Son*! Listen to *him*!

Moses and Elijah are two of the most significant figures of the Old Testament. God's law was given through Moses. Elijah was the great prophet of Israel. Here the consummate lawgiver and consummate prophet appear with Jesus, but God tells the disciples to listen to Jesus instead.

Jesus has supremacy, even over the great men God has used in the past. God wants us to honor him—and as we do so, we honor God.

One Thing to Think About: Do I listen to Jesus above every other voice?

One Thing to Pray For: Diligence to give Jesus the honor he is due

WEEK 45 – TUESDAY

Reading: Matthew 17:14-27

Not to Give Offense

The mountaintop moment of Jesus' transfiguration doesn't last long. On coming down from the mountain, a crowd greets him, complaining that the other disciples were unable to cast a demon out of a man's son. Jesus then gives another distressing prophecy about what awaits him in Jerusalem (Matt 17:22-23). This is followed by another round of complaining: *"When they came to Capernaum, the collectors of the two-drachma tax went up to Peter and said, 'Does your teacher not pay the tax?'"*(Matt 17:24).

Peter impulsively answers the question *"Yes"*(Matt 17:25). Jesus challenges this as he enters the house. *"'What do you think, Simon? From whom do kings of the earth take toll or tax? From their sons or from others?' And when he said, 'From others,' Jesus said to him, 'Then the sons are free'"*(Matt 17:25-26). Peter has spoken out of turn and Jesus is not required to pay this tax. The basis for his exemption is his status as "son." The royal family is exempt—and Jesus is certainly in the royal family.

"However, not to give offense to them, go to the sea and cast a hook and take the first fish that comes up, and when you open its mouth you will find a shekel. Take that and give it to them for me and for yourself"(Matt 17:27). Despite the fact that he is free, Jesus pays the tax anyway. He does so in a humorously bizarre way. He simultaneously affirms his status as God's Son (by pledging money in a fish's mouth) and his willingness to pay the unnecessary tax anyway.

Jesus' motive is *"not to give offense to them."* Very often Jesus' words and actions have troubled the Jews—on the Sabbath, or about tax collectors and sinners, or about hand-washing. Yet in this case, Jesus asserting his rights would have created a legitimate problem for them. Jesus shows that he is willing to be inconvenienced and misunderstood if it will help others come to faith. Some matters cannot be compromised, but on things that don't truly matter, Jesus will bend.

One Thing to Think About: What are some situations where it would be better for me to accept wrong than insist on my own rights?

One Thing to Pray For: Jesus' consideration of others

WEEK 45 – WEDNESDAY

Reading: Matthew 18:1-9

Become Like Children

The disciples ask Jesus to resolve their long-running dispute. *"At that time the disciples came to Jesus, saying, 'Who is the greatest in the kingdom of heaven?'"*(Matt 18:1). This is a golden opportunity for Jesus to endorse someone who is exactly what he wants in his kingdom—his poster child, the face of his ministry. They are looking for Jesus to mention a name. Instead, Jesus does a most unexpected thing.

"And calling to him a child, he put him in the midst of them and said, 'Truly, I say to you, unless you turn and become like children, you will never enter the kingdom of heaven. Whoever humbles himself like this child is the greatest in the kingdom of heaven'"(Matt 18:2-4). Instead of a disciple, Jesus praises a child. The greatest in the kingdom is whoever is humble like this child. Jesus says this in a time when children are viewed as lesser and unimportant—a time when children are told to grow up, but adults are never told to be like children.

The focus of Jesus' saying is humility: *"whoever humbles himself like this child"*(Matt 18:4). The disciples have shown the intensity of their pride by jockeying for status. This won't do. Little children, by contrast, are not constantly worried about besting everyone around them (unless such thoughts are planted there). They are not too proud to learn from others. They are cooperative rather than competitive. Without this humility, Jesus warns us that not only will we not be great, but *"you will never enter the kingdom of heaven"*(Matt 18:3).

One Thing to Think About: Am I like a child?

One Thing to Pray For: The humility Jesus expects in me

WEEK 45 – THURSDAY

Reading: Matthew 18:10-20

Conflict Resolution

As Jesus uses a child to teach the disciples about humility, he moves from the tragedy of causing a little one to stumble (Matt 18:6) to the problem of causing others to sin generally (Matt 18:7-10). Finally he gives his disciples a guide to resolving conflicts.

"*If your brother sins against you, go and tell him his fault, between you and him alone. If he listens to you, you have gained your brother*"(Matt 18:15). Jesus describes a situation where my brother *sins*—which is different from hurting my feelings or making me angry. When this happens, I "*go and tell him his fault, between you and him alone.*" I do this instead of calling my friends, families, or fellow-brethren. If he hears me, we can resolve the conflict without involving anyone else.

"*But if he does not listen, take one or two others along with you, that every charge may be established by the evidence of two or three witnesses*"(Matt 18:16). If this does not resolve the conflict and my brother remains in sin, I take others to reason with them. "*Witnesses*" here also stresses that these are people with knowledge of the sin. "*If he refuses to listen to them, tell it to the church*"(Matt 18:17). Only now is the wider community is involved in trying to reason the man out of his sin. "*And if he refuses to listen even to the church, let him be to you as a Gentile and a tax collector*"(Matt 18:17).

When someone sins against me, I need to tell him. I must develop the habit of going to a brother to resolve our conflicts. When someone comes to speak to me, I must choose to be reasonable and humble. If my brethren are concerned about my spiritual state, I must listen.

One Thing to Think About: Do I take sin as seriously as Jesus does?

One Thing to Pray For: Willingness to preserve peace in my relationships

WEEK 45 – FRIDAY

Reading: Matthew 18:21-35

Pity and Forgiveness

Jesus has just implied that he expects us to forgive our brother when he sins against us (Matt 18:15). Peter wants to know how many times this forgiveness is required. "*Lord, how often will my brother sin against me, and I forgive him? As many as seven times?*"(Matt 18:21). Jesus refuses limits. "*I do not say to you seven times, but seventy-seven times*"(Matt 18:22). Jesus then tells a story to better illustrate why forgiveness is appropriate.

A servant owes a king 10,000 talents—an extraordinary sum of money—and the bill comes due. "*So the servant fell on his knees, imploring him, 'Have patience with me, and I will pay you everything'*"(Matt 18:26). He begs only for patience. "*And out of pity for him, the master of that servant released him and forgave him the debt*"(Matt 18:27). Jesus specifies that the king forgives the entire debt out of pity. This newly forgiven servant then takes his fellow-servant (who owes a much smaller debt) and refuses to pity or forgive him. "*And should not you have had mercy on your fellow servant, as I had mercy on you?*"(Matt 18:33).

The central fact of my life is always God's forgiveness of my debt—not the relatively small hurts others have done to me. God wants us to feel *pity* for others when they hurt us—to see them entrapped and enslaved by what they have done, to see their desperation, to see our opportunity to set them free. Pity will require me to set aside my hurt and see that sin hurts the sinner in addition to the one sinned against.

One Thing to Think About: Are there people who need my forgiveness?

One Thing to Pray For: A heart of mercy like my God's

WEEK 46 – MONDAY

Reading: Matthew 19:1-15

Divorce

Jesus is asked a straightforward question on divorce and gives a straightforward answer. *"Is it lawful to divorce one's wife for any cause?"*(Matt 19:3). Is divorce lawful? Jesus goes back to the beginning (Matt 19:4-5), especially to the idea that marriage involves making two people into one. *"What therefore God has joined together, let not man separate"*(Matt 19:6). Jesus views marriage as God's work, not to be undone by man. Is divorce lawful? No.

It is notable that the Pharisees scramble in response to this. *"Why then did Moses command one to give a certificate of divorce and to send her away?"*(Matt 19:7). Jesus answers that Moses' command was not God's original intent (Matt 19:8) and restates his assertion, with the reason behind it. *"And I say to you: whoever divorces his wife, except for sexual immorality, and marries another, commits adultery"*(Matt 19:9). Jesus adds an exception—marriages involving sexual immorality—but the rule is clear: divorce and remarriage is adultery.

Jesus wants married people to stay married. If we are unwilling to keep that commitment, it is better not to marry (Matt 19:10). These are sobering words for the unmarried, who must count the cost of a major decision that can affect the rest of life and eternity. These are sobering words for the married, who must keep their promises, maintain this vital relationship, and be willing to sacrifice for the good of their mate.

One Thing to Think About: Am I honoring God's expectations of marriage?

One Thing to Pray For: God's help and blessing in my closest relationships

WEEK 46 – TUESDAY

Reading: Matthew 19:16-30

What Do I Still Lack?

The rich young ruler approaches Jesus as a remarkable prospect for the kingdom. *"Teacher, what good deed must I do to have eternal life?"*(Matt 19:16). Yet Jesus seems to resist him and his apparent eagerness to serve God. *"Why do you ask me about what is good? There is only one who is good. If you would enter life, keep the commandments"*(Matt 19:17). The response is brusque and dismissive. When pressed, Jesus encourages observance of the commandments. Finally the young man can reveal his heart. *"All these I have kept. What do I still lack?"*(Matt 19:20).

Jesus' manner with the rich young ruler has for a long time bothered me. Why would he repel a seeker? Why would he find fault with him calling him "good" or trying to keep the commandments? It is helpful to note that the man has come to Jesus asking *"what do I still lack?"*. There is something missing for him—something that no amount of wealth, law-keeping, and popularity can do for him. He comes to Jesus to hear the thing that is missing in his life—and Jesus does not disappoint him on this score. *"'If you would be perfect, go, sell what you possess and give to the poor, and you will have treasure in heaven; and come, follow me.' When the young man heard this he went away sorrowful, for he had great possessions"*(Matt 19:22). When read this way, it is clear that Jesus wants the young man to truly find the eternal life he is seeking. Wealth has become the problem for him—the thing he lacks that he cannot put his finger on—and Jesus recommends swift removal.

Each of us has a key issue that stands between us and God. Perhaps it is a moral flaw—sexual sin, addiction, anger, or evil talk. Perhaps it is a relationship—a family that rivals God, a boyfriend or girlfriend for whom we would compromise it all. Perhaps it is a love for some hobby, pastime, or otherwise innocent pleasure that grows out of proportion to its real importance. Jesus challenges us to make him the supreme Lord in whatever the key issue is.

One Thing to Think About: What do I still lack?

One Thing to Pray For: Gratitude for the clarity that Jesus brings to our flaws and needs

WEEK 46 – WEDNESDAY

Reading: Matthew 20:1-16

God's Right to Grace

Jesus tells a parable here that is prompted by Peter's question: *"See, we have left everything and followed you. What then will we have?"*(Matt 19:27). Jesus responds that all who sacrifice for Jesus will be repaid—yet that grace looks different for everyone.

In the story, workers work for different periods of time: some 12 hours, some 9, 6, 3, and 1. *"And when those hired about the eleventh hour came, each of them received a denarius. Now when those hired first came, they thought they would receive more, but each of them also received a denarius"*(Matt 20:9-10). When paid the same, they grumble and the master defends himself.

Jesus explains that God has a right to grace—even when we don't like it. First the master says *"Friend, I am doing you no wrong. Did you not agree with me for a denarius?"*(Matt 20:13). God's grace does not somehow deprive us, giving others a blessing at our expense. *"Am I not allowed to do what I choose with what belongs to me?"*(Matt 20:15). Since all the blessings are his, he can dispense them as he wants. *"Or do you begrudge my generosity?"*(Matt 20:15). Why would God's goodness make me angry?

We like grace when it is extended to us, but often we want something less than grace for others. It is then that complaints about justice and fairness spring up. God has a right to give grace—always.

One Thing to Think About: Are there people—especially those who have hurt me—that I resent God giving grace to?

One Thing to Pray For: A heart that celebrates God's grace

WEEK 46 – THURSDAY

Reading: Matthew 20:17-34

You Do Not Know What You Are Asking

James and John enlist their mom in their power play. *"Then the mother of the sons of Zebedee came up to him with her sons, and kneeling before him she asked him for something"*(Matt 20:20). Evidently they believe Jesus is more likely to grant the request if their mother is present. *"Say that these two sons of mine are to sit, one at your right hand and one at your left, in your kingdom"*(Matt 20:21). They assume that the most powerful positions in the coming kingdom of God will be granted to them—as long as they ask nicely.

Jesus refuses. *"You do not know what you are asking"*(Matt 20:22). Their request makes sense to them, but there is more to it than they realize. This may refer to their misconception of the kingdom as an earthly political power. But probably Jesus is referring to the fact that kingdom authority and honor work differently than they could possibly understand.

"'Are you able to drink the cup that I am to drink?' They said to him, 'We are able.' He said to them, 'You will drink my cup, but to sit at my right hand and at my left is not mine to grant, but it is for those for whom it has been prepared by my Father'"(Matt 20:22-23). Suffering is a reality for kingdom citizens—especially those who are given the greatest authority. Instead of honor, they suffer the greatest shame. At the head of it all is Jesus.

Jesus challenges our impulses to seek to have power over others. He shows us the better way—the way of humility, service, and quiet obedience to God. Though we may suffer, these are the marks of true greatness.

One Thing to Think About: Does it bother me that if I pursue humility, service, and quiet obedience, few will notice?

One Thing to Pray For: Contentment in simple service to Jesus

WEEK 46 – FRIDAY

Reading: Matthew 21:1-11

The Humble King

As Jesus approaches Jerusalem, the place where he will be rejected and killed, he makes detailed preparations. *"Go into the village in front of you, and immediately you will find a donkey tied, and a colt with her. Untie them and bring them to me. If anyone says anything to you, you shall say, 'The Lord needs them,' and he will send them at once"*(Matt 21:2-3). Jesus needs to enter in a certain manner and this clandestine mission will help.

Matthew makes clear what is motivating Jesus. *"This took place to fulfill what was spoken by the prophet, saying, 'Say to the daughter of Zion, "Behold, your king is coming to you, humble, and mounted on a donkey, on a colt, the foal of a beast of burden"'"*(Matt 21:4-5). Jesus is taking action to fulfill—down to a precise detail—the prophecy of Zechariah. Jerusalem's king would approach her on a donkey as a sign of his humility. The crowd certainly gets the message, shouting, *"Hosanna to the Son of David! Blessed is he who comes in the name of the Lord! Hosanna in the highest!"*(Matt 21:9).

Kings are not typically humble. Most rulers take great pains to flaunt their power and wealth. Jesus reveals himself as a very different kind of king—one who comes to suffer on behalf of others and does so without ostentation. As subjects of this great king, can we behave ourselves any differently? Is anything too lowly for us? Can we continue to seek power and wealth and hope to follow Jesus?

One Thing to Think About: Is there a part of me that wants Jesus to show more power and majesty here?

One Thing to Pray For: The humility to suffer shame—and pain—for God and others

WEEK 47 – MONDAY

Reading: Matthew 21:12-22

A House of Prayer

Upon entering the city Jesus proceeds immediately to the temple. He "*drove out all who sold and bought in the temple, and he overturned the tables of the money-changers and the seats of those who sold pigeons*"(Matt 21:12). The temple has become a commercial center. The activities Jesus challenges are legitimate in themselves. Money-changing and selling animals are both useful to helping people worship God according to Moses' law. The problem is not the practice, but its location.

"*He said to them, 'It is written, "My house shall be called a house of prayer," but you make it a den of robbers'*"(Matt 21:13). Jesus turns over the tables because this is such an egregious violation of God's expectation for the temple. God wants it to be "*a house of prayer*"—a place where people can gather to approach God. Instead, they have made it "*a den of robbers*"—a place where people gather to count their ill-gotten gain. Jesus appears furious that his countrymen have ignored God's purpose so completely.

God prescribes worship for us. It is good for us to worship him. Worship humbles, centers, and energizes us. Yet worship demands careful attention. Some things must be "left outside" while we worship—just as the moneychangers should have set up shop outside the temple gates. When we allow the mundane matters of life to interrupt communion with God, we anger our Savior.

One Thing to Think About: Does my worship keep God and his purposes foremost?

One Thing to Pray For: My worship to be sincere and pleasing to God

WEEK 47 – TUESDAY

Reading: Matthew 21:23-32

The Bottom Line

The chief priests and elders confront Jesus about cleansing the temple. He refuses to answer them because they don't have the honesty to answer his question about John the Baptist. *"What do you think? A man had two sons. And he went to the first and said, 'Son, go and work in the vineyard today.' And he answered, 'I will not,' but afterward he changed his mind and went. And he went to the other son and said the same. And he answered, 'I go, sir,' but did not go. Which of the two did the will of his father?"* (Matt 21:28-31). The chief priests respond correctly—the first son.

Now comes the shocker. *"Truly, I say to you, the tax collectors and the prostitutes go into the kingdom of God before you. For John came to you in the way of righteousness, and you did not believe him, but the tax collectors and prostitutes believed him. And even when you saw it, you did not afterward change your minds and believe him"* (Matt 21:31-32). These are strong words against religious leaders. Tax collectors and prostitutes—who obviously made poor initial decisions—change their minds and ultimately decide to do the will of God. But the chief priests never do obey God, even though they say the right things.

Jesus' story focuses on the bottom line. Initial responses are not nearly as important as ultimate obedience. It's not how we start but how we finish that makes the difference. Jesus also reminds us that it is not what we say that matters most, but what we do.

One Thing to Think About: Am I obeying God or merely saying the right things?

One Thing to Pray For: Diligence to finish well

WEEK 47 – WEDNESDAY

Reading: Matthew 21:33-46

The Stone the Builders Rejected

The Jewish leadership has responded with hostility to Jesus cleansing the temple. Jesus answers their negativity by telling a story that emphasizes the continual rejection of God by his people. A master of a house with a vineyard leases his property to servants. The key to the story is the fact that the owner sends servants to receive the fruit of the vineyard. *"He sent servants to the tenants to get his fruit. And the tenants took his servants and beat one, killed another, and stoned another. Again he sent other servants, more than the first. And they did the same to them"*(Matt 21:34-35). The servants reject their master by rejecting his messengers.

"Finally he sent his son to them, saying, 'They will respect my son'"(Matt 21:37). But instead of respecting the son, they *"took him and threw him out of the vineyard and killed him"*(Matt 21:39). The son becomes not only the most egregious rejection, but also the final one. Jesus then makes the application: *"Have you never read in the Scriptures: 'The stone that the builders rejected has become the cornerstone; this was the Lord's doing, and it is marvelous in our eyes'"*(Matt 21:42). This rejection was prophesied long before and has always been a part of God's plan. The servants in Jesus' story are the prophets—messengers through whom God has continually reached out to his people, only to be rejected. Yet now God has sent his Son —Jesus himself—and their rejection of him is the most terrible and significant of all. These Jews have written themselves into the story of God and his people in the most horrible way.

God can use all people. When people accept Jesus, they become incredible stories of God's grace and power. When people reject him, he can weave their rejection into something even more amazing and beautiful. God can make the rejected stone into the chief cornerstone.

One Thing to Think About: How have I seen God use people—regardless of their response to him?

One Thing to Pray For: A part (for good) in the great work God is achieving through Jesus

WEEK 47 – THURSDAY

Reading: Matthew 22:1-14

The Second Invitation

Jesus is still answering the rejection of the Jewish religious leadership and he has another story to tell. *"The kingdom of heaven may be compared to a king who gave a wedding feast for his son, and sent his servants to call those who were invited to the wedding feast, but they would not come"*(Matt 22:2-3). It is a gracious invitation to come and enjoy and celebrate, yet it is greeted with disdain. *"But they paid no attention and went off, one to his farm, another to his business, while the rest seized his servants, treated them shamefully, and killed them"*(Matt 22:5-6). The king is furious and destroys them (Matt 22:7).

But the story does not end here. *"Then he said to his servants, 'The wedding feast is ready, but those invited were not worthy. Go therefore to the main roads and invite to the wedding feast as many as you find'"*(Matt 22:8-9). There is another invitation. The king extends grace yet again. It is not his first choice, but his first choice *"were not worthy."* Even these must be properly attired (Matt 22:11-13), but the marvel is that they are invited at all.

This section of Matthew is very focused on the Jews' rejection of Jesus, but that is not all. He also talks about the kingdom being taken away from the Jews *"and given to a people producing its fruits"*(Matt 21:43). He tells the Jewish leaders that *"the tax collectors and prostitutes go into the kingdom of God before you"*(Matt 21:31). The second invitation means that God does not quit simply because some reject him. It reminds us of the tremendous grace of God—that God is simultaneously harsh to those who reject him and merciful to continue to invite.

One Thing to Think About: Have I ever rejected God's invitation?

One Thing to Pray For: Praise to God for his patience and grace

WEEK 47 – FRIDAY

Reading: Matthew 22:15-22

Render to Caesar

In the week before his crucifixion, several groups take their best shot at Jesus. Here the Pharisees *"went and plotted how to entangle him in his words"*(Matt 22:15). Their trap begins with flattery, complimenting Jesus' sincerity and objectivity. *"Is it lawful to pay taxes to Caesar, or not?"*(Matt 22:17). The difficulty here is that paying taxes to Caesar is incredibly unpopular among average Jews because it implies agreement with the occupying power. However, going on record as discouraging people from paying taxes to the Romans will make Jesus' teaching career a short one.

Jesus asks for a coin, then asks whose picture and name are on it. *"Therefore render to Caesar the things that are Caesar's, and to God the things that are God's"*(Matt 22:21). The coins are obviously Caesar's, since they bear his name and picture. Pay Caesar what already belongs to him. This does not somehow intrude on God's realm. Jesus here endorses paying taxes and validates the authority of governments to levy them.

But *"render...to God the things that are God's"* also means that we have similar obligations to God. There are things that belong to him (duties and expectations) that we can give to no other. My worship does not belong to Caesar. My unqualified service, the absolute priority of my time, my hope for tomorrow—these are things that I must give to God and no other.

We have political duties that we owe our nation. But let us never allow them to overcome our duties to God.

One Thing to Think About: Am I giving Caesar his due?

One Thing to Pray For: Clarity to keep Caesar and God in their proper places in my heart

WEEK 48 – MONDAY

Reading: Matthew 22:23-33

God Spoke to You

The Sadducees, who deny the resurrection, challenge Jesus with an elaborate story. A woman ends up married to seven brothers, each one after the previous dies. *"In the resurrection, therefore, of the seven, whose wife will she be? For they all had her"*(Matt 22:28). Jesus' answer is instructive.

"You are wrong, because you know neither the Scriptures nor the power of God"(Matt 22:29). The answer to their scenario is already there in the Scriptures. *"And as for the resurrection of the dead, have you not read what was said to you by God: 'I am the God of Abraham, and the God of Isaac, and the God of Jacob'? He is not God of the dead, but of the living"*(Matt 22:31-32). God speaks of himself as *presently* the God of dead people, meaning that Abraham, Isaac, and Jacob are still alive.

Jesus words this in an interesting way: *"have you not read what was said to you by God"*. The startling thing is that these words were *not*, in fact, spoken to the Jews of Jesus' day. They were spoken about 1500 years earlier to an entirely different generation of people. But Jesus' point is that when God speaks, he expects us to read and understand what he is revealing about himself—*even if he is not speaking directly to us*. Jesus speaks of Scripture as God's revelation to us.

For modern Christians, this makes reading the mail of the ancient Corinthians, Jeremiah's prophecies, and the desert musings of Moses much more relevant. God is speaking to us.

One Thing to Think About: Am I listening to God daily?

One Thing to Pray For: Deeper understanding of God by deeper knowledge of his word

WEEK 48 – TUESDAY

Reading: Matthew 22:34-46

The Most Important Commands

One last group challenges Jesus in this last week before his death. The Pharisees present Jesus with a common question among the rabbis of the day: *"Teacher, which is the great commandment in the Law?"*(Matt 22:36). Of all the (more than 600) commands of the Law of Moses, which is the most important? Jesus gives them two answers for the price of one. *"You shall love the Lord your God with all your heart and with all your soul and with all your mind. This is the great and first commandment. And a second is like it: You shall love your neighbor as yourself. On these two commandments depend all the Law and the Prophets"*(Matt 22:37-40).

All the expectations God has for man can be boiled down to *love*. That love has two directions—loving God and loving our neighbor (meaning our fellow-man). Loving God involves respecting his word and will for our lives, giving him honor for his goodness toward us, and pursuing his holiness by living well. Loving our neighbor involves showing compassion, learning to forgive, yielding to others, and doing no harm. The sheer breadth of these two commands is astounding; nothing lies outside their purview.

My difficulty with this text is not with any of the above, but with how deceptively easy love appears. I don't feel any particular ill will toward God or man, but that does not necessarily mean that I love. Love also means positive actions that may inconvenience me as they put others and their needs ahead of me. Love means that I accept God's will trumping mine because I trust him.

One Thing to Think About: How will I show love for God and for man today?

One Thing to Pray For: Strength to release my will in favor of God's—and others'

WEEK 48 – WEDNESDAY

Reading: Matthew 23:1-12

Exalting and Humbling

Having silenced his critics, Jesus turns to address the Pharisees and their deficient spirituality. First he talks *about* them—in the following verses he will address them directly. *"The scribes and the Pharisees sit on Moses' seat, so do and observe whatever they tell you, but not the works they do. For they preach, but do not practice"*(Matt 23:2-3). These men are the spiritual paragons of the day. They relish status—sitting on Moses' seat—but the things they tell others never seem to make it onto *their* to-do lists.

"They do all their deeds to be seen by others"(Matt 23:5). Jesus has an extensive list. They make broad phylacteries and long fringes as overt signs of goodness. They love honorable seats at public events. They expect to be called by formal, respectful names—rabbi, father, instructor. *"Whoever exalts himself will be humbled, and whoever humbles himself will be exalted"*(Matt 23:12).

Jesus outlines one of the dangers of honor. It starts innocently enough: people show respect to leaders because of their role in communicating God's word. Gradually it becomes a motivation (*"they do all their deeds to be seen by others"*). They grow to love all the trappings of their position and work to increase their power. Jesus calls this exalting themselves and promises that they will be humbled.

Religious corruption and status-seeking are not new. The answer is not to stop respecting anyone, nor is it to give up on God's word. The answer is to deliberately seek humility. *"But you are not to be called rabbi...and call no man your father...neither be called instructors...the greatest among you shall be your servant"*(Matt 23:8, 9, 10, 12). If we humble ourselves before God and others, it will be God who exalts us.

One Thing to Think About: Do I do my works of righteousness to be seen by people?

One Thing to Pray For: Deeper humility in my service to God and others

WEEK 48 – THURSDAY

Reading: Matthew 23:13-24

Straining Out a Gnat and Swallowing a Camel

Jesus heaps woes on the Pharisees for their hypocrisy and holy-sounding corruption. But one image stands above the rest for its preposterousness. *"Woe to you, scribes and Pharisees, hypocrites! For you tithe mint and dill and cumin, and have neglected the weightier matters of the law: justice and mercy and faithfulness. These you ought to have done, without neglecting the others. You blind guides, straining out a gnat and swallowing a camel!"* (Matt 23:23-24). In one powerful picture, Jesus sums up the Pharisees' zeal and its tragically misguided emphasis.

Gnats and camels are unclean according to Jewish dietary restrictions. Jesus pictures the Pharisees hard at work, attempting to strain tiny gnats out of their drinks. When they are successful, they swallow a camel—one of the largest unclean animals—instead!

Jesus parodies the way Pharisees focus all their attention on the minutiae and details of the Law while missing the point. They tithe meticulously—keep the Law scrupulously—can debate about every point of doctrine—yet they neglect justice, mercy, and faith. All of these things are important, but some of them are more important than others. They are *"the weightier matters."*

The Pharisees warn us of the danger of thinking that being religious—or being quite busy in our religion—is somehow a substitute for genuine service to God. God has given us this warning so that we can be certain our religious priorities remain in the right place—where his are.

One Thing to Think About: Do I tend to major in minors?

One Thing to Pray For: Wisdom and insight into what matters most to God

WEEK 48 – FRIDAY

Reading: Matthew 23:25-39

Clean Inside the Cup First

Jesus continues his denunciation of the Pharisees by highlighting the inconsistency between their words and behavior. *"Woe to you, scribes and Pharisees, hypocrites! For you clean the outside of the cup and the plate, but inside they are full of greed and self-indulgence"*(Matt 23:25). Cleaning only the outside of the cup is poor dishwashing. *"Woe to you, scribes and Pharisees, hypocrites! For you are like whitewashed tombs, which outwardly appear beautiful, but within are full of dead people's bones and all uncleanness"*(Matt 23:27). We can whitewash tombs, but they are still full of corruption and potential defilement for Jews.

Jesus is making a point about the difference between appearances and reality. *"So you also outwardly appear righteous to others, but within you are full of hypocrisy and lawlessness"*(Matt 23:28). The Pharisees are hypocrites because they act as if they are righteous people while they are really greedy, self-indulgent, unclean, and lawless. These are not sincere people occasionally stumbling; they are committed to faking it.

Jesus then gives advice: *"You blind Pharisee! First clean the inside of the cup and the plate, that the outside also may be clean"*(Matt 23:26). The way to eliminate corruption and hypocrisy is to *start within*. We start with being sincere and eliminating evil motives. We continue to serve God even when others don't notice. We don't focus on appearances because our hearts are given to God. As we clean the inside of the cup—as we are transformed from the inside out—the appearances take care of themselves.

Real life change may (or may not) be visible to others, but it will always happen from the inside out.

One Thing to Think About: Are there differences between the way I appear and the reality?

One Thing to Pray For: A clean heart that leads to a clean life

WEEK 49 – MONDAY

Reading: Matthew 24:1-14

The Beginning of the Birth Pains

As his disciples point out the beauty of the temple buildings, Jesus warns them that the temple will soon be destroyed. They probe: *"Tell us, when will these things be, and what will be the sign of your coming and of the end of the age?"*(Matt 24:3). This chapter contains Jesus' answer to when Jerusalem will be destroyed—along with some statements that hint at his ultimate return.

Jesus warns them about the effect certain signs might have on them. *"See that no one leads you astray. For many will come in my name, saying, 'I am he,' and lead many astray"*(Matt 24:4-5). *"See that you are not alarmed"* when there are wars. *"And then many will fall away and betray one another and hate one another"*(Matt 24:10) and *"the love of many will grow cold"*(Matt 24:12). *"But the one who endures to the end will be saved"*(Matt 24:13). It is important that the disciples not become discouraged by the difficulty of the era or the tribulations they themselves will suffer.

But particularly here, Jesus is teaching them not to assume that such things are a sign that Jerusalem's destruction is imminent. *"All these things are but the beginning of the birth pains"*(Matt 24:8). Just like labor pains, they are signs that something dramatic is coming but is not here yet. This image is common in the Old and New Testaments to describe the beginning of judgment. It also may be that Jesus is speaking of the consummation of the kingdom as the birth—and that conflict and chaos are inevitable as the kingdom grows toward its full stature.

What does this mean for us? While the events described here may have special application to the time before Jerusalem's destruction, they describe life in our time as well. We still need endurance (Matt 24:13) as we observe a world hostile to Jesus. We still must be prepared to have tribulation, threats, and hatred from others (Matt 24:9).

One Thing to Think About: Do I get discouraged by the fact that many people oppose the message of Jesus?

One Thing to Pray For: A calm, settled heart in the face of a chaotic world

WEEK 49 – TUESDAY

Reading: Matthew 24:15-35

False Christs and False Prophets

In response to the disciples' question about when Jerusalem will be destroyed, Jesus continues to speak in apocalyptic, judgment-style language. He warns them not to conclude that the destruction is imminent simply because many disastrous things begin happening (Matt 24:4-14). However, *"when you see the abomination of desolation spoken of by the prophet Daniel, standing in the holy place (let the reader understand) then let those who are in Judea flee to the mountains"*(Matt 24:15-16). This is the sign that cannot be ignored and it is time for disciples to escape.

There is a related danger. In the midst of this climate of world-shaking events, some will try to mislead and deceive. *"Then if anyone says to you, 'Look, here is the Christ!' or 'There he is!' do not believe it. For false christs and false prophets will arise and perform great signs and wonders, so as to lead astray, if possible, even the elect"*(Matt 24:23-24). The New Testament speaks in numerous places of false prophets (Matt 7:15), false teachers (2 Pet 2:1), and false brethren (Gal 2:4). The implication of attaching the term "false" to these titles is that they are not what they claim. They are to be avoided because the damage they can do is greater because of their claim of authenticity.

Jesus' apocalyptic language is filled with warnings because the events described here are scary. They can lead us to seek comfort in people or ideas that are not from God. They can lead us to work ourselves into an excited state, eager to grasp God's next move, and away from the quiet work of discipleship and obedience. Evil people will prey on us in our agitation if we allow it.

One Thing to Think About: How do I respond to uncertainty?

One Thing to Pray For: Wisdom and discernment in turbulent times

WEEK 49 – WEDNESDAY

Reading: Matthew 24:36-51

Like a Thief in the Night

After speaking so much about signs and responses in this chapter, it is strange to see Jesus change his language and speak about things *without* a firm date or sign. "*But concerning that day and hour no one knows, not even the angels of heaven, nor the Son, but the Father only*"(Matt 24:36). It is possible Jesus has changed his topic to speak about the end of time instead of simply Jerusalem's destruction. It is also possible that he is saying that even with all the information he has given, the specific day and hour remain unknown.

Jesus focuses on the uncertainty surrounding his return: "*For as were the days of Noah, so will be the coming of the Son of Man. For as in those days before the flood they were eating and drinking, marrying and giving in marriage, until the day when Noah entered the ark, and they were unaware until the flood came and swept them all away, so will be the coming of the Son of Man*"(Matt 24:37-39). This judgment will be sudden and unexpected. "*But know this, that if the master of the house had known in what part of the night the thief was coming, he would have stayed awake and would not have let his house be broken into. Therefore you also must be ready, for the Son of Man is coming at an hour you do not expect*"(Matt 24:43-44). Jesus expects his disciples to remain alert in anticipation of his return.

Repeatedly New Testament authors use the image of the thief in the night to emphasize the unknown nature of the second coming (Luke 12:39, 1 Thess 5:2-6, 2 Pet 3:10, Rev 3:3, 16:15). Jesus wants us to remember that his disciples not only look backward to his life while on earth, but also forward to the finishing out of God's plan for the world and his people. By definition, we won't know when that is, but Jesus expects us to be ready.

One Thing to Think About: What kinds of things distract me from being prepared for Jesus' return?

One Thing to Pray For: Vigilance as we wait for our savior

WEEK 49 – THURSDAY

Reading: Matthew 25:1-13

Ready and Waiting

Jesus teaches a parable to stress the vigilant preparedness he expects from kingdom citizens. *"Then the kingdom of heaven will be like ten virgins who took their lamps and went to meet the bridegroom"*(Matt 25:1). The virgins are part of the wedding party, awaiting the groom so that they can proceed to the wedding feast. *"Five of them were foolish, and five were wise"*(Matt 25:2). In this story, wisdom and foolishness are revealed by willingness to wait.

What is interesting is that Jesus' story has an understood expectation of waiting. *"As the bridegroom as delayed, they all became drowsy and slept"*(Matt 25:5). The groom may be delayed; will the virgins still wait? The foolish virgins, unprepared for this delay, run out of oil and are unable to borrow. *"And while they were going out to buy, the bridegroom came, and those who were ready went in with him to the marriage feast, and the door was shut"*(Matt 25:10). Because of their lack of preparation, they miss what they were waiting for. It is particularly tragic to hear their cry at the door: *"Lord, lord, open to us"*(Matt 25:11) and the groom's response, *"Truly, I say to you, I do not know you"*(Matt 25:12). Their foolishness makes all their waiting a waste.

Jesus makes the application: *"Watch therefore, for you know neither the day nor the hour"*(Matt 25:13). Jesus wants us to be ready and waiting. Because our deepest desire is to be with him in eternity and see the consummation of his kingdom, we are willing to wait as long as it takes.

One Thing to Think About: Am I ready and waiting for Jesus' return?

One Thing to Pray For: Jesus to come quickly

WEEK 49 – FRIDAY

Reading: Matthew 25:14-30

How Jesus Will Settle Accounts

Jesus is still telling parables that emphasize what will happen upon his return. This story—the parable of the talents—is confusing because Jesus uses the word "talent" to refer to money where we have a different use for the word. A master leaves and gives his servants each different amounts of money—one, two, and five talents—*"to each according to his ability"*(Matt 25:15). The intrigue of the story is in how these men will manage their master's money in his absence.

"He who had received the five talents went at once and traded with them, and he made five talents more"(Matt 25:16). The two-talent man has similar success. *"But he who had received the one talent went and dug in the ground and hid his master's money"*(Matt 25:18). The one-talent man does nothing with the money. When the master returns (think of Jesus' return), he *"settled accounts with them"*(Matt 25:19). The five-talent man and two-talent man are praised and given more responsibility. The master chides the one-talent man—*"You wicked and slothful servant!"*(Matt 25:26)—and gives his talent away and punishes him.

What do we make of the story? Jesus teaches us that each of us is given different amounts of money—which I believe represent opportunities to serve and be useful to God. These are given *"to each according to his ability."* What matters to Jesus is not how much we've been given, but what we do with what we have been given.

One Thing to Think About: Am I using my gifts and opportunities in a way that pleases Jesus?

One Thing to Pray For: Vision to remember that I will give account of my master's things

WEEK 50 – MONDAY

Reading: Matthew 25:31-46

You Did It to Me

Jesus tells a final parable emphasizing what will happen when he returns. *"When the Son of Man comes in his glory, and all the angels with him, then he will sit on his glorious throne. Before him will be gathered all the nations, and he will separate people one from another as a shepherd separates the sheep from the goats"*(Matt 25:31-32). Upon his return, Jesus establishes his power. His first act in this role is to judge the people and separate them into two groups. One of the groups will inherit the kingdom (Matt 25:34) while the other will depart to eternal fire (Matt 25:41). These fates should get our attention.

What separates the groups? Jesus (*"the King"*) explains: *"For I was hungry and you gave me food, I was thirsty and you gave me drink, I was a stranger and you welcomed me, I was naked and you clothed me, I was sick and you visited me, I was in prison and you came to me"*(Matt 25:34-36). The sheep are baffled: *"Lord, when did we see you hungry and feed you...?"*(Matt 25:37). Though they may be thankful for the commendation, they don't remember instances of Jesus hungry, naked, or imprisoned. *"Truly, I say to you, as you did it to one of the least of these my brothers, you did it to me"*(Matt 25:40). What we do for Jesus' people we do for Jesus. The goats are those who see Jesus' people in the same need and do nothing, thus slighting the king.

Like the parables of the virgins and the talents (Matt 25:1-30), this parable stresses what disciples do while awaiting Jesus' return. Jesus wants us to care for his people—meeting needs, reaching out, and sacrificing. No one is too lowly to deserve our care. What we do to others is truly done to him—and will be a part of our judgment when he returns.

One Thing to Think About: Are there people that I hesitate to serve? Does Jesus' statement *"you did it to me"* change my attitude?

One Thing to Pray For: Diligence to truly serve others who are in need around me—especially those belonging to Jesus

WEEK 50 – TUESDAY

Reading: Matthew 26:1-16

Thirty Pieces of Silver

After this long set of speeches, Matthew returns us to the matter at hand. Jesus is to die in a just a few days. *"Then the chief priests and the elders of the people...plotted together in order to arrest Jesus by stealth and kill him. But they said, 'Not during the feast, lest there be an uproar among the people'"*(Matt 26:3-5). They are afraid that a public arrest and execution will agitate the people.

"Then one of the twelve, whose name was Judas Iscariot, went to the chief priests and said, 'What will you give me if I deliver him over to you?' And they paid him thirty pieces of silver. And from that moment he sought an opportunity to betray him"(Matt 26:14-16). Judas fits their need perfectly. He is willing to betray Jesus, ensuring a quiet arrest. We are not told what leads Judas to turn on Jesus, but his love of money (John 12:6) must be at the heart of it. For thirty pieces of silver he walks away from the greatest relationship he could ever have and begins the series of choices that will end his life.

There is something ironic about the fact that Mary gives up a flask of *"very expensive ointment"*(Matt 26:7) to honor Jesus while Judas gains thirty pieces of silver to betray him. It is in giving up that we please Jesus—and in seeking to gain more that we dishonor him.

There may be times where we lose our spiritual steam and contemplate giving up on Jesus, like Judas. In such moments we are particularly susceptible to the temptations of greed, lust, pride, and self-indulgence. Whatever our thirty pieces of silver may be, we must choose better than Judas.

One Thing to Think About: What is my thirty pieces of silver? What would I be willing to give up my faith for?

One Thing to Pray For: A heart to sacrifice to honor Jesus

WEEK 50 – WEDNESDAY

Reading: Matthew 26:17-29

My Body and My Blood

Jesus eats the Passover with his disciples and the usually celebratory event is somber. *"Truly, I say to you, one of you will betray me"*(Matt 26:21). The disciples are saddened by this pronouncement. *"And they were very sorrowful and began to say to him one after another, 'Is it I, Lord?'"*(Matt 26:22). He finds a way to tell Judas that he knows about his betrayal without the other disciples picking up on it.

"Now as they were eating, Jesus took bread, and after blessing it broke it and gave it to the disciples, and said, 'Take, eat; this is my body'"(Matt 26:26). Jesus takes one of the elements of the Passover meal and invests it with special significance. He will soon offer his body as a sacrifice and wants them to associate the coming betrayal and death with the bread they eat. *"And he took a cup, and when he had given thanks he gave it to them, saying, 'Drink of it, all of you, for this is my blood of the covenant, which is poured out for many for the forgiveness of sins'"*(Matt 26:27-28). As they share the drink, he wants them to think about the blood about to be poured out. Jesus willingly goes to his death, allowing his blood to be shed to forgive many people.

Eating the bread and drinking the fruit of the vine connect them to Jesus and his sacrifice. As they partake, they share in something whose significance they do not yet comprehend. When we emulate them in partaking of the body and blood of Jesus, we join them in sharing in the sacrifice and the forgiveness it affords.

One Thing to Think About: Do I think about the pain and difficulty of Jesus sacrificing his body and pouring out his blood for me?

One Thing to Pray For: Discernment to see the importance of Jesus' sacrifice

WEEK 50 – THURSDAY

Reading: Matthew 26:30-46

I Will Never Fall Away

Having finished the ominous Passover meal with his disciples, Jesus warns them: *"You will all fall away because of me this night. For it is written, 'I will strike the shepherd, and the sheep of the flock will be scattered'"*(Matt 26:31). Jesus here emphasizes that his death will also mean trouble for them. They *"will all fall away because of me."*

"Peter answered him, 'Though they all fall away because of you, I will never fall away'"(Matt 26:33). Peter—perhaps unwittingly—contradicts Jesus. He sees himself differently from the other disciples. *They* may fall away, but *I* never will. Jesus presses the point: *"Truly, I tell you, this very night, before the rooster crows, you will deny me three times"*(Matt 26:4). Peter is persistent in negating Jesus: *"'Even if I must die with you, I will not deny you!' And all the disciples said the same"*(Matt 26:35).

There is something chilling in the confidence that leads Peter to say *"I will never fall away."* He feels his commitment to Jesus and love for him outstrips the other disciples. Different rules apply to him.

It is easy to pile on Peter for this brashness, especially in light of his denial later this night. Yet we act the same way when we believe "it'll never happen to me." We recreate this spirit when we feel we're above correction—when we condescend to others and feel our faith is better than theirs—when we refuse to examine ourselves. *"Therefore let anyone who thinks that he stands take heed lest he fall"*(1 Cor 10:12).

One Thing to Think About: What if I'm wrong?

One Thing to Pray For: Humility to see myself honestly

WEEK 50 – FRIDAY

Reading: Matthew 26:47-58

Twelve Legions of Angels

Judas leads the armed crowd out to the Garden of Gethsemane and signals Jesus to them by giving him the kiss of greeting. *"Then they came up and laid hands on Jesus and seized him. And behold, one of those who were with Jesus stretched out his hand and drew his sword and struck the servant of the high priest and cut off his ear"*(Matt 26:50-51). Even after all the statements about his coming death, the disciples appear surprised and uncertain at this moment. They respond with violence as they see Jesus at a disadvantage.

"Then Jesus said to him, 'Put your sword back into its place. For all who take the sword will perish by the sword'"(Matt 26:52). Jesus rebukes the show of force. His warning is that violence will beget violence. His kingdom will not be spread this way (John 18:36). This likely disorients the apostles, who have recently all agreed that they would die for him (Matt 26:35). Now we see that they must have been imagining a physical battle.

"Do you think that I cannot appeal to my Father, and he will at once send me more than twelve legions of angels? But how then should the Scriptures be fulfilled, that it must be so?"(Matt 26:53-54). Jesus is not in this position because of he is unable to help himself. He can easily call down angels to remove the threat. Jesus suffers in this moment and allows himself to be captured because *he chooses it*. He must follow through with God's plan—the Scriptures must be fulfilled—sin must be atoned for. It is complete devotion to the Father's will—and absolute love for us—that shines here.

One Thing to Think About: How much must God love me?

One Thing to Pray For: Absolute willingness to follow the Father's will

WEEK 51 – MONDAY

Reading: Matthew 26:59-75

I Do Not Know the Man

After his arrest, Jesus is taken to the home of the high priest. "*And Peter was following him at a distance, as far as the courtyard of the high priest, and going inside he sat with the guards to see the end*"(Matt 26:58). Peter believes that this is the end for Jesus. He has already tried to fight for Jesus tonight—only to be rebuked—but now he waits "*to see the end*" just outside.

Yet the accusations soon come as the servants take notice of him. "*You also were with Jesus the Galilean*"(Matt 26:69). "*This man was with Jesus of Nazareth*"(Matt 26:71). "*Certainly you too are one of them, for your accent betrays you*"(Matt 26:73). These accusations do nothing more than connect Peter with Jesus, yet this is precisely the connection that Peter wants to avoid in this moment.

His denials escalate. "*I do not know what you mean*"(Matt 26:70) becomes "*I do not know the man*"(Matt 26:72), while his final denial includes cursing and swearing (Matt 26:74). The escalation reveals Peter's increasing panic. It is only later, when the intensity of the moment has dimmed, that Peter will realize what he has said—and weep bitterly.

Peter's denials are a reminder that pressure can expose our faith. As tempting as it is to criticize Peter here, we must acknowledge the difficulty of this situation—especially because of his confusion. While we lament his denial, we also must remember that we can similarly deny Jesus when the pressure is on.

One Thing to Think About: What situations or people might lead me to deny Jesus?

One Thing to Pray For: Dedication through the challenges of life

WEEK 51 – TUESDAY

Reading: Matthew 27:1-10

Bringing Back the Silver

The wheels are in motion for Jesus to be crucified today. All of this began with Judas' betrayal. Judas appears not to have realized that this would ultimately lead to Jesus' death. *"Then when Judas, his betrayer, saw that Jesus was condemned, he changed his mind and brought back the thirty pieces of silver to the chief priests and elders, saying, 'I have sinned by betraying innocent blood'"*(Matt 26:3-4). Seeing Jesus condemned to death leads to intense regret. Judas tries to undo his deed by bringing back the silver.

The Jewish authorities respond angrily to Judas' effort at remorse: *"What is that to us? See to it yourself"*(Matt 26:4). This seems to drive Judas over the edge. *"And throwing down the pieces of silver into the temple, he departed, and went and hanged himself"*(Matt 26:5). In frustration and despair, he throws down the money that meant so much to him the day before. Judas is sorry for what he has done, but it is clear that the leaders will not turn back from their course. All is lost for Judas. He sees no reason for hope and feels he cannot live with himself.

All people have done things we deeply regret. Judas illustrates the danger of semi-repentance. He brings back the silver sincerely, but he is unwilling to face the reality of a world where sin cannot be undone. No matter his course, he will always be a traitor. Even his suicide does not change this reality. True repentance will mean accepting a world where our reputation is tarnished, our relationships are damaged, and our self-esteem is lowered.

One Thing to Think About: Are there sins I hesitate to acknowledge and correct?

One Thing to Pray For: Godly sorrow that leads to true repentance

WEEK 51 – WEDNESDAY

Reading: Matthew 27:11-26

Pilate Washes His Hands

Pilate is in a bind. The Jews bring him this man Jesus with vague, unsubstantiated charges. The man does not defend himself. It is clear he should be released, but Pilate doesn't want to anger the Jewish leaders. He has an idea. He will make the *people* choose. "*Now at the feast the governor was accustomed to release for the crowd any one prisoner whom they wanted. And they had a notorious prisoner called Barabbas. So when they gathered, Pilate said to them, 'Whom do you want me to release for you: Barabbas, or Jesus who is called Christ?'*"(Matt 27:15-17).

The problem is that his brilliant idea doesn't work. "*Now the chief priests and the elders persuaded the crowd to ask for Barabbas and destroy Jesus*"(Matt 27:20). When the crowd barks back that they want Barabbas—the notorious prisoner—to be released and Jesus crucified, Pilate asks in desperation: "*Why, what evil has he done?*"(Matt 27:23). The crowd drowns him out.

"*So when Pilate saw that he as gaining nothing, but rather that a riot was beginning, he took water and washed his hands before the crowd, saying, 'I am innocent of this man's blood; see to it yourselves*'"(Matt 27:24). Pilate wants it noted for the record that he is against their act and that this crucifixion is over his protest. He brings water to accentuate the point, literally washing his hands as he abdicates responsibility. There is a problem. Washing his hands does nothing to change Pilate's role in this and his utter failure to stop an injustice that is his duty to man and God.

Pilate reminds us that there are times when our words and gestures are hollow if not combined with action. If we do not stop injustice and evil when we have the opportunity, it doesn't matter what we say. Bemoaning sin is not the same as preventing it—in ourselves and others. It is yet another weakness of man that takes Jesus a large step closer to the cross.

One Thing to Think About: Do I ever talk instead of acting?

One Thing to Pray For: Courage to do what I know is right

WEEK 51 – THURSDAY

Reading: Matthew 27:27-44

He Saved Others; He Cannot Save Himself

After Pilate instructs that Jesus be beaten and then crucified, the Roman soldiers gather around and mock Jesus. They strip him and put fancy clothes on him, make a crown of thorns, and place a scepter in his hand. They beat him and spit on him and mock him. Jesus says nothing.

He walks out to the place where the crucifixion will take place. Over his head reads the charge: *"This is Jesus, the King of the Jews"*(Matt 27:37). It is a taunt and a warning to other Jews who might try to gain followings against Rome. *"And those who passed by derided him, wagging their heads and saying, 'You who would destroy the temple and rebuild it in three days, save yourself! If you are the Son of God, come down from the cross'"*(Matt 27:39-40). They have heard of Jesus. Perhaps some of them previously followed him. Yet seeing him in his present position, they mock. Jesus says nothing.

Jesus' enemies also gather to mock. *"So also the chief priests, with the scribes and elders, mocked him, saying, 'He saved others; he cannot save himself. He is the King of Israel; let him come down now from the cross, and we will believe in him. He trusts in God; let God deliver him now, if he desires him. For he said, "I am the Son of God"'"*(Matt 27:41-43). Jesus' entire ministry is ridiculed. Who can he save now? Whose son is he now? How close is he to God now? *"And the robbers who were crucified with him also reviled him in the same way"*(Matt 27:44). No one can pass up the opportunity to mock Jesus. Jesus says nothing.

Matthew highlights the shame Jesus experiences as he dies. His death means more than simply the end of his life. It is also—by every worldly appearance—the end of his entire movement and all that he taught. Yet in this pivotal moment, Jesus endures such shaming patiently and without challenge. It is a dark moment and hard to watch.

One Thing to Think About: Can I suffer shame without retaliation?

One Thing to Pray For: Faith in God that endures humiliation

WEEK 51 – FRIDAY

Reading: Matthew 27:45-56

My God, My God, Why Have You Forsaken Me?

Jesus hangs on the cross. He is the subject of ridicule from all sides. Matthew does not mention any of his friends or followers around the cross as he dies. "*And about the ninth hour Jesus cried out with a loud voice, saying, 'Eli, Eli, lema sabachthani?' that is, 'My God, my God, why have you forsaken me?'*"(Matt 27:46). Even this cry is misunderstood by the watching crowd, which assumes he is calling for Elijah (Matt 27:47). It is the last thing Matthew records Jesus saying before he dies—ridiculed, forsaken, and misunderstood.

"*My God, my God, why have you forsaken me?*" is a biblical quotation. It takes us back to Psalm 22, which contains many descriptions of the suffering of the author. "*All who see me mock me; they make mouths at me; they wag their heads; 'He trusts in the LORD; let him deliver him; let him rescue him, for he delights in him!'*"(Psalm 22:7-8). These words are almost verbatim the words of those who mock him on the cross (Matt 27:43). The psalmist describes pain, hunger, and others gambling for his clothes. In such a state, he cries out to God. Why have you forsaken me?

What is fascinating about Jesus mentioning this psalm of faithful lament is that David is rescued by God (Psalm 22:21-24). Jesus laments his suffering but trusts that God will rescue. His words point us to this ancient prophetic psalm and remind us that suffering is not the end of the story. God will hear his cry and rescue. Jesus dies, but God has not forsaken him.

One Thing to Think About: Have I ever felt forsaken by God?

One Thing to Pray For: Trust that God hears his people—including me

WEEK 52 – MONDAY

Reading: Matthew 27:57-66

Joseph of Arimathea

Jesus has just died. As they rush him down from the cross, "*there came a rich man from Arimathea, named Joseph, who was also a disciple of Jesus. He went to Pilate and asked for the body of Jesus. Then Pilate ordered it to be given to him*"(Matt 27:57-58). Mark tells us that Joseph is "*a respected member of the council, who was also himself looking for the kingdom of God*"(Mark 15:43). This means he is part of the Jewish ruling body that condemned Jesus. Luke adds that Joseph "*had not consented to their decision and action*"(Luke 23:51). The composite picture is of a sincere man living as a follower of Jesus in hostile territory.

"*And Joseph took the body and wrapped it in a clean linen shroud and laid it in his own new tomb, which he had cut in the rock. And he rolled a great stone to the entrance of the tomb and went away*"(Matt 27:59-60). Joseph proves his devotion to Jesus by taking his body. It is a gruesome errand that would leave him ceremonially unclean. He places Jesus in his own new tomb, identifying himself with Jesus. His act is a strong (though quiet) protest to the injustice of the Sanhedrin.

Joseph's act is all the more touching and powerful when we remember that he has no expectation that Jesus will rise from the dead. The gospels are full of these quiet acts of devotion, like the woman who anoints Jesus with her ointment or the widow who puts two mites into the treasury. When we do small acts of kindness, they are noticed by God—and never forgotten.

One Thing to Think About: Do I believe that God notices my quiet acts of kindness and faith?

One Thing to Pray For: A heart of sacrificial devotion to Jesus

WEEK 52 – TUESDAY

Reading: Matthew 28:1-10

He Is Not Here, for He Has Risen

The Sabbath is now past. Jesus' tomb—borrowed from Joseph of Arimathea as an act of kindness—is sealed with a large stone and a guard. Early in the morning, two of the women approach the tomb, likely to remedy the poor job of tending to the body that Joseph has done. *"And behold, there was a great earthquake, for an angel of the Lord descended from heaven and came and rolled back the stone and sat on it. His appearance was like lightning, and his clothing white as snow. And for fear of him the guards trembled and became like dead men"*(Matt 28:2-4). This is the last thing any of them expected.

"But the angel said to the women, 'Do not be afraid, for I know that you seek Jesus who was crucified. He is not here, for he has risen, as he said. Come, see the place where he lay"(Matt 28:5-6). They are looking for Jesus—but Jesus is gone! He is not here, but the reason has nothing to do with robbers or conspiracies. Jesus has risen! The women see where Jesus lay before—but no longer. *"Then go quickly and tell his disciples that he has risen from the dead, and behold, he is going before you to Galilee; there you will see him"*(Matt 28:7). Suddenly their errand—their hope—their lives have changed.

This is the moment at the heart of the Christian faith—the moment that has changed human existence since it occurred. With these words, the possibility of life after death for all people opens up.

One Thing to Think About: Does Jesus' resurrection change the way I view my own death?

One Thing to Pray For: Thanksgiving for the empty tomb

WEEK 52 – WEDNESDAY

Reading: Matthew 28:11-20

Make Disciples of All Nations

Matthew fast-forwards us to a scene where the eleven meet Jesus in Galilee. *"And when they saw him they worshiped him, but some doubted"*(Matt 28:17). Amazingly, some are still struggling with believing in Jesus even as they see and talk with him again. Jesus directs their attention to the future in which they will fully become the preaching fleet he has trained them to be.

"All authority in heaven and on earth has been given to me. Go therefore and make disciples of all nations, baptizing them in the name of the Father and of the Son and of the Holy Spirit, teaching them to observe all that I have commanded you"(Matt 28:18-20). Jesus wants them to make preaching efforts to *"all nations,"* not excluding anyone because of their race. This will take many years to be fully realized. He also wants them to *"make disciples"*—helping them build a relationship with Jesus that mirrors theirs. The amazing thing is—just as when Jesus sent them on the Limited Commission (Matt 10:5ff)—they will do this even though Jesus will not be physically present.

Christian preaching *makes disciples*. Those who accept the gospel do more than simply agree with facts about Jesus or have a transaction with him. They become his followers. The first step is *"baptizing them in the name of the Father and of the Son and of the Holy Spirit"*(Matt 28:19). Baptism is a commitment to follow Jesus. Then their preaching moves on to *"teaching them to observe all that I have commanded you"*(Matt 28:20). Disciples rearrange their world around observing Jesus' commands.

One Thing to Think About: Am I a *disciple* of Jesus?

One Thing to Pray For: Opportunities to help make disciples for Jesus

WEEK 52—THURSDAY

Reading: John 14:1-11

Show Us the Father

As Jesus prepares the disciples for his departure, he points them to his Father. *"In my Father's house are many rooms"*(John 14:2) and *"no one comes to the Father except through me"*(John 14:6) and *"If you had known me, you would have known my Father also"*(John 14:7). All this talk about the Father prompts a request from Philip: *"Lord, show us the Father, and it is enough for us"*(John 14:8). This comment makes me chuckle. What exactly is Philip asking for? Does he want Jesus to open up heaven for him to peek in? And then Philip insists that this is all he needs—just this "small" thing will be *"enough for us."* His expression may be awkward, but we understand Philip's desire: help us understand God more deeply. Give us more.

Jesus is taken aback. *"Have I been with you so long, and you still do not know me, Philip? Whoever has seen me has seen the Father. How can you say, 'Show us the Father'? Do you not believe that I am in the Fathe rand the Father is in me?"*(John 14:9-10). Jesus and the Father are so unified in thought, purpose, and character that when we see Jesus, we see the Father. Jesus brings God down to a level where we can understand him. John insists that while no man has ever seen God, Jesus *"has made him known"*(John 1:18). The Hebrew writer declares that Jesus is *"the radiance of the glory of God and the exact imprint of his nature"*(Heb 1:3). Paul writes that *"in him all the fullness of God was pleased to dwell"*(Col 1:19). When we see Jesus, we gain a glimpse of God himself.

We have spent the year working through the gospel accounts of the life of Jesus. It is natural for us to want more. We have unanswered questions and uncertainty. We know there is truth here, but we wish it was closer and simpler. We stand with Philip: Jesus, can't you just *show us* the Father? Jesus' response helps us. In his wisdom, God has not chosen some great, show-stopping event to reveal himself. He has *become a man and lived in a way that we can relate to*. When we read about Jesus, hear his cries, see his compassion, meditate on his wisdom, *we are observing God*. These are not words to be mastered, but a life-giving revelation we return to again and again.

One Thing to Think About: What have I learned about God from Jesus this year?

One Thing to Pray For: A deeper knowledge of God—as he has revealed himself

WEEK 52—FRIDAY

Reading: John 20:24-31

That You May Believe

Thomas requests more evidence before he is willing to believe the accounts that Jesus has risen from the dead. Even the witness of his friends is insufficient. *"Unless I see in his hands the mark of the nails, and place my finger into the mark of the nails, and place my hand into his side, I will never believe"*(John 20:25). Thomas flounders in his unbelief for eight days until Jesus makes another visit. Warmly, Jesus invites him to inspect his scarred body for himself. *"Put your finger here, and see my hands; and put out your hand, and place it in my side. Do not disbelieve, but believe"*(John 20:27). In this moment, Thomas moves from skeptic to believer. *"My Lord and my God!"*(John 20:28).

But Jesus wants to make a lesson from Thomas' posture. *"Have you believed because you have seen me? Blessed are those who have not seen and yet have believed"*(John 20:29). The vast majority of the people who believe in Jesus will not have the opportunity to examine Jesus as Thomas has. Even people contemporary with the apostles more than likely never have any physical contact with Jesus. (*"Though you have not seen him, you love him,"*1 Pet 1:8). But this doesn't have to be the end of their hopes for faith. Not everyone has to examine Jesus' body to believe. Jesus blesses those with the faith to overcome this lack of firsthand evidence. Faith—vibrant, serious-minded, life-giving faith—is possible for those who never saw Jesus in the flesh.

John has written about all Jesus did *"so that you may believe that Jesus is the Christ, the Son of God, and that by believing you may have life in his name"*(John 20:31). Ordinary people who read about Jesus can become believers and gain the life he brought down from heaven. We have spent the year tracing Jesus' life. The stories are powerful and fascinating. The teachings are brilliant and incisive. The crucifixion is at once breathtakingly horrific and unspeakably wonderful. The question is not whether these things are worthy of our thought. The question of importance—for now and eternity—is simple: Do you believe?

One Thing to Think About: What would keep me from believing in Jesus?

One Thing to Pray For: The rich gift of life for *"those who have not seen and yet have believed"*

A Note from the Author

Thanks for reading *A Year with Jesus*! I would greatly appreciate your feedback on the book. Would you take a moment to review the book on Amazon? Amazon reviews ensure that more people find *A Year with Jesus* and also help me know what readers find helpful or problematic about the book. You can review by searching for the book on Amazon's site and scrolling down to the "Write a review" button.

For more information about other titles, visit my website at jacobhudgins.com.

Thanks!

Jacob Hudgins